D0783742

Boyle's Lore

Boyle's Lore
Katie Boyle

Edited by
Frances Kennett

... to all those TVTimes
readers without whom
this book would never
have been written ...

Weidenfeld and Nicolson/ITV Books

Jointly published by
Weidenfeld and Nicolson with ITV Books

George Weidenfeld and Nicolson Limited
91 Clapham High Street, London SW4 7TA

Independent Television Books Limited
247 Tottenham Court Road, London W1P 0AU

First published 1982
ISBN 0 297 78148 0

Printed in Britain by
Butler & Tanner Ltd, Frome and London

Illustrated and designed by Heather Sherratt

Cover photograph by Godfrey Argent

The Power of the Dog, by Rudyard Kipling,
is reproduced with the kind permission of
the National Trust and Macmillan, London.

Contents

Acknowledgements

So many people have contributed to this book that it seems unfair to mention some and not others. But I do want to thank all the readers who have written to me over the years, giving me a fund of knowledge, wisdom and humour which I am delighted to pass on. Many organisations, charitable and otherwise, have supplied details of their work, and spent considerable time dealing with my specific enquiries, so to all those and everyone else who has played a part in the 'Dear Katie' letter page, I can only express my general but heartfelt gratitude. But there are a few stalwart friends to whom I could always turn. Thank you to Julia Clements, Linda Cook, Miriam Davis, Veronica Gillespie, Janet Mills, Kitty Little and the late Buster Lloyd Jones.

My thanks go also to Heather Sherratt and Behram Kapadia of Weidenfeld and Nicolson for all their hard work to make the book look so attractive; to John Doyle of ITV Books for his constant editorial advice and patient encouragement; and to Stephen du Sautoy, who had the idea for the book in the first place and virtually bludgeoned me into producing *Boyle's Lore*. Then finally, though probably foremost, to Franny Kennett. From the moment when she first brandished a giant pair of scissors over twelve years' worth of 'Dear Katie' pages, through those hours when she used her editorial skills and incredible talent to extract sense from my illegible handwritten pages, and with infinite patience telephoned to check and re-check facts, I knew *Boyle's Lore* would see the light of day. I only hope she enjoyed her hard work as much as I have appreciated it.

While every effort has been made to check the facts, names, addresses and telephone numbers given in this book, there are bound to be changes that have passed unnoticed. I would be delighted to receive any corrections and additional information to set the record straight.

Introduction

This book is a celebration of a long-standing friendship between Katie Boyle and the readers of *TV Times*; since 1970 Katie has received sacks full of letters every month, and answered an enormous cross section of inquiries, from all kinds of emotional problems to mothers' concerns over household tasks, from children's queries about pets and hobbies to old-age pensioners' questions about money and medicine.

Few people perhaps realise the amount of concern that goes into a letters page in a weekly magazine. As well as those letters that are published, Katie personally writes to as many individuals as she possibly can, each month, in her own inimitable style – that special mixture of sound practical advice, humorous commentary on life's wrinkles, and a good spoonful of encouragement. In return, readers have given her hundreds of useful snippets of information on house-cleaning tactics, wiles and ways with difficult neighbours or family members, in addition to their hilarious anecdotes of holidays, high-days or down-in-the-dumps cures.

This book is a compilation of some of the best letters and answers that have appeared in Katie's pages since her correspondence began in 1970. Not only that, but it contains a valuable collection of useful addresses, telephone numbers and book lists to help readers put ideas into practice for themselves.

Katie Boyle is uniquely suited to her role as *TV Times*'s 'Dear Katie', because there is so little in her nature that gives in to life's obstacles. Born in Italy, the child of a fascinating Italian aristocrat, the Marchese Demetrio Imperiali dei Principi di Francavilla, and an exquisitely beautiful Yorkshire girl, Dorothy Ramsden, her upbringing was unconventional and presented her with a fair share of life's troubles from the start: her parents' divorce, when she was five years old, and two stepmothers during her girlhood. It was not until after the war, when she started her career as a model, that Katie settled in England, eventually making use of her natural aptitude for languages by compèring the Eurovision Song Contest on a number of occasions, and giving laughter and pleasure to countless audiences on television and radio quiz programmes and shows.

The letters page reflects Katie's great enthusiasm for life and illustrates her capacity to learn and to change with the times. It is fascinating to see how the page has evolved over the years. At the start, being very much the glamorous star of television, Katie dealt primarily with problems of beauty, grooming, etiquette and life's funnier corners. In time, as she became more involved with her readers' lives, the mix altered; her own experience of bereavement and her continuing zest for life added to the wisdom and sympathy of her replies. Katie is the first person to admit that she does not know a fact, or is wrong to have taken a particular step, and it is just this honesty and grit that wins her popularity and respect. The proof of this can be seen in the number of people who write to Katie again and again, for years after they have received their first response. She remembers people and problems intimately, her natural curiosity and warmth ensuring everyone attention and understanding.

But above all, Katie brings fun and sparkle into everyday affairs. In her letters page she does not 'agonise' over people's complexes and deficiencies, nor does she ever talk down to her readers. Instead, she will always try to suggest a remedy, a new slant, a funny perspective on the problem.

Katie, too, can remember hard times, with no money, no friend at hand to turn to, and no future worth speaking of. Yet she never lost faith that with time, somewhere, a chink would appear in the prevailing gloom. When people are locked into impossible circumstances, they need to know that others have survived and that there is always a way out. Having every obvious advantage does not always provide the answer: a positive attitude is far more important. That belief, and her genuine kindness are the qualities which make Katie Boyle's letters page a delight to read and a continuing success.

Frances Kennett

1
Life's Philosophy

Boyle's lore – please note, it's L-O-R-E, not LAW, but even so there may be many of you wondering why I should consider laying down even a lore. Let me explain at once that there is nothing patronising, superciliously conceited or even know-allish about this endeavour of mine. Simply, I have an absorbent approach to life; I love learning and try to remember what I have learned. I enjoy passing on any information which could be helpful – and I have been lucky enough to meet experts in many fields, from those who have been highly technically trained to those who have acquired knowledge over the years from a close contact with nature. Many differently talented people have given me a variety of values and perspectives with which to view life's problems.

Apart from muddling through my own medley of mistakes and by trial and error reaching some useful conclusions, I have spent my professional days with people who work in fashion, beauty, health and housekeeping, to mention but a few areas, and that has helped me to have a practical outlook.

From an emotional point of view, I think I can also come under the heading of 'experienced'. (This will come as no surprise at all to those of you who have read my autobiography.) I must confess that a letter which wounded me greatly came from a gentleman who asked why on earth I should consider myself qualified to understand or even put a constructive point of view to any human emotion because, said he, I had been born with a gilded silver spoon between my infant lips and had obviously known no greater disappointment than a nanny removing a favourite toy from my reach! Nothing could be further from the truth. On the contrary, you can be quite certain that apart from envy there cannot be one basic human emotion that I have not experienced and, being full-blooded, impulsive and intuitive in all my reactions, I try to respond to my readers' problems with honesty and understanding. Besides, different backgrounds make little difference to the reactions we all have to the blows that life deals us, and therefore I hope I shall always be capable of putting myself in the place of others.

There is one point I want to make clear, though – I do not dole out advice with a capital A. I try to stick to my own heartfelt opinions, because an objective point of view from someone who cares but who is not involved can be very useful.

Sometimes the offer of a humorous comment can puncture that 'trapped' sensation we so often experience. I like to feel my role is that of a catalyst, someone who starts the 'victims' off on a new train of thought, so that possibly, with a confidence catch released, they can deal with their problems more easily.

Time and again while reading back over the letters of the past eleven years and more, I have noticed that our basic beliefs and values have not altered that much, although the way that you or I have suggested we deal with some of our problems may have. It is fascinating to see how, although many problems are voiced differently by each generation as it comes into its own, they are essentially the same human predicaments that really change very little over the years. Your way of expressing them, and many of my replies, put the matter in a multitude of ways, simply because we instinctively keep up with and adjust to an ever-changing world.

I have learned that those people who have or who are willing to develop an ability to communicate, who have consideration for others and a sense of humour, and lace the whole lot with a healthy dose of common sense, will also hold the key to living life to the full. That is really what we are here to do, surely? And besides, many of the letters here reveal an extraordinary strength and warmth of humanity, which have inspired me, not just when I have had my own troubles, but on peaceful days too, because they offer a glimpse of better-loving natures that each one of us would do well to take to heart.

You cannot bring about prosperity by discouraging thrift. You cannot strengthen the weak by weakening the strong.

You cannot help the wage earner by pulling down the wage payer. You cannot further the brotherhood of man by encouraging class hatred.

You cannot help the poor by destroying the rich. You cannot keep out of trouble by spending more than you earn. You cannot build character and courage by taking away a man's initiative and independence.

You cannot help men permanently by doing for them what they could and should do for themselves.

Abraham Lincoln, 1865

Incidentally, the origin of the phrase 'My name is Mud' comes from the moment in the theatre when Abraham Lincoln was assassinated. A doctor named Mudd leapt forward to assist the murderer who fell and injured himself when he attacked the President. Going against the current flow of feeling, the doctor's announcement of his name made him less than popular!

You helped my husband and myself and prevented the break-up of our marriage when you put me in touch with Alcoholics Anonymous. My husband is now recovering. They showed me that many other men and women shared the same problems, and that saved me from insanity. They also restored my faith in God and He has been a great strength and help to me. Without your help and good advice this would never have happened and I sincerely want to thank you. I would like the address of the Calix Society, a Catholic Organisation which helps recovering alcoholics and their families.

Mrs J. W., Southampton.

I'm delighted you feel that I've helped you in some way but I believe that the real 'help' comes from within ourselves, from the strength and determination to find a solution to our problems when we go in search of assistance. I'm sure a lot of people would like to have this address: The Calix Society, The Rev. Isaac McLaren, St James, 232 Woodhall Avenue, Coatbridge, Strathclyde, NML5 5DS.
P.S. Al-Anon can be reached at 61 Great Dover Street, London SE1 4YF (01 403 0888), and The Calix Society has a separate address for England now: Father David Tobin, Grace Dieu Manor, Whitwick, Leicester LE6 3UG.

I shut my eyes, count the steps to the kitchen and smile. I know how many steps there are to the toilet. 'No', I shout to my husband, 'don't put the light on. Think of all the low electricity bills.' He laughs. It is a funny sensation when you close your eyes and walk about, then open them again and look at the lovely flowers in the garden or chase the cats from the birds. All this is 'our game' for I am a 'learner'. In a few more months I shall lose my sight, and all will be darkness. But I have at least seen the beauty of this world for many years.

Mrs V. Howlett, Canvey Island, Essex.

What a remarkable woman you are. There is not a hint of self-pity in your letter. Your courage is a real lesson and inspiration, and I hope it will make some of the 'moaners' of the world think. One thing is certain, you can 'see' far more with your failing eyes than many can with perfect sight. I think you're wonderful and I'm sure you're husband does too.

The years pass quickly, the visions flit by,
Thousands of happenings trouble my eyes,
Unwanted arguments, unwanted fights,
Much wanted sleep on those sleepless nights.

Wine, women and song,
The times you do wrong,
The people you hurt, the ones that you love,
In the life you fit into like a well-worn glove.

Life is long, life can be hard,
Don't fight, don't argue, be on your guard,
Join together, let's be as one,
Then on our happiness will be no setting sun.

This poem is by my schoolboy son. Unfortunately he speaks the truth. Although my husband is a wonderful person he is also very jealous, especially when he drinks, and he can be violent. My son did not show me this poem – I found it; but I can't help but be proud as I think it shows good feeling.

Mrs C., Cleveland.

I was deeply touched by your son's poem. He must have been influenced by your own patience and courage, because, in spite of his troubles there is love in every line, not bitterness. Violence from parents is extremely damaging to a child, even though these fathers may not be unloving but more like 'mixed-up kids' themselves. You can protect yourself and the boy: Women's Aid came into being to help women with this sort of problem, so write to Chiswick Women's Aid, 369 Chiswick High Road, London W4 (01 995 4430) and they will send you the address of their nearest counsellor.
P.S. The director, Mrs Anne Ashby, tells me that her organisation is now known as Chiswick Family Rescue, because she found their help being directed to all family members, not just the wives. Both men and women can

Mrs Doris Davis, a Salvation Army collector from Southampton reminds me, never let children answer the door and innocently admit, 'Mum and Dad are out.' Another useful protection when out at night is a special type of torch which makes a loud noise. Called Alarm with Light, it's available from Presents of Sloane Street, 129 Sloane Street, London SW1.

contact her for advice and referral to help nearer their homes. The Chiswick Centre also offers a refuge for women and children from violent situations. Alternatively, women can contact the National Women's Aid Federation, 374 Gray's Inn Road, London WC1 (01 837 9316) for similar help.

Impulsively I said to the lady next to me in the tea-shop: 'Aren't you nice and slim?' She said I'd made her day and we started chatting. We shared a table and I enjoyed my pot of tea more than usual with someone new to talk to. Don't you think it's a pity that our reserve stops us from talking to people because we don't know them? It isn't difficult to strike up a conversation because there are so many subjects which can be used. I spend lots of time alone and a few minutes' chat will certainly brighten my day – and maybe someone else's too.

Mrs C. Grimstead, Edgware, Middx.

Recently an elderly couple moved into our street. I think they're in their middle 60s. They are very reserved and don't go out much, no newspapers or milk are delivered and I have been told they have no living relations. I am worried about what would happen if both of them became ill. Is there anything I can do without appearing to be interfering?

Mrs P. C., Birmingham.

This couple may particularly enjoy their own company and not want to mix, but I do appreciate your concern for their welfare. You could go to your local Social Services office and explain the situation, leaving the couple's name and address. Or you could ask your local vicar to pop round and welcome them to the parish. If they want to join in community life they will, but they might be quite content simply with each other.

Reading the letter about new people moving into a street and the neighbour wondering how to make contact without interfering, I think I have solved the problem. When new people moved into our street I sent a card giving our names and simply saying welcome to the street. The new neighbours soon sent a card to say hello. This is a simple way of breaking the ice without actually pushing yourself into their homes. I hope many readers will find they make new friends this way.

Mrs J. Hands, Blaydon-on-Tyne, Tyne and Wear.

Can you tell me whether it is necessary to have been christened to be married in church?

Miss K. Barnfield, Devon.

It used to state in Canon Law that you had to be baptised in order to be married in church, but when the law was revised that particular canon was left out. Baptism (christening) signifies entry into the Christian faith. The House of Bishops of the Church of England have stated recently that in order to be married by common or special licence, at least one partner must have been baptised or christened.

It is true that people who wish to marry in the Church of England need to have been baptised, but other denominations follow differ-ent practices. The Roman Catholic church has its own regulations and free churches usually do not require either party to have been baptised before a marriage can be solemnised. The Congregational denomination, which I serve, differs from the Church of England in this as in other matters.

The Rev. Janet H. Wootton, Suffolk.

I have been separated from my husband for five years and would like to get a postal divorce. There are no children involved and I don't want anything from my husband except my freedom. What can I do?

Mrs B. J. S., London.

You can get the forms you need from Oyez Stationery Co, 237 Long Lane, London SE1. At the same time ask for a copy of leaflet PIP which tells you how to apply for divorce by mutual consent, after two years' separation, and which gives you the address of local Divorce Courts. In your particular case the do-it-yourself divorce is probably the answer, but I'm sure you know that it's not allowed where children's rights have to be protected, or where there are problems over sharing the possessions and claims for maintenance.

I am a single man of 26 and I don't seem to be able to find a lady friend of my own age. I work in a food factory with lots of women, but most of them are married. Another problem is that I am very shy and unsure of what to say to girls. All my old mates have married so I'm left on my own. When I go to a disco and see the girls standing in groups of five or six I can't summon the courage to ask one of them to dance. I'm so lonely, what can I do?

J. K. B., Grimsby.

As you're so agonisingly shy I'd really take things step by step. First, make contact with the very young or very old. Working Men's Clubs, Old People's Whist Drives and Children's Homes all run outings and parties where I'm sure your help would be most welcome. You'll find it's much easier to communicate with people who need your help and this in turn will gradually build your confidence. The International Friendship League has members all over the country and their main aim is to encourage friendships. They arrange get-togethers between groups of people over a cup of tea and a meal. Write to them at The International Friendship League Hospitality Service, 3 Creswick Road, Acton, London, W3 9HE – and tell them that you are especially shy. Do try to take the first step to help yourself because you'll find the next steps become progressively easier. Soon those disco girls will hold no fear for you!

Many who read your column must fear they will never meet Mr Right, but I implore them not to give up hope. I spent many dances as a wallflower, not being asked for one dance all evening, but it didn't stop me from going out. At 34 I suddenly met my Mr Right and we married a year later. At 40 I gave birth to my first child and at 42 to my second. As an older mother I appreciate the time at home and don't feel that I've missed out on any pleasures or experiences. I had plenty of time to do all I wanted before I settled down.

Mrs M. P. T., Exeter.

I am divorced with two children and would like to talk to someone in the same situation as myself. I have heard of an organisation called Gingerbread, but don't know how to get in touch with them. I'm sure lots of people would be glad of the information.

Mrs A. D., Norwich.

You need to get in touch with any one of the following organisations which have been established especially to help the thousands of people in your position: The Gingerbread Association for One-Parent Families, 35 Wellington Street, London WC2; The National Council for One-Parent Families, 255 Kentish Town Road, London NW5 2LX, and The National Council for the Single Woman and her Dependants, 29 Chilworth Mews, London W2 3RG.

I am 35 and have been a widow for five and a half years. I have three daughters aged 11, 10, and five. I do a job one day of the week, which has given me new friends, a break from routine, extra money and more confidence. My problem is that I would like to meet a man in my own age group with whom I could make an honest and lasting friendship. I attended a new club for lonely people – about 50 women and three men turned up. Surely there must be lots of lonely, sincere men around somewhere – but where?

Mrs R. P., Leeds.

I can imagine your loneliness, and the responsibility for three youngsters must lie heavily on your shoulders at times. You may like to know of Gingerbread (address at the end of this chapter) and another suggestion which could involve you socially is the Solo Clubs, Head Office, 7/8 Ruskin Chambers, 191 Corporation Street, Birmingham 4 (021 236 2879). Write to them enclosing a sae for details of your nearest group. If you would like to contact a marriage bureau, an excellent one is Heather Jenner, 124 New Bond Street, London W1 (01 629 9634). She will tell you which of her branches is nearest to you. Also, how about paying a visit to your local Citizens' Advice Bureau and asking for a list of local drama, political and social clubs? We are less likely to feel lonely when surrounded by people who share our interests.

For the past three years I have been going through the menopause. I have suffered so much that I feel I don't even know myself. I love my husband and family very dearly and have tried to explain what is going on, but it's very difficult for them to understand that all I want to do is go to bed and sleep my life away. I have been to my doctor and privately to a specialist, who don't seem to be able to help me. Can you give me any advice on what to do next as I am getting desperate?

Mrs D. A., Shipley, Yorks.

The menopause is a perfectly normal change in a woman's hormone pattern as she leaves her child-bearing years behind, and some women sail through without a care in the world. Perhaps if you tried to view this change from another angle it might help to minimise your problem. In many ways it can be a boon, giving you a chance now to enjoy a physical relationship with your husband without the fear of pregnancy, and no longer to suffer the inconvenience of a monthly period. But if the menopause really is more than you can cope with, you may be one of the many women who might benefit from Hormone Replacement Therapy. This isn't a step to take lightly and many doctors are reluctant to interfere with this natural phase in life. Go back to your doctor and ask him to put you in touch with a sympathetic gynaecologist. St Thomas's Hospital in London is well-equipped to deal with this problem, as are two hospitals near you – the Female Infirmary at the Sheffield Hospital and the Jessop Hospital for Women. I also think you may feel happier just reading more about what's going on in your body. The National Marriage Guidance Council publish booklets such as The Menopause: Questions and Answers. Living Through Middle Age, *another book you may find helpful, and* Women: The Middle Years *are also on their list of titles. You will find the address of your local NMGC in the telephone directory but if you have any difficulty write, enclosing a sae, to The Bookshop, The National Marriage Guidance Council, Little Church Street, Rugby, and ask for a full list of their publications. Personally, I was lucky enough to sweep through the menopause without really noticing it, and armed with only a fan to subdue those hot flushes. We're not all the same, I know, but I do think the right attitude of mind can help – and above all a lack of fear.*

I am a divorced woman living alone with a child from my first marriage. It broke up because I told my husband that I had had an incestuous affair with my uncle in my early teens. He was disgusted. I have now met a man who loves me and I love him. Yet I cannot bring myself to commit myself to a permanent relationship because I feel I should tell him. Not to admit would be living under false pretences. What can I do? Can you give me a short answer?

J. K., Yorks.

Yes I can: just simply, shut up. That incident is now buried in the past, and not only is it self-indulgent to rake it up, it is positively destructive. Look upon your vow of silence as an expiation, as this is the hardest thing for you to do.

I am 37 and have been happily married for 18 years. I have two teenage children. My problem is that over the last seven years the craving to have another baby has nearly driven me mad. The trouble is that we kept putting off having another child because we were in a bad way financially and didn't think the additional strain would be fair on either the children or ourselves. Recently things have improved and I now have an interesting and well-paid job. I expected this to occupy me fully, but I still can't stop wanting to have another child. Even though I know it's impractical I really can't get the idea of a baby out of my mind.

Mrs A. C., Derby.

The urge to have a baby isn't unnatural and every woman gets broody from time to time. But your obsession might spring from misguided and hidden feelings that now your children are older they don't need you so much and a baby would fill the gap because it would be entirely dependent on you. But in fact the children you already have do still need you – growing up doesn't mean they're growing away from you. And then there's your husband. How would he feel about being tied down to the 'nappy routine' again, not to mention the extra and permanent financial burden? I believe that in your case you should analyse very carefully the reasons why you want another child, and also consider your other two children as well as your husband before you succumb to that urge to have a brand new baby.

I am 10 years old and have two sisters who are both older than me. I am easily hurt and sometimes one of my sisters calls me names and makes me cry. When this happens my other sister joins in which makes me worse. Do you think there's anything I could do to help myself?

Miss L., Worcs.

You're a very grown-up young lady because you say you want to 'help yourself' and I'm sure you can. When your sisters start calling you names make yourself very busy doing something else – read, sing, or play. Do anything, but think about what you're doing so that you can ignore them. If you feel you must explode occasionally, then do, but if they find they just cannot annoy you, they'll gradually stop bothering to tease you.

I overheard a conversation between two women bemoaning the fact that now their children had gone away to college, they no longer expected to have any say in their lives. May I offer a word of comfort to parents with similar doubts? When you let go of your children you regain them in a very special way. I left home five years ago but my relationship with my mother has matured into something very special. She is always an anchor of security to help me with my problems and share my triumphs. I love to return home on visits because I gain the strength to carry on the day-to-day battle of living in a large city. Friends in the same situation feel as I do.

Miss E. Butterworth, Birmingham.

You recently published a letter from a 16-year-old girl who wanted to continue a romance with a boy who had seduced her. You advised her to make friendships not romances. I'm afraid you have given your age away! This is irrelevant today as advice to all but the most sheltered of girls. I am amazed you can be so innocent. In my work as a teacher I see plenty of this 'teen scene'. Most girls are under pressure to go on the pill, and some are regular mistresses by the time they are 16, seeking abortions by the age of 17. I have grown-up sons and daughters and realise that this situation hasn't occurred from choice on the girls' part. Girls are pushed into relationships, with clinics handing out the pill and boys believing that a physical relationship is their right. In future, when you give the same advice, why don't you also mention that the girl will be called a coward, a lesbian, a baby – and will be friendless both in male and female circles?

Mrs J. White, Head of Religious Education Dept, Rochester, Kent.

I welcome the chance to make it clear that I totally stand by the advice I gave. The tone of your letter suggests you've had more than your share of disillusionment where young people are concerned – and you have my sympathy, but I also know that there are many sensible teenagers all over the country who are successfully resisting the pressures you talk of. And doing so with the help of caring, understanding parents. We adults must provide more guidance – not less. I would agree that moral arguments don't bear much weight with youngsters these days but most are willing to listen to sensible practical advice. Apart from not being emotionally equipped to handle sexual relations, many young girls are not mature enough physically. One doctor told me of some serious internal problems that can arise. And let's not forget that VD is on the increase among young people and can have serious long-term effects reaching any off-spring they may have. What we need to imbue into our daughters is that they have a choice – control over their own bodies – that they don't have to give in to pressures of any kind and the popularity gained from giving in can be very short-lived. Self-respect comes from following your own beliefs, not from following the herd.

When children ask the famous question, 'Where do babies come from?' please tell the truth. I hear so many of my friends telling

***

I have tried to develop the ability to live in the present, and to enjoy life to the full. I would never want to thrust all my memories under the carpet, and would hate to forget a great many of them, but if you live in the past you will be sad that you cannot bring the good parts back, or become bitter because you could not change it.

Living in the future means sacrificing the value of today for something you cannot know about, can do nothing to control and which may not even be yours. Make prudent plans, of course, but accept your own day now, as a continuous link between what has happened and what lies ahead. I am sure that how we have been affected by the past makes us the kind of people we are today. For instance, I am too self-protective to harbour grudges – anyone who has done me a bad turn has probably forgotten it anyway, and if I cling on to it I am only gnawing at myself, and that hurts. I find that by leaving yesterday behind, and by feeling the reality of today more fully, I become better equipped to cope with the surprises of tomorrow.

***

their children ridiculous stories, and when they get older, the children hear the wrong information from friends which may well frighten them. The child could grow up not trusting the parents' advice, and seek it elsewhere. When we went out shopping recently, my small daughter asked me where babies came from. I told her we'd have a chat when we got home. Waiting in a chemist's shop she quietly whispered: 'It's all right now, we won't need to have that chat – the lady in front is having one weighed so I know you buy them here.' It made me laugh, but I did put her straight when we got home.

Mrs L. Bryan, Leeds.

Your daughter's observations were charming. I do agree that parents should answer their children's questions as honestly as possible, and there are several publications around that make the task easier. The National Marriage Guidance Council (see page 28) publish an extensive booklist on sex education and other sensitive subjects. Claire Rayner has written The Body Book, *by André Deutsch. An easy-to-understand text and colourful, clear illustrations take young readers and parents alike through all the situations and problems that may arise to perplex children. Claire also produces various leaflets for the* Sunday Mirror *on sexual and other personal problems. You can get in touch with her, enclosing a sae at PO Box 125, Harrow, Middx., HA1 3XE.*

I have found out that my Mum is having an affair with a married man, and worst of all, my Dad does not know. I feel I ought to tell him, but am afraid it might affect their marriage. I am 14. Could you advise me?

G., Edinburgh.

This is the moment in life to learn that silence is golden. I understand you want to tell your father but it would make things worse and you do not actually know what private events have led your mother to take this course. Appearances are not always what they seem, and right or wrong seldom belongs solely to one partner. Your part is to be as kind as you can to both your parents, and if possible keep your knowledge a secret. If you must talk to someone, make it your mother, not your father.

Please could you tell me where I can get information about sexually transmitted diseases?

S., Leicester.

There is an excellent book suitable for men and women called Sexually Transmitted Diseases *by Dr John Kenyon Oates which you can obtain by writing to Women's Health Concern, 16 Seymour Street, London W1H 5WB.*

You wrote to a mother a few weeks ago about post-natal depression – it was so much more helpful than that usual 'snap out of it' reaction which is impossible to do. I wonder if you have heard of the National Childbirth Trust with their post-natal support groups? These have been going for quite a while now but not everyone knows about them. They are run by other mothers which is in itself helpful because you are an equal, not a patient. Part of being depressed is the feeling of inferiority and I think these groups overcome this. The headquarters are at 9 Queensborough Terrace, London W2 3TB. They can put anyone in touch with her nearest group. It's best to send a sae.

Mrs T. Twelftree, Yeovil, Somerset.

P.S. Another useful address for women who need very special help is The Stillbirth Association, 15a Christchurch Hill, London NW3 1JY (01 774 4601).

I have often read on problem pages how adopted children try to trace their natural parents. I was an adopted child and searched in vain until I finally found my natural mother. It was only then I realised that my adoptive mother had been the person who had loved me and cared for me all my life and seen me through all my childhood illnesses and scrapes. I loved her more from that moment on. But it took about 10 years to heal the rift I had driven between us. Besides which, my natural mother was happily married to a man who knew nothing of me and this nearly broke up their marriage. So I hope other adopted children will stop and think before they try to find their natural parents.

Cathy, Essex.

I'm really sorry that your success in tracing your natural mother led to so much misery all round. I have always felt that it is the birthright of everyone to know, if possible, his or her parents and I am glad the law now makes it easier to obtain this information. I've always found that the most successful and loving relationships between adoptive parents and children are those that are honest and open. No adopted child should have to feel guilty about wanting to find a natural parent and, if support and guidance are given by the adoptive parents, the loving ties between them can only be strengthened. So I'd say to any adopted child wanting to trace a natural parent: involve your adoptive parents and let them see that your love for them is as strong and unchanging as ever, and, if the search is successful, proceed with a good deal of sensitivity and caution.

Since I saw a programme about vandalism it occurred to me that as a mother for 20 years and a school nurse for five, I might pass on some useful advice to parents of younger children. It could prevent a child from becoming 'disadvantaged' – the type presumed responsible for vandalism. It's this: do listen to your children's criticisms and arguments – they may have a good point to make. Parents who ignore a child's point of view end up with a frustrated, resentful and often violent child on their hands. Don't throw away your children's books or toys, however shabby, without their permission – they won't respect other people's property if you don't respect theirs. Don't allow them to be at an unnecessary disadvantage at school because of poor vision, hearing or speech defects which may well be treatable. So make use of school medicals, and meet the school doctor if you can. Remember, they deal with behaviour problems as well as physical illness. My own children will probably say I should have followed all this advice myself. I wish I had.

Mrs J. P. Lyall, Chelmsford, Essex.

'If only youth knew, and old age still had the chance.' No doubt this saying will echo through further centuries. But the advice you give is constructive and understanding.

Who knows where he gets it from but our son (10 years old) is brilliantly clever. This isn't a prejudiced parents' opinion but comes from his headmaster and his schoolteachers. They refuse to put him into a class with older boys even though they know he is far too advanced for his own. The result is not only a very bored little boy but also a rather naughty one with endless energy because he seems to need so much less sleep than other children of his age. My husband and I are utterly exhausted and at a loss to know how to cope with this problem.

N. K., London.

Despite your present quandary yours is an exciting problem. Get in touch with the National Association for Gifted Children, 1 South Audley Street, London W1 (01 499 1188). This 25-year-old organisation has 50-plus branches all over Britain and was founded in order to give extra bright youngsters a chance to come up against equally intelligent ones and find stimulating competition on their own level. (Remember to enclose a sae when writing to the Association for further information and addresses.)

The physical energy you describe often goes hand in hand with a very high IQ and once your son becomes mentally outstretched that physical facet will fall into place – but don't ever expect to have a sleepyhead around the house.

It sounds as though you and your husband have lots of pride in your son and fun to look forward to in the years ahead. Enjoy them to the full.

I live in an old house which has been converted into separate apartments and I share the communal areas with an elderly couple. They are good neighbours and very kind. Recently their television set broke down and when the old lady asked me if she could come and watch mine in the evenings I was quite happy to agree. Unfortunately our tastes in programmes could not be more different and after several evenings of sitting watching her choices I found myself planning excuses not to let her in. Being a Christian and feeling guilty at thinking this way, I made my decision – I would do all those little jobs around the flat which I'm always putting off, while she watched the programmes she wanted to see. Her TV set is now repaired and although I am pleased to be able to watch my own favourite programmes again, I feel happy that we remained good friends. I've also managed to complete those horrid little jobs I had been postponing for so long.

Mrs J. M. W., Hove, Sussex.

What a lot we can learn from your letter. I can only gasp with admiration at your self-discipline. I think I would have been tempted to make those excuses to keep the old lady out. But you have demonstrated how forbearance can overcome a short-term problem and if you had made your neighbour feel unwelcome, you would eventually have come to regret it. Ill-feeling between people is difficult

to amend and doing without television for a while is a small price to pay for a friendship intact.

While awaiting treatment in a rehabilitation centre I saw a woman who was obviously depressed after the amputation of her leg. Nothing could be done to please her. We were left alone for some time but all my conversational gambits failed to get any response. I saw I couldn't help her in any way, and I gave up and started walking along the practice bars. Suddenly she asked me: 'Will I be able to walk like that?' and of course I could tell her from my own experience that she would. My actions, not my words, had given her that desperately needed ray of hope for the future.

G. Browning, Tunbridge Wells, Kent.

Your action was exactly the right approach – the impossible becomes the feasible if you set the example rather than preach it.

I never realised how difficult life could be for disabled people until I became one myself. But the compensations seem enormous. Traffic stops for me, people open doors, other disabled people smile and pass the time of day. I'm always given the most comfortable seat in a person's home – and no one expects me to help with the washing-up. Best of all, I can gently nod off to sleep when I feel like it without being considered rude. Top all this with having a smashing husband and I consider myself fortunate, in spite of my physical limitations.

Mrs G. Jones, Truro, Cornwall.

Could I suggest that everyone who knows a disabled person makes at least one day in the year a special day for them? Visit them at home or in hospital, or take them out for a few hours to give both parents or guardians and the handicapped person a complete break. Caring for the disabled is admirable, but much appreciated also is the giving of time and the personal love this would demand. I can assure such givers they will be rewarded beyond their highest expectations.

T. M., Yorks.

I have had many letters asking how people can be of active help and have been in touch with the International Year of Disabled People, 26 Bedford Square, London WC1B 3HU. Here are some suggestions that could make all the difference to someone's lifestyle. Offer to do the shopping for someone who has difficulty getting about, or drive them to the shops. Help a family with a handicapped child and give the parents some time off-duty. Learn how to push a wheelchair, guide a blind person or speak clearly to the partially deaf. Also support the work of those concerned with disability – contact your local Council of Voluntary Service or Association of Disabled People. Learn more about different disabilities and their effects by ordering the Labelled Disabled *leaflet from RADAR, the organisation that carries on the work of IYDP, now: Royal Association for Disability and Rehabilitation, 25 Mortimer Street, London W1N 8AB (01 637 5400).*

Last summer I lost my little three-year-old daughter in a crowded shopping centre. It must be the nightmare of all young mothers. Never again. She now wears a clear plastic identity tube available at all pet shops, with her name, address, date of birth and telephone number in it, attached to her clothes. The details can so easily be altered when she goes to stay with her grandmother or when we are on holiday.

Mrs G. F. Smith, Surrey.

Another method is to make a bracelet by writing the child's name and address on a piece of paper and then sticking it in between two strips of clear tape to make it waterproof and smudgeproof.

While my husband and I were away recently visiting my sick sister our house was flooded. The police had to break in and on examining my address book they were able to identify my daughter's phone number from all the other local numbers because I put all my family's relationships to me in brackets after their names. It certainly paid dividends on that occasion.

Mrs Hilda Kerma, Southampton.

Recently you awarded your Letter of the Week to a reader who suggested that serial numbers of valuables be kept at hand. You might like to know that there is a scheme operated by local police stations whereby people can obtain a ready-printed card for this purpose. Under another scheme called Be A Good Neighbour you keep details of any old or infirm persons near you who may need help at any time. I hope that more readers will take advantage of these helpful schemes.

Eric Bristow, Surrey.

Since my husband is in the Royal Air Force and we have to move around, my daughter often has to live away from home. She is a sensible girl and looks after herself, but we would like to help her with a present of luncheon vouchers.

Mrs K. Saunders, Glamorgan.

I'm sure many parents whose children have left home worry about them not eating properly. You can buy luncheon vouchers in demoninations of between 5p and £1; £20 worth of vouchers costs £20.69 from Luncheon Vouchers Ltd, 50 Vauxhall Bridge Road, London SW1V 2RS (01 834 6666). The big advantage of giving vouchers is that you know they will be spent filling tummies, whereas money could tempt a girl to buy a new pair of shoes instead.

I have an idea to help nervous people who live alone. I have recorded the sound of a dog barking loudly on my cassette player and when the doorbell rings I switch it on and shout 'Quiet, Rex' as I walk to the door. It gives me confidence and I am sure would-be burglars will think twice if they imagine being bitten by my fierce Alsatian dog.

Mrs I. M. D., Weybridge.

We have a lovely laburnum tree in the garden, but it's causing me some concern. My daughter is only one year old and is showing a lively interest in the seed pods which contain the poisonous laburnum seeds. I would be interested to know the incidence of laburnum poisoning. Should I chop down the tree and sacrifice the beauty of the flowers for peace of mind?

Mrs Veronica Clarke, Malvern, Worcs.

According to the Poisons Centre at one of London's top hospitals, laburnum seeds do not contain a deadly poison. Their record shows only rare cases of severe poisoning. Apparently the content of the poison in the seeds varies tremendously – three from the same pod could be eaten with no effect and at worst might produce sickness and diarrhoea. In your case I would take sensible precautions, fencing around the laburnum, and if you have to leave your child alone in the garden then put her safely in a playpen. This way you can keep both your beautiful tree and your peace of mind.

Good neighbours are worth their weight in gold, and I'm particularly grateful to one of mine because she really opened my eyes to life. Like everyone I have down days, and in spite of the fact that I'm happily married with a family, I used at one time to become very sorry for myself. On one such day a few years ago my neighbour asked me to visit a hospital for the terminally ill. I wasn't keen, as I felt I had enough problems of my own. How wrong I was. It made me realise I was lucky, and I saw also that there was a great need for extra hands to help the overworked nursing staff. For the past few years I've been going back twice a week, helping the League of Friends by taking the refreshment trolley around or simply talking or reading to patients who don't have many visitors. I can also do a number of jobs that the nurses have little time for, such as arranging flowers and plumping pillows. It's the best cure for depression I've found, and makes me appreciate the good things of my life even more.

Mrs J. J., Devon.

Here I am relaxing in a sun-lounger in a garden, adding a little more to my golden tan.

My expensive-looking cream dress looks good and shows off the fashionable brown and cream beads of my long necklace. My hair is freshly washed and set and I feel great. Am I a wealthy lady of leisure? No, just a 63-year-old gran, widowed three years ago after 44 years of extremely happy marriage. I have taken a part-time job preparing tea for three delightful children aged 12, 10 and seven years whose parents are at work from Monday to Friday. I normally work afternoons only. My dress from the Oxfam shop cost 25p and my hair was set at half-price (pensioner's rate). I feel so contented as I sit here in the sun and it's lovely to feel needed again.

Mrs K. H. Gunn, Wakefield, Yorks.

Most of us have problems galore, but I think we'd feel happier and cope with them more easily if we had your approach to things. Your life is undoubtedly 'half full' rather than 'half empty'. Thanks for writing and cheering us up.

Two years ago I was involved in a driving accident, in which a 17-year-old boy was killed. Although the coroner absolved me from responsibility, I blamed myself. For months it preyed on my mind. Finally a doctor told me that the sooner I accepted the boy was dead, the sooner I could begin to live again. He said that although death is a tragedy, it is also the will of God. Those few words helped me to face life again. Perhaps they will help others.

Mrs C., W. Yorks.

Many people find their retirement spoiled by unthinking friends and relatives descending for a holiday without considering the extra cost to pensioners. Feeding even one or two extra people over a week or just a weekend

can be a real worry. My three daughters have each solved this problem individually. One hands over her week's housekeeping money when she arrives and leaves me to do the shopping. Another brings round ready-baked pies and cakes, then pays for extra groceries when I shop. The third goes to a cash-and-carry the day before her departure and re-stocks my cupboard with my usual weekly purchases plus those bulk buys I can't usually afford. A leaving gift of a plant or flowers is a kind thought – but it really doesn't help refill a pensioner's purse or pantry. I hope that some people take my daughters' good examples and make a practical gift.

C. B., Barnstaple, Devon.

Having been a businesswoman all my life – and enjoyed every minute of it – I dreaded my retirement. So many women seem to drop into a depression after giving up a busy life that I determined this wouldn't happen to me. I love cooking so I took a part-time job as a cook for a while. I also joined our local senior citizens' club so that I still meet new people. At present I am working as a charwoman and I'm really enjoying life. So please don't stick in a rut when you retire. Life can begin at 60.

Mrs Betty Jenkin, Newcastle-upon-Tyne.

We have had some splendid holidays in the past and have travelled extensively. Now we're retired and can no longer afford to go away anywhere; instead we have do-it-yourself holidays. For a couple of weeks each year, we allow ourselves no more than one and a half hours for shopping, cooking, and household chores. After that the prospects are endless. If the weather is good, we enjoy our garden or take a gentle walk in the nearby parks and have a lunchtime drink at the local pub. We take the bus to other towns and have also visited some places of interest in the area. In the evening, finances allowing, we go to the cinema or perhaps out for a meal. There are endless possibilities for enjoyment and our do-it-yourself holiday is a real but inexpensive treat.

Mrs G. Gibson, Gloucester.

You might also be interested to learn about an organisation called the National Federation of Old Age Pensioners' Association, who offer lots of information and help to pensioners and also publish a very useful booklet called Your Pension, *giving details of benefits and clarifying many problems concerning pensioners. Further details can be obtained from the NFOAPA, 91 Preston New Road, Blackburn. The Pre-Retirement Association (of Great Britain and Northern Ireland), 19 Undine Street, London SW17 8PP, is able to help many people both preparing for retirement and coping with it when it happens. The Association is able to give advice on all aspects of retirement, and it also publishes a magazine, entitled* Choice, *details of which can be obtained by writing to the above address.*
P.S. *The address of* Choice *itself is Bedford Chambers, Covent Garden, London WC2E 8HA.*

I am wondering if there is a leaflet one can obtain which lays down all the procedures to be carried out when someone dies. For example, whom do you see first? When do you contact the undertaker, solicitor and so on? Sorry if this is a morbid subject, but I do hate leaving loose ends untied. We have made our wills and I thought if I could leave such a leaflet in the deed box it would save any unnecessary confusion.

Mrs M. A. Doyle, Ormskirk, Lancs.

Death becomes a morbid subject only for those who treat it as such. We all have to die one day and your practical approach will save your loved ones a great deal of extra stress when the time comes. Which magazine publishes a clear, sympathetic and very helpful booklet on all the procedures and formalities following a death. Write for details to the Consumers' Association, Caxton Hill, Hertford SG13 7LZ, and ask for their publication, What To Do When Someone Dies.

I think I speak for a lot of old people when I say how worried I am about the cost of a funeral today. I understand it can be as much as £300 and I would hate to burden any of my family with it. I am 84 and can't possibly save that amount out of my pension. Can my daughters be forced to pay the extra expense?

Mrs A. K., London.

Thank you for bringing up this seldom-discussed subject. Apart from the booklet mentioned in the previous answer which will be of general help, you may like to know that no one can be forced to pay for a funeral unless they arrange it themselves and assume liability for the funeral director's account. If there is no one able and willing to pay for the funeral the local authority will arrange and pay for a perfectly decent 'no frills' send-off.

When I lost my husband, you sent me a short paragraph by Canon Scott Holland. I was very deeply touched and now that a friend of mine has been widowed I want to copy out the words for her but I have put it away in such a safe place that I have lost it. Those words are much more wonderful than I could write myself and if you send another copy it will not get mislaid.

Mrs H. F. Hughes, Cirencester, Glos.

I have been asked many times to quote the lines that Henry Scott Holland wrote on the death of a loved one. I have since discovered that Holland (1847-1918) was a Canon of St Paul's and one of the most vigorous and practical theologians of the last 100 years. Instead of teaching us that in the midst of life we are in death, he reminds us that in the midst of physical death we also have spiritual life. But while we are submerged in grief we cannot become aware of the continuing presence of our loved ones. I'm quite certain that these lines, below, will always give great comfort.

****

Death is nothing at all. I have only slipped away into the next room. I am I and you are you. Whatever we were to each other, that we are still. Call me by my old familiar name, speak to me in the easy way you always used. Put no difference into your tone, wear no forced air of solemnity or sorrow .... What is death but a negligible accident? Why should I be out of mind because I am out of sight? I am waiting for you, for an interval, somewhere very near just around the corner. All is well.

Henry Scott Holland

****

Useful Addresses

Chiswick Women's Aid,
369 Chiswick High Road, London W4. (01 995 4430)

National Women's Aid Federation,
374 Gray's Inn Road, London WC1. (01 837 9316)

The Calix Society (to help Catholic ex-alcoholics and their families),
Rev. Isaac McLaren, St James's, 232 Woodhall Avenue, Coatbridge, Strathclyde NML5 5DS.

The Calix Society (UK),
Father David Tobin, Grace Dieu Manor, Whitwick, Leicester LE6 3UG.

Al-Anon (to help alcoholics and their families),
61 Great Dover Street, London SE1 4YF. (01 403 0888)

The International Friendship League,
Peace Haven House, 3 Creswick Road, Acton, London W3 9HE. (01 922 0221)

The Gingerbread Association for One-Parent Families,
35 Wellington Street, London WC2. (01 240 0953)

The National Council for One-Parent Families,
255 Kentish Town Road, London NW5 2LX. (01 267 1361)

The National Council for the Single Woman and her Dependants (women caring for older relatives),
29 Chilworth Mews, London W2 3RG. (01 262 1451)

Solo Clubs,
7–8 Ruskin Chambers, 191 Corporation Street, Birmingham 4. (021 236 2879)

Heather Jenner Marriage Bureau,
124 New Bond Street, London W1. (01 629 9634)

Oyez Stationery Co (for postal divorce details),
237 Long Lane, London SE1.

The National Marriage Guidance Council,
Little Church Street, Rugby CU21 3AP. (0788 73241)

Women's Health Concern,
16 Seymour Street, London W1H 5WB.

The Stillbirth Association,
15a Christchurch Hill, London NW3 1JY. (01 774 4601)

National Childbirth Trust,
9 Queensborough Terrace, London W2 3TB. (01 221 3833)

The National Association for Gifted Children,
1 South Audley Street, London W1. (01 499 1188)

RADAR: Royal Association for Disability and Rehabilitation,
25 Mortimer Street, London W1N 8AB. (01 637 5400)

Luncheon Vouchers Ltd,
50 Vauxhall Bridge Road, London SW1V 2RS. (01 834 6666)

National Federation of Old Age Pensioners' Association,
91 Preston New Road, Blackburn.

The Pre-Retirement Association of Great Britain and Northern Ireland,
19 Undine Street, London SW17 8PP.

Choice magazine (advice in preparation for retirement),
18 Bedford Chambers, Covent Garden, London WC2E 8HA.

Further Useful Addresses

National Housewives Register,
South Hill, Cross Lanes, Chalfont St Peter, Bucks. (02407 3797)

PHAB – Physically Handicapped and Able-Bodied Clubs (for both able and disabled young people to meet and mix),
42 Devonshire Street, London W1N 1LN. (01 637 7475)

Child Poverty Action Group,
1 Macklin Street, London WC2. (01 242 3225)

The Disabled Living Foundation,
346 Kensington High Street, London W14. (01 602 2491)

National Association for Mentally Handicapped Children,
86 Newman Street, London W1P 4AR. (01 636 2861–2867)

Family Therapy Practice Centre,
198 Sylvan Road, London SE19 2SA. (01 653 6395)

Invalid Children's Aid Association,
c/o Thomas Coram Foundation for Children, 40 Brunswick Square, London WC1. (01 837 8488)

Turning Point (to help rehabilitate alcoholics and drug addicts),
8 Strutton Ground, London SW1P 2HP. (01 222 6862)

Association of British Adoption Agencies,
27 Queen Anne's Gate, London SW1H 9BU.

Adoption Resource Exchange (hard-to-place children, not babies),
40 Brunswick Square, London WC1. (01 837 0496)

Homosexuality: London Friend,
274 Upper Street, Islington, London N1 2UA. (01 359 7371)

Che: Campaign for Homosexual Equality,
274 Upper St, London N1 2UA. (01 359 3973) In Ireland, contact **NIGRA**, PO Box 44, Belfast BT1 1SH.

Gay News (fortnightly magazine, news and information),
1A Normand Gardens, Greyhound Road, London W14 9SB.

Gay Switchboard (what's on in London, accommodation problems, advice, referrals to other groups out of London). (01 837 7324)

Help the Aged,
8-10 Denman Street, London W1A 2AP. (01 437 2554)

Age Concern,
Bernard Sunley House, 60 Pitcairn Road, Mitcham, Surrey. (01 640 5431)

Mothers in Action,
Munro House, 9 Poland Street, London W1V 3DG. (01 734 3457)

Brook Advisory Centres (office and central clinic, for all kinds of gynaecological help: they can offer referrals),
233 Tottenham Court Road, London W1P 9AE. (01 580 2991)

London Pregnancy Advisory Service,
40 Margaret Street, London W1N 7FB. (01 409 0281)

The Mothers' Union,
Mary Sumner House, 24 Tufton Street, London SW1P 3RD. (01 222 5533)

The Association for Post-Natal Illness,
7 Gowan Avenue, Fulham, London SW6.

Prisoners' Families,
The Circle Trust, 25 Camberwell Grove, London SE5. (01 703 6545)

The Samaritans (befriending the suicidal),
Crypt of St Stephens, 39 Walbrook, London EC4. (01 626 2277-9000)

The Migraine Trust,
45 Great Ormond Street, London WC1N 3HD. (01 278 2676)

The Phobics Society,
4 Cheltenham Road, Chorlton-cum-Hardy, Manchester M21 1QN. (061 881 1937)

Headway (for families of head-injured patients),
17-21 Clumber Avenue, Sherwood Rise, Nottingham. (0602 622382)

Useful Reading

These books were all in print when this book was being prepared, though do remember that even if a bookseller can no longer supply you, it might be possible to order an out-of-print book through your local public library. If your local bookshop doesn't have one of these titles and it is in print, then you can also write directly to the National Marriage Guidance Council, Book Department, Herbert Gray College, Little Church Street, Rugby CU21 3AP, enclosing a sae, and they will send you details of how to order, a price list, and a complete booklist.

Adolescent Disturbance and Breakdown, Moses Laufer (Penguin).
Growing Pains - a study of teenage distress, Edna M. Irwin (Macdonald and Evans).

Boys and Sex, Wardell B. Pomeroy (Pelican).

Girls and Sex, Wardell B. Pomeroy (Pelican).

So Now You Know About Sex, Dr Elizabeth Penrose (Family Doctor Booklet).

So Now You Know About VD, R.S. Morton (Family Doctor Booklet).

Making Sense of Sex, Helen Kaplan (Quartet Books).

Make It Happy, What Sex Is All About, Jane Cousins (Penguin).

The Body Book, Claire Rayner (André Deutsch).

Sex and Life, Brian Ward (Macdonald).

Getting Married in Church, M. Batchelor (Lion Guides).

The Birth Control Book, Howard I. Shapiro (Penguin).

Becoming Orgasmic: A sexual growth programme for women, J. Herman and L. & J. Piccolo (Prentice Hall).

Men and Sex, Bernie Zilbergeld (Fontana).

Shyness, Philip G. Zimbardo (Pan).

My Secret Garden, Nancy Friday (Quartet). (Women's sexual fantasies.)

The Art of Sensual Massage, Gordon Inkeles and Marray Todris (Allen & Unwin).

The Menopause; Questions and Answers, S. Beedell (Arlington Books).

Women: The Middle Years, Margaret Smith (BMA).

Love and Sex After 60, Robert M. Butler and Myrna Lewis (Harper & Row).

Publications from the NMGC (samples only: the complete list is much fuller). These are inexpensive little booklets, under £1 variously, which will offer a start in helpful advice.

Sex in Marriage
Alone Again

The First Year of Life
Where Do Babies Come From? (for 9-12 year olds.)
Parents are Forever (parents and children in divorce.)
Marriage and the Law – where do I stand? (for separation and divorce being considered.)
Divorce: What Shall We Tell The Children, Peter Mayle (W.H. Allen.) (Also available from the National Council for One-Parent Families.)

The NMGC also supplies the **Which?** guides, published by The Consumers' Association. Further details can be acquired direct from **Which?,** c/o The Consumers' Association, Caxton Hill, Hertford SG13 7LZ (Hertford 57773). Some useful current titles include:

Which Guide to Your Rights
Living Through Middle Age
Earning Money at Home
What to do When Someone Dies
Wills and Probate
Pregnancy Month by Month
The Newborn Baby

Further useful titles on family health, child care and life's problems come from the Family Doctor publications produced by the BMA. These are generally available in chemist shops, bookshops and libraries, but if you come across a title mentioned that you would like to read in detail, write enclosing a sae to Family Doctor Publications, BMA, Tavistock Square, London WC1H 9JP (01 387 9721). These small books are very inexpensive, starting at less than £1, and give clearly expressed informative sources.

2
Health and Beauty

I sometimes wonder why we should be so presumptuous as to try to decree who is beautiful and who is not. After all, when a person, be it a man or a woman, is labelled a 'raving beauty' or 'devastatingly handsome' there's always a militant camp which swears that he or she leaves them absolutely cold. And beauties who do keep their looks often seem to acquire a slightly sour expression in their old age, as if regretting that they ever had to leave their prime behind them.

'Attractive' is a description I would value far more. Attractiveness seems to have a much wider appeal because its boundaries are so flexible and can never be limited by age – an attractive person has an indefinable and individual quality, never confined by the straight teeth, small nose and large eyes rule-book. Such a person possesses an aura, something that draws people to them. But when all is said and done, even 'attractiveness' can be a source of argument, because it too is based on opinion, and is a blend of what appeals to you personally plus that elusive, all-essential element of feeling special, which only comes to life when it meets its brother or sister ingredient. The right chemistry is what makes the world go round, and makes everyone capable of being deeply beautiful, from the inside out.

For me, despite the modern vogue that favours the tousled, unkempt look (and not forgetting a well-known and exceedingly wealthy Romeo who used to cable his current lady love: *Am coming home next week, don't wash*), cleanliness goes hand in hand with attractiveness. Clean we can all be. While I would be mad to map out a make-up plan in this book because there is nothing that dates a face more than last year's way to apply shadows, pencils and blushers, it is a fact that actual skin care does not change all that much.

Our skin cells will continue to regenerate regularly, helped by a proper diet, and it's only logical that if we can slough off the dead surface cells and give a chance to the new cells to develop smoothly, we shall always minimise the dangers of clogging pores, hence spots, dry and flaky patches and sallow complexions from the left-over, tired old cells.

In other words, the 'cleanse, stimulate and nourish' formula remains the only basic skin care routine to follow, adapted to individual complexions by choosing the products which suit them best.

At whatever time, and under whatever circumstances you go to bed, take that make-up off. Even if you belong to the soap and water brigade as I do, start by using a cream or milk remover – all brand removers are made specially to dissolve our 'gilding' ingredients. Left overnight, your make-up (or even the day's dirt without it) will clog your pores, dilate them, and so encourage an orange-peel complexion, plus spots. Never leave your mascara on. Apart from anything else, nothing is more ageing and unattractive to anyone (including the milkman) than the sight of baggy panda eyes first thing in the morning. Now wash with soap and water if you like the freshness this induces, but whether you do or not, you should always use a freshener for a final cleanse and brace. A skin freshener contains no alcohol and is mild enough for dry skins. A skin tonic is alcohol-based and ideal for greasy skins, particularly younger ones. If it stings when used neat, dilute it by adding a few drops straight from the bottle on to a pad of cotton wool wrung out in water.

Spread on a face mask every so often; this can be a real face-saver on a 'morning after' and the perfect reviver if you are going out and feel depressed by your looks after a long hard day. There are numerous excellent masks on the market for all different types of skin, but I could recommend my own simple home-made version, which is a half and half mixture of kaolin and magnesium carbonate, mixed into a paste with calamine lotion (all readily and cheaply available from local chemists). You can make enough for three or four packs and store it in an airtight jar for a fortnight or so. Spread the mask on generously and try to think serious thoughts while it sets – the effect is lost if you break into a grin. After 15 minutes or so, ease off the hardened pack with cotton wool drenched in tepid water, taking care not to drag your skin. Always stick to tepid water on your face: water which is either too hot or too cold encourages broken veins.

The third stage of a regular facial routine should be to nourish the skin – on the little and often principle, because it can only absorb a small amount of 'food' at one time. You can probably save pounds by cutting down on the actual quantity of creams you use. But it is essential to keep skin soft and moist so that the inevitable 'expression' lines of time don't set in harshly. An extra skin-feeding session should also be held before stepping into the bath, so that the steam opens up the pores and speeds up the process. Skins must be nourished throughout the day with a film of moisturiser, or even a light night cream, under make-up, but let it dry well before applying a foundation, otherwise it will not blend in smoothly. Apply extra moisturiser round your eyes and over your neck during the day if you can, because for some reason these two areas dry out more during the day than during the night. A last tip: a tumblerful of hot water first thing in the morning – as you totter from bed to bathroom – and last thing at night works wonders. Disgusting, but effective!

I personally prefer to use cosmetics and beauty-care products which are made from natural ingredients. More and more people today are exploring this field because they prefer to avoid the risk of allergies, or simply because they do not wish to use products based on animal ingredients (which is my own reasoning). Some helpful addresses are included on page 50 for those who wish to look into this subject more fully.

Beauty is more than a question of make-up – in fact this is the least important and most evanescent aspect of looking your best. What you eat has a pronounced effect on your skin. Cigarette smoking, alcohol, late nights and an irregular diet will produce a face that would certainly not inspire a Trojan army. No one should feel that they are too plain or too vain not to pay great attention to making the best of their appearance. It is an aspect of self-value which can have the most uplifting effect, if you set about a 'beauty programme' with determination and regularity. None of this need cost a fortune: there is no call to spend unwisely on expensive products.

If you have time to spare, start by trying out some simple home remedies (several excellent ideas are contained in the letters which follow). If your arms and thighs are rough and blotchy, your circulation needs a boost, buy a loofah and give yourself a good rub down while you steam in a hot bath. If you have hard patches of skin on your elbows, knees or heels (and what working woman hasn't), use any clear, cheap oil – sunflower, sesame, nut or corn – and rub it into your skin *before* getting into the bath. Work it in while soaking, then just wash with soap as usual. Tie up a handful of oatmeal bran in a muslin bag (use an old nylon stocking if muslin doesn't fall readily into your grasp) and float that in the water to help soften it. It is quite extraordinary how an improvement in the texture of your skin encourages you to improve on other specific problems, such as shedding a few upholstering pounds, or brightening up a jaded complexion. The following pages offer you personal care tips, exercise plans, and diet information, for the time when you decide to stop nature taking its unwitting course, and tend more carefully your own little patch of self!

They've invented false hair, false teeth, false eyelashes – even artificial limbs. When are they going to come up with a false face – yes, a complete mask to hide all those tell-tale wrinkles, and especially bags under the eyes?

Mrs M. Wright, Worcester.

Well, plastic surgeons have pretty nifty knives these days and it takes the smallest of operations to get rid of those bags if you're really fed up with carrying them around. But first pay a visit to your GP and find out if your kidneys are a bit sluggish. Infused teabags allowed to cool down, then placed on closed lids should help to reduce the morning-after-the-night-before baggy look, and if the swelling is due to drying, I know of no quicker remedy than to peel and grate some raw potato, wrap it up in gauze, lie down and press the packed gauze to your closed eyes. Don't forget to rinse off the potato starch with lots of cool water after a quarter of an hour or so. And remember that all types, shapes and sizes of girl appeal to the equally varied opposite sex. The heavy-eyed Lauren Bacall types have masses of devoted admirers.

Working late in the hotel trade and often on duty again at 8 am the next day, I find my eyes puffing up and feeling irritated. Does the answer lie with make-up or should I try, say, a sauna bath for a general tone-up? I don't want to seem vain but I like to look smart and well-groomed for my job.

Mrs J. Fairclough, Plymouth.

There is nothing vain about wanting to make the best of oneself. Puffy red lids could spell a slight infection or an allergy to certain kinds of make-up. Ask your doctor because certain drops could clear up this condition in a few days. Sauna baths are stimulating and a marvellous skin toner and cleanser – try one and see if you enjoy it.

I am 16 and feel very self-conscious because I have most unflattering, deep brown-red freckles covering my face mostly around my eyes. In these days when a clear natural complexion looks best, I find these not only a disadvantage but extremely upsetting. Could you recommend a way to get rid of these freckles or recommend some make-up to disguise them?

J. Lewis, Ryde, Isle of Wight.

I'm afraid pigmentation is almost impossible to change with creams and potions. Your sunnier climate could be responsible for your freckles so the protection of a large floppy hat on sunny days may slow down any increase. Two friends of mine who haven't a freckle between them now, have these vital tips. Mix a teaspoonful of freshly grated horse-radish with a tablespoonful of milk. Leave to stand for an hour before using daily as a face mask, night and morning, for two weeks. Cover fresh elderberries with cold distilled water and leave to stand overnight. Strain and wash your face with the liquid. Continue daily until the freckles diminish. I guess the texture of your skin is beautiful, so don't be discouraged – wear colours which tone with it, such as greens, golds and blues. In general I don't think you need worry too much if you combine these applications with a careful watch on the dress colours you choose.

Could you please help me with a beauty problem which I know I share with many girls? I have the embarrassment of having hair around my nipples. I cut them with nail scissors as I have heard plucking them is not advisable, but it grows back to a dark stubble. Could I use a mild hair-removing cream in this area?

Miss E. A., Dagenham, Essex.

This isn't an unusual problem. A little facial hair-removing cream, used occasionally, should do no harm at all and the effect of this can be reinforced by Hair Stop Jelly – for the face. This is a 12-year-old Swiss product now obtainable direct from Beauchamp Marketing Ltd, 111 Fulham Road, London SW3 6RP. After using a depilatory, daily application of Hair Stop makes the hair grow finer and finer. It is expensive, but after a few months it needs to be applied only once a week.

Some time ago I read in a newspaper of a lady consultant who specialised in make-up to cover facial birthmarks. I have lost her name and address, so can you help me, as I would like to take my daughter to see her?

Mrs C. B., Boston, Lincs.

The lady you're referring to is Mrs Doreen Savage Trust, who worked hard for 12 years to establish a Camouflage Service within the National Health Service to help people with facial and bodily disfigurements. However, since this inquiry was first received, the situation has improved on a national level enormously. The British Red Cross Society has branches in each county, and attached to each is a Beauty Care Organiser or Welfare Officer who organises voluntary help in her area, concerned with beauty care and cosmetic camouflage. There are also cosmetic camouflage specialists trained by the Red Cross at many hospitals. A GP can put patients in touch with this service and the patient is advised as to what creams to use and how to apply them.

Covermark is a useful preparation, distributed by Medexport, and available from 76 Wells Street, London W1P 3RE (01 580 6375). If you contact this address, Medexport will advise you whether a visit or two is necessary to show you how to apply the product, or refer you to a suitable specialist for advice. If you feel that a private con-

sultation would be useful, contact Stephen Glass Face Facts, 76 George Street, London W1 (01 486 8287), who will be able to advise individual cases.

Can you recommend something that will make my eyelashes grow? They are practically non-existent. I have tried false ones, but I can't get used to them. I have also tried mascara with filaments in but this is not much good either as one has to have something to put it on.

Mrs E. A. Charles, Llanelli, Camarthen.

Smear castor oil on your lashes – it helps prevent the ends from drying and breaking off and will darken them too. But make sure you remove all trace of it at night or you could wake up with puffy lids.

★★★★★★★★★★★★★★★★★★★★★★★★★★★★★★★★
★ *For those who find it difficult to apply mas-* ★
★ *cara to an even depth, here is a very simple* ★
★ *tip. Look down into the mirror and brush the* ★
★ *eyelashes upwards – it works every time.* ★
★★★★★★★★★★★★★★★★★★★★★★★★★★★★★★★★

I read recently about vitamin E cosmetics, but the newspaper concerned did not say where to buy them. Some American friends visiting London at the moment think the oil and cream are fantastic; in America even young girls are using them for blemishes, vaccination marks, etc. Surely someone is selling them in this country?

Mrs P. de Courcy, London W2.

According to Dr Alloys Tappel, American food researcher and Professor at the University of California, vitamin E can delay the ageing process of the body cells. When eaten in the form of wheat germ (you can get this at any health food store) sprinkled over your food, it is nerve-nourishing and energy-giving as well as supposedly increasing sexiness and fertility. Used on one's skin, vitamin E helps to heal and eradicate scars.

Your local chemist shop may well stock one of the new products containing vitamin E, but should you have any difficulties, write to Tiki Cosmetics, enclosing a sae for details and prices (they make a high potency vitamin E oil which is good for skin massages, besides other beauty products containing the vitamin and herbs). Alternatively, try Hymosa Products Ltd (addresses at the end of this chapter). If you want to economise, you can always enrich any cream you have by stirring one or two vitamin E capsules straight into it.

I have heard recently of a new type of leg make-up which doesn't come off in the water. I've tried several beauty counters but no one seems to have heard of it.

Miss G. Brown, Bow, London E3.

Any of the quick-tanning products such as Ambre Solaire's Duotan will help give you a permanent tan that doesn't come off in water. If you want a cover cream you can use Max Factor's Pan Cake in a range of eight shades or Elizabeth Arden's Covering Cream in Light, Medium or Dark. They will not come off in water if you don't rub them and you can help them stay on by dusting lightly with powder to set them before you go in the sea. Incidentally, these cover creams can be used very effectively on birth marks or stretch marks anywhere on the body. If you want to swim in your usual make-up, put it on, then wring out a pad of cotton wool in cold water and press it gently over your face and neck. Not only will the effect be glowingly natural but it should stay put even if you dive in the water.

Is it possible to find out how many choices of spectacles are available through the National Health Service? Some opticians seem very off-hand about them and only stock two or three styles. I have asked many people and they all say the same – there is no choice. Is it because there is not enough profit for the optician, or are there only a few to choose from? I am a widow on a pension and have to consider very carefully every expense.

Ursula Payne, Andover, Hants.

How I hate off-hand, unhelpful people, and there seems to be a crowd of them around. There are, in fact, six styles of NHS spectacle frames to choose from. A few look rather alike but the plastic frames are available in six colours – light-brown mottles, flesh, crystal, black, and ice blue, and there are quite a few shades of 'gold'-rimmed professor-like ones, too. Ask your local area health authority for details of NHS glasses, including styles and prices, and then take this along to an optician.

P.S. The DHSS tell me now that you should apply to your local Family Practitioner Committee if you have any queries about optical, dental, or GP services. A further useful address is the Association of Optical Practitioners, Bridge House, 233 Blackfriars Road, London SE1 (01 379 7016). Miss Susan Conrad will give all the advice she can – this is the

political and protective body for the ophthalmic and optical profession, so they should be able to give you good advice and information.

Please can you recommend something to cure sore and tender fingertips? This letter is a last resort. Visits to doctors, creams, lotions – I've tried them all. The soreness sometimes goes away for a while. Handling nylon or ironing is a misery. I'm 45 and have been told that perhaps it is because I am a vegetarian, but I have only had this trouble for a year and I've never eaten fish or poultry.

Mrs M. Wardle, Tipton, Staffs.

Your vegetarian diet shouldn't really be causing you the trouble but your circulation might need checking by your GP. You might, for example, have a touch of Raynaud disease which could cause this problem. You don't say whether you cut your nails a bit too short, or too close to the quick down the sides. If this is so, dip your fingertips daily into a little surgical spirit to harden the outer skin, then before you go to bed each night massage castor oil well into those nails and pads and wear a pair of shortie cotton gloves so you don't mess up the bedclothes. Never use glycerine on your nails as this is a mineral oil and could do them more harm than good.

Just lately, I have noticed that the skin on my neck is getting very dry and tending to wrinkle. And though I am not putting on weight elsewhere, I am developing something I never had before – a double chin. I suppose these are the inevitable signs of age (I am 45) and that I shall just have to grin and bear them, but can you suggest anything?

Mrs Pat Steel, Brentford, Middx.

Congratulations to a lady who is prepared to admit her age, and face up to dealing with it.

For some reason the skin on one's neck dries out at a high speed, so to remedy that crêpey texture – which is a real tell-tale sign when it comes to age – the skin must be fed nightly with skin food and protected during the day with frequent applications of moisturiser.

At bedtime, follow this routine as often as possible. Grease your neck thoroughly. I find sunflower oil or any other vegetable oil excellent. Then crumble a man-sized tissue into a ball, and with this rub the skin firmly, but always gently, until it's really warm and a healthy shade of pink. Now that the blood has come to the surface, join your thumbs and forefingers and go all over your neck with a firm pinch and push movement. Push, never pull, or you'll stretch the skin and use up irreplaceable elasticity. Most necks are very thirsty and absorb any excess grease. So this nightly beauty routine won't ruin the sheets.

For a sleeker jawline and to remove that double chin, smooth the oil up from your neck on to your face, then tuck your chin into your neck as far as possible and give that extra bulge of flesh a good going-over with that same firm pinch and push movement as you used on your neck. This time take bigger wodges of skin between your finger and thumb. Now raise your chin to its usual position (held straight with tips downwards) along the jawline from chin to earlobes, pressing up firmly on the actual jawbone. Repeat this a number of times. Finally, pinch and push the flesh along the edge of the jawbone too.

This odd-sounding routine showed results on my own face within 10 days. Never attempt to pinch and push your neck and chin(s) until you have creamed or oiled the skin.

Unless the man in your life has a reliable sense of humour, I would keep your beauty treatments out of sight. They could prove a bit too traumatic for him!

★★★★★★★★★★★★★★★★★★★★★★★★★★★★★
To reduce the risk of scarring when drying the skin of chicken pox patients, use a hair-dryer on a warm setting instead of a towel.

F.D. Hacket, Camborne, Cornwall.

I de-frost my freezer using a hand-held hair-dryer.

Mrs E. M. Fletcher, Port Erin, Isle of Man.

If your hairdryer has a cold setting, this can be used for drying nail varnish quickly.
★★★★★★★★★★★★★★★★★★★★★★★★★★★★★

I am a fashion buyer in a large retail store and my nails are flaking away in layers. They look so unsightly. Is there a cure?

Miss S. B., Cleveland.

My nails are continually splitting and break-ing, even though I wear rubber gloves to do housework. I've tried various nail-hardeners. Can you suggest anything to help?

Mrs L. D., Chelmsford.

Can you help me to stop biting my nails? I chew them all the time.

Mrs R. H., Harrogate.

I can offer no overnight miracle cure for flak-ing or splitting nails. It was not until I had finished my third bottle of Healthcrafts Nail Formula capsules that I began to notice a real improvement in my nails. These capsules can be bought at health stores or acquired by mail order (see address list). To do chores, I always smooth on hand cream and wear cotton gloves inside rubber ones. As for compulsive biters, the best incentive is to meet a romantic man who wants to kiss your hand.

P.S. For those who live in the London area or can travel for an appointment, Miriam Davies offers individual advice, which includes infor-mation on diet, occupational hazards, and health problems. She also prescribes some of her own products. Contact her at 16 Whistler Walk, London SW10 0EP (01 351 2820).

I can't even switch on my TV set without damaging my nails. They flake and break con-tinually at the slightest contact and never seem to grow to any length. I'm always care-ful to wear rubber gloves in the kitchen and garden, and massage my nails when I cream my hands. Is there anything more I can do?

Mrs D. Cole, Coventry.

Yes. Make up a large bottle of surgical spirit and castor oil (approximately one dessert-spoonful of castor oil to a pint of the spirit). Shake it up well and keep a small jar of this concoction by your hand basin. Every time (and I mean every time) you wash your hands, dry them, then dip your fingertips into the jar and blot lightly with a tissue. The smell's pretty pungent – but you should see a marked improvement within a week to 10 days. Water encourages destructive 'bodies' to lodge in your nail and this odd mixture neutralises their effect.

I have always worn brightly-coloured nail varnish, but have recently noticed that my nails have lost their natural whiteness and are yellowy-brown. Can you suggest anything to remove the ugly stains?

Miss C. Aylin, Norwich.

It would seem that your nails have dried out, so you must leave off your varnish for a while to allow your nails to breathe and be nour-ished. There are a number of excellent nail treatment creams available: Sally Hansen's, or Proteinnail – available from Boots chemists. Massage the cream in – always be-fore washing your hands and before going to bed. Also buff your nails to boost your circu-lation, but remember, if you go backwards and forwards the nail will become too hot and split. Leave off varnish for as long as you can, and when you wear it again, remember to apply a base coat. It is kinder to add an extra coat or two of varnish between manicures rather than to use an oily polish remover more than once a week.

★★★★★★★★★★★★★★★★★★★★★★★★★★★★★★★★★★★★
★ *Nail varnish lasts longer if you keep it in the* ★
★ *refrigerator. It's also a good idea to wipe* ★
★ *round the inside of the lid with a cotton* ★
★ *wool-tipped stick dipped in nail varnish re-* ★
★ *mover, so that the screw-top doesn't become* ★
★ *jammed on to the bottle after use.* ★
★★★★★★★★★★★★★★★★★★★★★★★★★★★★★★★★★★★★

I seem to remember hearing that a cube of jelly once a day is good for your nails. I work in a pharmacy and women often ask for a remedy for splitting nails. Can you help, please?

Mrs R. E. Tomkins, Ipswich.

Flaking and brittle nails seem to be one of the ills of our time. I've found three or four kelp-and-pollen tablets a day more effective than a daily jelly cube. The tablets should be combined with Proteinnail Cream massaged into the nails and cuticles after washing the hands. But whatever the remedy, the results take months to show and treatment must be kept up. Proteinnail Cream can be bought from any branch of Boots chemists, and Pollen-Plus tablets containing pollen and kelp are obtainable from Dietmart Mail Order (address at the end of this chapter).

I've got this terrible complex about washing my hair – sometimes as often as two or three times a week. It's always been slightly greasy and I've heard it said that frequent washing makes it more greasy, but I still end up in the bathroom washing it yet again. I'm 17 and my hair is quite long.

Christine Denney, Norwich.

Every time you wash your hair and rub your scalp you stimulate your sebaceous glands which pour out grease. So go easy on your scalp when shampooing – try just to wash your hair *and be careful, too, when you brush your hair; tugging at or scraping the scalp merely stirs up the problem. A rigid diet will help: no fats, no cheese, no fried food of any kind. And the more rabbit-style salads you eat the better. A sulphur-based shampoo should also help. You can buy one called Selsun but your doctor could give you a prescription for one containing a larger quantity of sulphur. For fine greasy hair use Wella Set or brown ale as a setting lotion.*

To make a cheap and completely natural hair colorant, take a handful of blackberry leaves and the same amount of sage leaves. Boil them together in a pint of water for about 15–20 minutes. Allow to cool, then strain the juice into a jar, squeezing the leaves to extract all the juice. The straw-coloured liquid doesn't look like black hair dye, but it darkens the hair quite considerably when it's combed in. This recipe is used in the country, and has been for centuries, but with the advent of modern chemicals, women are forgetting the old recipes with natural ingredients. Since the discovery that some hair dyes may be harmful I think that there will be a demand for these natural means to change hair colour. I'm delighted with the results.

Miss F. C. Murray, Dalneigh, Inverness.

My husband was recently in hospital with a very bad skin rash. I have since found that this is because he is allergic to my hair, or the dye I use for it. After using many dyes and rinses, I find he is allergic to them all. My hair is beginning to go grey, mousy and dull. Do you know of anything I can use that won't affect my husband?

Mrs Jean Green, Grantham, Lincs.

If your husband is allergic to hair try wearing an all-hiding bed bonnet – a pretty frilly one, mind you – or keep your distance. Let's hope

he is allergic to something in the products you use. Try those made from natural ingredients which health stores either stock or can get for you. For instance, instead of dyeing your hair, use Sesonol's Organic Grey Gone. Follow the instructions carefully and gradually the grey will be restored to a natural colour. To improve the condition of your hair and give it a gloss, get one of Tiki's Herbal Shampoo packs, with a jar of matching herbal conditioner. Watch your diet, too: cut down on carbohydrates, eat as much fruit and raw vegetables as you can and take either H-Pantoten tablets, Orovite vitamin B/C or if you can't get these, kelp (seaweed) tablets each day. You should notice an improvement in a few weeks. These products are available at health stores.
P.S. Sometimes skin allergy reactions can be more simply treated. A non-specific skin rash,

Pruritus

I know exactly what pruritus sufferers go through with this itching because at times, and for no apparent reason, I suddenly get it too. I have even raised weals on my thighs, arms, tummy or wherever this 'pruritus' has attacked me.

No prescription given to me by a doctor helped one iota, then, on one occasion, by accident and because I was in such a state of irritation, I poured too much eau de cologne over myself. First it burnt when it touched the scratch marks, then in a matter of a few minutes the itching had subsided almost everywhere, and where it hadn't I just sprinkled more cologne on, until it did.

I soon discovered that the cheapest cologne does the trick, and when I ran out of that once, I grabbed my husband's Menthol and that too worked beautifully. I do hope that my method will be the answer to others with a similar problem.

which your doctor may describe as pruritus can be a cause of tremendous discomfort (see above).

While browsing through a book of herbal remedies, I found a lotion to keep one's hair free of grease. The recipe is as follows: 1 sprig of marjoram, 1 teaspoon of salt, 4 drops of castor oil, ¼ pint buttermilk, 1 cup of beer, 1 egg yolk and ¼ pint of water. Bring water and salt to boil, add marjoram, mint, castor oil and beer and simmer for five minutes. Leave mixture to cool. Strain and add buttermilk and egg yolk. Use the lotion in small quantities, then rinse. I used it and passed it on to my friends who found it invaluable.

Mrs P. Linden, Manchester.

The best way to clean up hairbrushes is to soak them in a mixture of warm water and bleach – a teaspoon to a pint of liquid. Bristle brushes that have become too soft can sometimes be renovated if you soak them in vinegared water for several minutes.

Shoebrushes need soaking too once in a while to get rid of the build-up of dirty wax polish in the bristles. Here's a good way to avoid a sink rimmed with stubborn polish-bits at the end of the day: pour warm soapy water into a (watertight!) plastic bag, and let the brushes soak in that for a few hours. Then all you need to do is tip out the water and throw away the bag.

Bleaching and perming plays havoc with my baby-fine hair. I want it soft and shiny and ash-blonde but I need the body a perm gives.

Mrs P. Windle, Bristol.

I'm afraid that perming and bleaching still cannot be combined without drying out the hair. But you can minimise the damage by using 20 Volume Peroxide for the bleaching, such as Born Blonde Lightener by Clairol, and then putting on a non-peroxide-based toner, such as the Born Blonde Colorant. If in any doubt it is always best to consult a good hairdresser for expert advice on perming. Why not let your perm grow out and then achieve the body with a small hair-piece? Oil – castor, coconut, olive, almond – combed through your hair and then steamed into it by wrapping a wrung-out hot towel round your head for 10 minutes or so will recondition your hair but remember two points. (1) If your hair is bleached, oil will strip off the colour; (2) pour shampoo on to your oiled head and rub in before adding any water otherwise you'll find the oil difficult to remove. Lifetex is an excellent re-conditioner (available from hairdressers usually), because it lifts the outer scales and nourishes the hair, but regular use of a conditioner after each shampoo will restore lustre, too. If you need advice, write to Jo Clair, Clairol Division, Bristol Myers, Stonefield Way, South Ruislip, Middlesex HA4 0JN. (01 845 5541)

I have been on a diet and am reaching my goal weight but due to wearing a long-line bra and corset I have a brown ring round my middle. We go on holiday in a few weeks time and I want to wear a bikini but won't be able to until this problem is solved.

Mrs G. A. May, Newcastle-upon-Tyne.

When you're in the bath, scrub the brown mark energetically with a loofah using Innoxa's Skin Shampoo 41 or their Medicated Soap 41. A top layer of brownish dead skin should flake off in a few days. Don't worry – we have several layers, so there's plenty to spare. Towel dry, then, with a generous pad of cotton wool well dampened with Innoxa Solution 41, go over the darkened area, rubbing firmly. A facial mask applied round your middle and allowed to dry before washing it off will also help brighten dingy skin. After doing this a few times you could use an overnight tanner such as Quick Tan, or an instant one such as Sudden Tan or Piz Buin's Self Tan – take your pick, but when you put it on leave out the brown belt area completely. You'll find that quick-tanning products spread more easily if you apply a thin film of oil first. For your holiday and for the future, why not change over to shorter bras and compensate with better posture? You'll walk taller and more gracefully and feel much more comfortable.

P.S. Reading this letter reminds me to offer some general advice on measuring and choosing a bra.

41

The tape should be slipped around above the breasts, under the armpits. This will give you the 36 or 38 inch bit, then, depending on whether you carry all before you or have a broad back, you can gauge what size of cup you need.

Berlei's Minimiser model, which goes up to a double D, is a good make, and Selfridges of Oxford Street say that their most popular bra, going up to a 46 E fitting, is Doreen by Triumph. This style comes in a long length too, from 36 to 48 double D fitting.

My own choice is a French Empreinte, wired underneath each cup with a definite separation in the middle. Rose Lewis, 40 Knightsbridge, London SW1 (01 235 6885), is one of the few importers of this range to England. But remember that bra buying is a strictly personal and not a postal purchase: Rose Lewis only sells bras after an individual fitting.

The address of Berlei is Berlei House, Bath Road, Slough SL1 4AT (75 34505), and Triumph International is at 91 New Bond Street, London W1Y O6J (01 629 0866).

I was bothered with rheumatism and was always in pain, until I tried this treatment: I began by putting a handful of salt in a warm bath and relaxing in it for five minutes until my pores were opened, then I massaged myself with a generous helping of table salt until my body tingled. For a facial I mixed a little salt with olive oil in equal proportions and gently massaged my face and throat. The olive oil soothes the skin, whilst the salt removes impurities. I am 61 years old and I still have no wrinkles and I never need make-up.

Mrs C. Hamill, Coatbridge, Lanarks.

I think you must also have a rubbery textured skin and a very pleasant unworrying nature which hasn't furrowed your face over the years. All the same it's interesting how many people have gone back to natural remedies. You can use cooking salt, sea salt, or even Epsom salts – they're all effective, but make sure the bath water isn't too hot. After your facial, a final wipe over with a half and half mixture of rosewater and witch hazel will take away any left-over tacky feeling on your skin.*

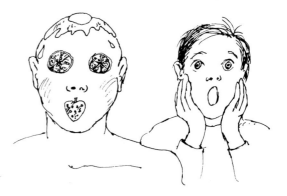

I've been searching for a recipe for a home-made face pack. My mother half-remembers one which contained oatmeal and egg white, but she cannot remember the other ingredients. Perhaps you can fill the gap. Also, have you any other recipes for home-made face packs? I love to experiment.

Barbara Field, Hackney, London E9.

The juice of a lemon should lace the oatmeal and egg white into a good face pack, but I rely on the following well-proven one: a half and half mixture of kaolin powder and magnesium carbonate worked into a smooth paste with calamine lotion. I find it more economical to put the kaolin and magnesium carbonate in large jars and more practical to mix about three dessertspoonsful of each with the calamine lotion and keep it in a screw-top jar. This can be used daily on a greasy skin, or once every 10 days or so for a dry skin. If you browse round your local library you should find several good books with recipes for home-made cosmetics; a few suggestions are given in the booklist at the end of this chapter.

Here's a tip for getting rid of dandruff or an itchy scalp. Simply put two teaspoonsful of rosemary leaves (fresh or dried) and two tea-spoonsful of sage into a teapot. Add boiling water and let it infuse. When it's cool pour over your head. Rub castor oil or coconut oil into your scalp, leave for 10 minutes then wash off. It will leave your hair shiny and manageable. After using any kind of oil to condition or treat your hair always apply the shampoo neat, before adding water, other-wise you won't get the grease off.

Miss Clare Knight, Cheltenham, Glos.

I wondered if you knew of a brand of tanning aid containing natural ingredients.

Sally Simons, Burnham, Bucks.

For a natural tanning product it would be hard to beat either Alo's Fashion Tan, made from the Aloe Vera *plant, or Claire Swann's Sun Lotion. Not only does it help to bronze the skin without burning but, on my skin anyway, it seems to have the added advantage of preventing any freckling effect. All Claire Swann's products contain a wide assortment of herbs, including rose oil which is made from rose petals. These kinds of special beauty products cannot be mass-produced, so you won't find them in health shops. For a list of these natural products and their prices write to Mrs C. Swann, 14 Ferncroft Avenue, London NW3.*

Could you recommend some natural beauty products I could make myself, as well as those I can buy in the shops? I would also like to know if there is a book on the subject becuse I'm a vegetarian and would like if possible to carry my feelings about using natural non-animal products through to cosmetics.

Mrs F. Bakers, Yorks.

Among many excellent books on the market are: Your Health and Beauty Book *by Clare Maxwell-Hudson, published by Macdonald and Jane and* Natural Appeal *by Suzy Kendall and Pat Wellington, published by Dent. Both books contain simple 'kitchen' recipes, and both firms also have a range of products available by mail order. Send a sae to Clare Maxwell-Hudson Cosmetics Ltd, PO Box 457, London NW2 4BR, or to Kendall Wellington and Co., 1 Balfour Place, London W1Y 5HR. Both firms will send details.*

I'm 27 and must have nearly bought a chemist's shop trying to get rid of blackheads. What can I do?

Mrs S.P., Ipswich.

Open pores and blackheads follow each other in a vicious circle: open pores encourage blackheads, and blackheads stretch open pores. The essential thing with a blackhead-prone skin is to keep it oil free and scrupu-lously clean. Kathleen Corbett, 21 South Mol-ton Street, London W1 (01 493 5905), makes a strong grease solvent and open pore lotion. Use it only on the oily part of your skin and counteract any resulting dryness with a touch of moisturiser.

If you're determined to clear them up your-self, then do be gentle. Coax blackheads to the surface of the skin with a pad of cotton wool soaked in hot water – then wind a clean tissue around the tips of your fingers and gently ease out. Keep your nails completely sheathed and don't force a stubborn black-head out, try again to loosen it. Go very steady with metal extractors. Always use an astringent (or even a touch of surgical spirit) after this session to help shrink the open pores.

About two years ago you recommended some slimming tablets which contain an ingredient similar to cider vinegar. I took some and they worked wonders. But unfortunately I lost the address of the manufacturers and the bottles have been thrown out. I'm having to fight the battle of the bulge again and wondered if you could remind me where I can get these tablets – and how much they cost. They were the only thing that worked for me after years of trying to lose weight.

Mrs S. Kelly, Surbiton, Surrey.

Yes, these 'combination' capsules of lecithin, cider vinegar, kelp and vitamin B6 do help to speed up the metabolism and make it easier to shed the poundage but don't for one moment stop counting calories. I believe I mentioned Cida Ho, made by Carter Bros, Glen Laboratories, Shipley, Yorks BD17 7AQ, but there are some other versions of the same mixture called Formula 3 + 6 made by Food Supplement Co, and Ciderslim B6 which is a Healthlife product. All are obtain-able from Dietmart, Unit 18, Goldsworth Park Trading Estate, Woking, Surrey GU21 3BJ.

I've always tried to look smart but in the last year or two I've put on a lot of weight. My legs get swollen and my doctor has told me this is due to both weight and diet. I feel I need vitamins and hope you will advise me. I would like to take honey, but it seems to disagree with me. Is it available in capsule form? I have been told you take 'youth pills'. If this is true can you tell me what they are?

Mrs A. Jackson, Whitstable, Kent.

I have to smile at some of the rumours that go around about me. I would say I looked 'lively' rather than 'youthful'. And as for pills, I take daily two or three Healthcrafts Super Vitamin E capsules, and six Celaton CH3 Tri-Plus tablets, made by Celaton Laboratory Research Ltd, 128 High Street, Edgware, Middx. If honey affects you so so badly, honey capsules are unlikely to be any more compatible. Maybe your system doesn't need as much honey as other people's – and it's no good pretending honey doesn't add to the inches – so by-pass it. An excellent all-round vitamin supplement comes in Gev-E-Tabs. All these products should be available from your local health shop.

I remember some years ago reading of your remedy for burns on legs, never imagining I would need the treatment. Now I find after spending much of Winter (and Spring) in front of the fire I have scars which look very unsightly. Can you help, as with Summer coming I want to get rid of them?

Mrs J. Pickard, Birmingham.

Playing with fire tends to leave its trace – but this kind can be remedied. Mix the juice of a lemon, the white of an egg and enough mag-nesium carbonate to make a smooth paste. Spread this over the scar marks and let it set – then wash it off with lots of tepid water. Repeat as often as necessary. If your skin has become like parchment, and flaky, put some moisturising cream on under the mask.

I have a small daughter and because of all the washing I do my hands have become very rough. The hand creams I have tried do nothing for them. Can you please suggest a good but inexpensive hand cream?

Mrs B. Scholfield, Rochdale, Lancs.

You need to buy a lanolin-based cream then add sweet almond oil and/or castor oil so it becomes an ultra-nourishing concoction. But remember to massage some into your hands every time you've washed and thoroughly dried your hands – one application at night won't help your poor skin at all. And remember to wear cotton-lined rubber gloves when you do all that washing.

★★★★★★★★★★★★★★★★★★★★★★★★★★★★★★★★

Before working on his car engine, my husband smears the smallest amount of margarine into his hands. This prevents grease from becoming ingrained and is much cheaper than an expensive barrier cream.

Mrs J.L. Thomas, Crayford, Kent.

I always scrape my nails over a softish piece of soap before gardening. A quick scrub with a nail brush afterwards removes all the dirt.

Mrs G. Schofield, Derby.

A splash of 50 vol peroxide in a small bowl of hot water adds to the effect of pumice stone and nail brush.

★★★★★★★★★★★★★★★★★★★★★★★★★★★★★★★★

For a good, natural anti-wrinkle face lotion mix together one tablespoon of glycerine, one of rosewater, and three of honey and blend

for 45 seconds in a liquidiser, or use a rotary whisk. Put the mixture into a jar with a lid and it will keep for six months in a cool place.

Mrs B. McGrath, London SE22.

I agree that's an excellent concoction and for other recipes I suggest you get a copy of the paperback, Feed Your Face *by Dian Dincin Buchman, published by Duckworth. It is a fascinating book and I'm sure you'll want to try some home-made natural beautifiers.*

I'm only 35 but was horrified on holiday to notice I was going flabby. In particular, under my arms, on the inner thighs, and across my tummy. Are there any exercises I can concentrate on to get these areas firm again before it's too late? If I start now I should be all set for next year!

Miss E. Danby, Southampton.

I've seen some impressive results on underarm flab on people who over the past 10 months have persevered with the following exercise devised by beauty culturist Esther Fairfax. Stand straight with your feet slightly apart, lift your arms to shoulder height and stretch them out from either side. Now clench your fists and, keeping your arms absolutely taut, make small backward circles with your arms. Of course, the faster the circles, the more taut the arms, and the more frequent the exercise, the sooner you'll see the results. P.S. For all you want to know about spot reducing there are two books out written by Esther Fairfax, the first called Help Yourself to Health *published by Macdonald and Jane's, and the second,* The Reluctant Keep Fitter, *published by Whittet Books. If speed is what you're after, try* F40: Fitness in 40 Minutes a Week, *by Dr Malcolm Carruthers and Alistair Murray, a Futura paperback.*

I followed the *Yoga for Health* TV series and would like to keep up the exercises. Can you recommend a book on the subject?

Mrs H., Co. Tyrone, Ulster.

There is no doubt that a supple and slim body keeps its youthful bounce, which in turn must keep you feeling good. But just as you should never jerk into an exercise (the yoga attitude of coaxing your spine to be a little more flexible each day can be taken up whatever age and shape you are) don't launch into an exercise schedule so strenuous that you could never keep it up. The book Yoga For Health *by Richard L. Hittleman, published by Hamlyn, explains the importance of breathing correctly and gives exercises which can improve your physical and mental well-being. Practise the exercises you are personally in need of and which are best suited to you.*

Since I had my second baby I cannot stand the sight of myself in the mirror. I'm a mass of stretch marks. How can I get rid of them?

J. Somerfield, Redbourne, Humberside.

There's an effective treatment to prevent scarring from recent minor burns, including sunburn, grazes, cuts and spot scars, that might

Shape-up here

Stomach-flattening and waist-slimming exercises

Lie flat on your back, legs stretched out on the floor with a cushion between your feet. Slowly raise legs still holding the cushion. Don't bend your knees. When your legs have reached right angles to your body very slowly lower them again. The strongest pull is when you are about a foot from the floor.

Lie flat on the floor and, unless you can do this exercise easily, tuck your feet under the edge of a low chair. Place hands on thighs and very slowly raise your head, shoulders and gradually your body until you are sitting upright. Take a deep breath and go down again slowly trying to touch the floor with each vertebra separately. Repeat five or six times. Finally try it without a chair.

Stand with arms wide apart above head, feet apart and knees stiff. Swing down so that right fingertips touch left toe and the left arm swings away back and above your head. Swing your left arm down to touch your right toe and continue pendulum fashion beginning with 10 times and working up to 20 times. Inhale as you touch left toe, breathe out as you touch right toe.

To remove a 'spare tyre'

Stand with your feet apart and parallel, hands clasped above your head. Bend as far as possible to the right side, keeping your hips steady. Straighten and bend to the other side.

Stand erect with feet together. Put your right arm up over your head and curl your fingers round your left ear. Now bend over to the left as far as you can go as though you want to touch the floor; straighten up and repeat with other hand. Don't bend forwards or back-wards as you go to the side.

Lie flat on your back with hands stretched above your head. Push left leg down as far as possible and your left arm up as far as you can. Relax and push the right arm and leg. Breathe in as you push, and out as you relax.

To reduce a large seat

Stand erect, arms by your sides. Now tighten your buttocks as hard as you can, tuck your tail underneath hard and pull your tummy muscles in and up towards your ribs and spine. Then relax buttocks and tummy and tilt your tail out as much as you can. Repeat standing, and then on all fours.

Sit on a hard floor, back straight, arms out-stretched forwards and legs spread out. Now in little 'hitching' movements bump across the floor from one side of the room to the other. Without turning round, bump back again to where you started. Be careful to bump along and not slide.

Sit on the floor, knees up to chin, hands clasped around knees, then rock backwards as far as you can so that your shoulders are on the floor and your seat is in the air. Rock forwards to sitting position again, and repeat.

Hip and thigh reducers

Lie on the floor, legs straight, arms out-stretched at shoulder level. Now raise your right leg to a right-angle with the knee stiff. Keeping your shoulders flat on the floor, lower your leg over to your left side and try to touch your left hand. Raise your right leg and lower back into position then repeat with left leg to right side. Count four and do one movement on each count, stretching hard every time.

Lie on a hard floor, on your left side supported by your elbow, then raise your legs off the floor. Swing your right leg out and your left leg back, then reverse and repeat in a rhythmic scissors movement. Lie on your right side and repeat.

help, called Alo Burn Ointment, a gel made from the natural oils of the Aloe Vera *cactus plant. It is available direct from Malcolm Lyons, 63 Sloane Avenue, London SW3 3DH. A more expensive hand-made treatment is a regenerative cream made of 100 per cent pure plant extract, which helps to prevent scars and eliminate stretch marks during preg-nancy. Face Cream 'M' comes from Marguer-ite Maury, Suite 101, Park Lane Hotel, Pic-cadilly, London W1A 4UA. Getting rid of stretch marks after birth needs patience. A holiday in the sun and swimming in salt water will help, but you could also invest in a French product called Helancyl, made from an ex-tract of ivy. You have to scrub every day under the shower using a special massage kit for months, but eventually you will notice the improvement.*

My job has finally got me down – my two feet are virtually flat. My arches can't stand up to the endless hours of running around and standing at work. Of course I have to keep going, but it's so painful. Have you any remedy for this as I know you **are** often on your feet all day?

Joanna Drown, Wolverhampton.

A great friend of mine cured this very problem by rolling a golf ball under each foot and gripping it firmly with the toes. Apparently

47

it's excruciating to begin with, but persevere and it does work.

I've sprained my ankle badly and the swelling is taking ages to subside. I've got rather good legs so I wonder if you know of some way to get rid of the swelling?

Mrs B. Jones, Leeds.

Mix a white of an egg, and three tablespoons of vinegar into a paste with a handful of flour. Put this mixture on some greaseproof paper. Place some gauze against the swelling, then overturn the paste on to it, and bandage tightly over the greaseproof paper. Keep wrapped up as long as possible – overnight would be ideal – and by morning you should have returned to more normal proportions.

Being cursed with a sensitive skin, I react very badly to all insect bites and stings and even an anti-histamine cream seems to have little effect. I was therefore delighted to find in an ancient 'household hints' book that the cure is to rub a slice of raw onion gently on the bite. Shortly after reading this I was badly stung by a wasp, ran for my onion and found it soothed the pain immediately and reduced the swelling. I can recommend this hint for the most sensitive skins, and hope that it will be of some use to all your many readers.

Miss A. V. Stacy, Sutton, Surrey.

P.S. Equally effective is hydrotherapy: to counteract stings hold whatever part was stung under running cold water – I know this works ever since I sat on a wasps' nest! I have proven it time and again, since I seem to make a habit of treading on drowsy wasps on summer holidays.

I have two good tips for pregnant mums, which both worked for me. To prevent stretch marks, every night from 3–4 months onwards before getting into bed, rub olive oil into your skin. (I haven't any marks at all.) To stop morning sickness, eat a dry cream cracker before getting out of bed, even to spend a penny, and also before having a cup of tea or anything else. Also, if you have that queasy feeling during the day, eat a dry cream cracker. I used to keep a tin of them in my office drawer at work, and it really worked.

Mrs D. Bussell, Bournemouth, Dorset.

I do plenty of walking because I have two small children, not yet at school, who need fresh air and exercise. But my heels have become so hard that my husband will not let me put my feet on him at night. By Winter, I must either soften these heels or buy a hot water bottle. Help!

Mrs Irene Sparham, Sutton-in-Ashfield, Notts.

Before going to bed, soak your feet in hot water to soften the skin. Dry well, then squeeze about 10 drops of fresh lemon into a teaspoonful of lanolin cream and massage well into your heels. After a week or two of this treatment they should be soft again and you can back up that nightly treatment by rubbing some baby oil on before you put your tights on in the morning. Wear a pair of socks in bed to avoid greasing the sheets. Until your feet are soft enough to suit your husband again, his comment will probably be, 'Bless your little cotton socks.' That can't be bad.

I am 84 years old, and when I was young my Dad and Mum had some old fashioned remedies; there were eight children. First, for a sore throat, a small piece of butter rolled in sugar was sucked. For a stiff neck we'd be given a woollen sock to wind round our necks and off to bed. For a chesty cold we would wear a piece of brown paper with heated

Russian tallow applied to our chests, and it would be kept on for two days till the warmth made us better. For a toothache a deep saucer would be filled with brown sugar, vinegar and pepper, and we'd put our faces in it till our skin was hot, and then we'd go straight to bed, keeping the heat in our faces on the pillow and by morning the relief was great. For earache we would take a small piece of onion from the centre or the core, and heat it up and apply it to the ear while warm – it gives a lovely feeling. We were a big family and I've passed on most of my remedies; we couldn't afford doctors in those times but we got through. Please excuse my writing as I have arthritis and I've just had my wedding ring sawn off. With an old fashioned name, yours truly,

Mrs Alice Harriet Amelia Morrissey, Lowestoft, Suffolk.

Useful Addresses

Beauchamp Marketing Ltd (makers of Hair Stop Jelly),
111 Fulham Road, London SW3 6RP.

Medexport (makers of Covermark),
76 Wells Street, London W1P 3RE.
(01 480 6375)

Stephen Glass Face Facts,
76 George Street, London W1. (01 486 8287)

Tiki Cosmetics (vitamin E oil and other products),
Shipley, Yorkshire BD17 7AQ.

Hymosa Products Ltd (Vit-E Creme and other products),
39 Wales Farm Road, London W3 6XH.
(01 992 8656)

Innoxa (for Innoxa 41 range of anti-acne products),
202 Terminus Road, Eastbourne, East Sussex BN21 3DF. (0323 639671)

Rose Lewis (bra and lingerie specialist),
40 Knightsbridge, London SW1.
(01 235 6885)

Berlei (for a range of large-size bras),
Berlei House, Bath Road, Slough SL1 4AT.
(75 34505)

Triumph International (for a range of large-size bras),
91 New Bond Street, London W1Y O6J.
(01 629 0866)

Clare Maxwell-Hudson Cosmetics (natural cosmetics),
PO Box 457 London NW2 4BR.

Kendall Wellington and Co (natural cosmetics),
1 Balfour Place, London W1Y 5HR.

Claire Swann (natural cosmetics including tanning products),
14 Ferncroft Avenue, London NW3. (01 435 9581)

Kathleen Corbett (beauty treatments, including acne),
21 South Molton Street, London W1. (01 493 5905)

Dietmart (for Ciderslim B6 and other Health-life products),
Unit 18, Goldsworth Park Trading Estate, Woking, Surrey GU21 3BJ.

Carter Bros (for Cida Ho and other health products),
Glen Laboratories, Shipley, Yorks BD17 7AQ.

Miriam Davis (nail treatments),
16 Whistler Walk, London SW10 0EP. (01 351 2820)

Healthcrafts (Nail Formula and other natural products),
Healthways House, 45 Station Approach, West Byfleet, Surrey KT14 6NE. (Byfleet 41133)

Sesonol Hair Products (including SF12, hair colour restorer, and other organic hair food products),
Specialist Factors Ltd, PO Box 14, Worthing, Sussex BN12 4QR.

Malcolm Lyons (Alo Burn Ointment),
63 Sloane Avenue, London SW3 3DH.

Marguerite Maury (**Face Cream 'M'**),
Suite 101, Park Lane Hotel, Piccadilly, London W1A 4UA.

Helancyl
Concept Pharmaceuticals Ltd, Russell House, 59-61 High Street, Rickmansworth, Herts WD3 1EZ. (87 79388)

Clairol Hair Products,
Jo Clair, Clairol Division, Bristol Myers, Stonefield Way, South Ruislip Middx. HA4 0JN. (01 845 5541)

Further Useful Addresses

A. Nelson and Co Ltd (homoeopathic products),
215-223 Coldharbour Lane, London SW9 8RU.

Culpeper Ltd (herbal products),
Hadstock Road, Linton, Cambridge CB1 6NJ, and 21 Bruton Street, London W1X 7DA.

Martha Hill Beauty Care (natural cosmetics),
The Old Vicarage, Laxton, near Corby, Northants NN17 3AT. (Bulwick 259)

Almay (Hypo-allergenic cosmetics),
PO Box 17, 225 Bath Road, Slough SL1 4AW.

Beauty Without Cruelty (natural cosmetics),
37 Avebury Avenue, Tonbridge, Kent TN9 1TL. (0732 365291)

The Body Shop (mail order for oils and other natural products),
1 Crane Street, Chichester, West Sussex PO19 1LH.

Faith Products (herbal cosmetics),
52-56 Albion Road, Edinburgh EH7 5QZ (031 661 0900)

Creighton Cosmetics (natural cosmetics),
Creighton Laboratories Ltd, Water Lane, Storrington, Pulborough, Sussex RH20 3DP. (Storrington 3452)

Yin Yang Natural Products Ltd,
45 Chalton Street, London NW1 1HY. (01 387 0456)

Clarins (a range of balancing cosmetics for out-of-sorts or hypo-allergenic skins),
Ligne Douceur, c/o Joan Collings, 85 Pennine Drive, London NW2 1NN. (01 458 2172)

Alo Cosmetics (for Alo Fashion tan),
1 Belmore Parade, 768 Uxbridge Road, Hayes, Middx UB4 0RU. (01 573 6057)

Food Supplement Company (for all kinds of vitamin and health products),
Seymour House, 79/81 High Street, Godalming, Surrey CU7 1AW. (Godalming 28021)

Micheline Arcier (aromatherapy treatments),
7 William Street, Knightsbridge, London SW1X 9HL. (01 235 3545)

Eve Taylor's Institute of Natural Therapies and Aesthetic Treatments,
22 Bromley Road, Catford, London SE6. (01 690 2149)

Ginseng (and other health products),
Mr Healthy-Buy, 2 Commercial Street, Shipley, W. Yorks BD18 3SR.

Mary Chess (perfumes, oils essences),
7 Shepherd Market, London W1Y 7HR. (01 629 5152)

Floris (beautiful soaps, perfumes, oils),
89 Jermyn Street, London SW1Y 6JH. (01 930 4136)

Aspall Cyder House,
Aspall Hall, Stowmarket, Suffolk IP14 6PD. (0728 860 510)

Hofels Pure Foods (natural supplements, sea salt, etc),
Woolpit, Bury St Edmunds, Suffolk IP30 9QS. (0359 40592)

Healthilife Ltd (makers of Ciderslim B6 capsules),
Customer Service Dept, Nesfield Street, Bradford BD1 3ET.

Joan Price's Face Place (make-up lessons, special treatments),
33 Cadogan Street, London SW3 2PP. (01 589 9062)

Power Health Foods Ltd (makers of Wolo products),
Power House, 4 Kirkland Street, Pocklington, Yorks YO4 2DE. (075 92 2595)

Vessen Ltd (suppliers of Biostrath, Animastrath and Tiger Balm),
Mansen House, 320 London Road, Hazel Grove, Stockport, Ches. SK7 4RF. (061 483 1235)

Danièle Ryman at Mme Maury (aromatherapy),
Suite 101, Park Lane Hotel, Piccadilly, London W1. (01 493 6630)

The Yoga For Health Foundation,
Ickwell Bury, Biggleswade SG18 9EF. (North Hill 271)

The Keep Fit Association,
16 Upper Woburn Place, London WC1H 0QG. (01 387 4349)

Weight Watchers (UK) Ltd,
635/7 Ajax Avenue, Slough, Berks SL1 4DB. (Slough 70711)

Useful Medical Organisations

The British Homoeopathic Association,
27a Devonshire Street, London W1N 1RJ. (01 935 2163)

Homoeopathic Development Foundation Ltd,
19a Cavendish Square, London W1M 9AD. (01 629 3204)

British School of Osteopathy,
London SW1. (01 930 4640)

The British Acupuncture Association,
34 Alderney Street, London SW1.

Hypnotherapy Centre,
67 Upper Berkeley Street, London W1H 7DH. (01 262 8852)

Hypnotherapy Consultations,
7a Chepstow Villas, London W11 3EE. (01 229 4726)

The Vegetarian Society,
53 Marloes Road, Kensington, London W8 6LA. (01 937 7739)

Women's Therapy Centre (for advice on anorexia, and any women's problems),
6 Mellor Gardens, London N7. (01 263 6209)

Useful Reading

Your Health and Beauty Book, Clare Maxwell-Hudson (Macdonald and Jane's).
A Woman's Book of Natural Beauty Secrets, Clare Maxwell-Hudson (Autumn Press/ Thorsons Publishing).
Natural Appeal, Suzy Kendall and Pat Wellington (Dent).

Kitty Little's Book of Natural Health and Beauty, Kitty Little (Penguin).
Feed Your Face, Dian Dincin Buchman (Duckworth).
Help Yourself to Health, Esther Fairfax (Macdonald and Jane's).
The Reluctant Keep Fitter, Esther Fairfax (Whittet Books).
F40: Fitness in Forty Minutes a Week, Dr Malcolm Carruthers and Alistair Murray (Futura paperback).
Yoga For Health, Richard L. Hittleman (Hamlyn).
The Face and Body Book, edited by Miriam Stoppard (Pan).
The Best of Good Health, Phoebe Phillips and Pamela Hatch (Pitman Publishing).
The Health and Fitness Handbook, Miriam Polunin (Windwood).
Vogue Natural Health and Beauty Book, Bronwen Meredith (Condé Nast).
Vogue Body and Beauty Book, Bronwen Meredith (Condé Nast).

For health books (only for devotees, because you need to open an account to get the best discount arrangement): **Newman Turner Publications Ltd,** Unit 18, Goldworth Park Trading Estate, Woking, Surrey GU21 3BJ. The same address also applies for Dietmart, the largest and most comprehensive suppliers of health foods and health products to those who have difficulty in obtaining goods locally. Write for a list of their supplies.

3
Social and Entertaining

One of my aims in putting together this book is to try to make life more enjoyable all round – from a practical point of view of course, but also and far more importantly, in loosening up attitudes to living. I write, not from a moral standpoint, but to dispel any unnecessarily hidebound approach we may have towards each other in everyday life, especially in that very important part of our lives – socialising. I do not intend that we should ride rough-shod over everyone else. I think the people I dislike most are those who concentrate wholly upon their rights and ignore their responsibilities. On the contrary, one of my firmest beliefs is that if we have a deeply-rooted sense of consideration for others and adopt good manners as second nature, these two factors will always help to smooth down the most ruffled feelings and as a result make life much easier for us. Good manners have little to do with rules, and much more to do with a caring and sympathetic approach to people. For instance: an acknowledgement with a smile as I slow down to let someone walk over a pedestrian crossing, even though it is their *right* and I should, starts the day more pleasantly for both of us, whereas an aggressive stalk across the white bands, to a screeching of brakes and a muttered curse from behind the steering wheel, sets an unpleasant tone to my morning.

In just the same way, to face a social occasion, whether it be just a get-together in your own home or a splashy wedding, rigid to the gills with fear and wondering what is incorrect or proper, is likely to turn something that could be great fun and well worth remembering into a tormented ordeal. Try not to be hamstrung by rules and so-called etiquette – just approach events with a thought for everyone's enjoyment rather than obeying what was 'laid down' in some long-forgotten tome about how things were done or not done. The Princess of Wales is a perfect example of this instinctive and unselfconscious behaviour. The way she pulls down a woolly cap over a youngster's head, kneels to be on a child's level for a kiss, or dives to rescue a precious camera so as to restore it to its owner – all these actions in no way detract from her dignity, but endear her to everyone. These spontaneous examples of 'good manners' make life pleasant for everyone around her.

The success of a social event really does come down to goodwill and the atmosphere created by the organiser – which brings me to the vexed question of money. It is much better to admit frankly (not apologetically) that a certain style of entertaining is beyond your reach, and plan something that you can achieve without breaking the bank, rather than strain every nerve and feel pinched in more senses than one. I know what I am saying from personal experience – because pennies were far more in evidence than pounds when I first married. Yet we had some hilarious parties, with huge bowls of spaghetti laced with garlic, oil and fresh basil, sprinkled with Parmesan and swilled down with soda-watered plonk, which I fondly imagined gave it a bit more style! Replace any feeling of 'It must be a success, I've spent so much!' with 'I think I've thought of and done everything so now we can all have fun.' Otherwise, that inner panic can destroy a party before it has even begun. Similarly, there are no rules about mixing guests. It might seem logical to invite only one age-group for a teenage birthday party, or for formal adult drinks, but I have always found that a sprinkling of all generations makes a thoroughly enjoyable gathering and it is a good way of bridging the generation gap.

Elsa Maxwell, an international hostess of the Thirties, renowned for the stunning success of her parties, always used to include a group of reputed 'local bores' among her guests. She made sure that they were all placed at the same table and, invariably, from that group came the loudest laughs, because they were all on similar wavelengths!

A lot of thought has to go into throwing a party, whatever the size and scale. Always remember that this is *your* party, to be given in *your* way. People come to it firstly because they like you, and enjoy your company, and secondly to meet other people they know or want to know. I find it makes for an easy atmosphere to mix a few well-known friends, some talkers, some listeners, and a smattering of new people you think might share your interests or who are friends of friends. If you are inexperienced and unattached and the whole business is proving too daunting, then why not take an ally into your confidence and compliment him or her by saying; 'I'll be dreadfully nervous/busy/shy without you to back me up – you're so good at talking. How about looking after the drinks, or coming a bit earlier?' You may not need that support when the time comes, just because it will be there.

Soft music suits the quiet start of an evening, but remember to turn it down or off so nobody has to fight it to talk. Dancing will come later! If you're planning a buffet, stick to food you can scoop out of the dishes with large spoons and eat with a fork – rather than fiddling with disjointing *petits poussins*. Try to arrange to have plenty of sturdy tables for glasses and ashtrays, and napkins galore. Resist the temptation to split up threesomes and foursomes who are chatting happily, just because you have read somewhere that the good hostess gets her guests to circulate!

As for your clothes – wear something you can bend easily in and resist the glamour of flowing sleeves which dip into the food and knock over the glasses. If two people turn up in the same dress, bring them together and say you find it hard to decide which one looks the nicer. There is no need to be nervous about anything – you cannot be hanged for something that has gone wrong and you can often use mishaps endearingly to your own advantage to get a laugh against yourself. Remember you will always be forgiven for making mistakes, but seldom for always being right. A twitchy, nervous hostess makes for a twitchy atmosphere, whereas a relaxed, warm, friendly feeling is catching.

The other evening at a party I made the most tremendous gaffe. I thought you would sympathise with me, as I remember that when you were on a TV panel game, you mentioned a singer's 'terribly phoney Italian accent' only to discover that he was Italian born. Apart from feeling that I could have crawled under a rock, there was not much I could do. Is there a graceful way of extracting oneself from this sort of situation?

Mrs M. Paines, Shirehampton, Bristol.

I'll never forget that excruciating moment. It didn't even help later to be told that the young man, though born in Italy, had lived for years in England, so had in fact a British lilt to his mother tongue – I still put both feet into things. But nine times out of 10, it relieves tensions all round if I bring the gaffe out into the open and turn the laugh on myself. Besides, I never find a convenient rock to crawl under!

I would like to try my hand at shaking a cocktail. It's my girlfriend's 21st birthday soon, and I would love to be able to rattle a concoction in the way that barmen in old films do. Is there an easy way to find out how to mix such drinks?

J. Henry, Bucks.

I am told that making authentic cocktails is an art and some connoisseurs prefer certain drinks stirred and not shaken. But if you want to have fun and impress your friends, I should write for advice to The Cocktail Shop, 5 Avery Row, London W 1 X 9 H A (01 493 9744). It has a lot of original do-it-yourself ideas, and even offers a mail-order service. And look out for their cocktail calculators – one hundred cocktails at your fingertips in alphabetical order.
P.S. You might be interested in less-alcohol

cocktails too from time to time. Try The Blender and Juice Book, by Maurice Hanssen, available by post from Dietmart House, Unit 18 Goldsworth Park Trading Estate, Woking, Surrey GU21 3BJ. There's also How to Mix 100 Cocktails (non-alcoholic drinks) from Foulshams & Co Ltd, 837 Yeovil Road, Slough, Berks.

Can you provide the answer to a question which often pops up at the dinner table? Why has a wine bottle got a concave base? Is it for the sediment, or to assist in the carrying, or to preserve the bouquet of the contents, or to strengthen the bottle?

Mrs P. Goddard, Rugby, Warks.

As you uncork your bottle of Christmas wine you can explain that when all glass bottles were hand-blown the thicker, concave base gave the glass strength. Also, when it came to stacking the bottles in wine racks the neck of each bottle (and they were shorter in those days) could rest in the hollow of the bottle above. Apparently the correct way to pour wine then was with the bottle resting along the palm and fingers and with the thumb in the 'punt' (the proper name for the concave base). Try it and you'll see how comfortably the bottle balances and how evenly you can pour out the wine.

****
A decorative tip when you next have guests in the summer – serve them drinks in frosted glasses. Dip the rims of the glasses in lemon juice then in castor sugar and keep them in the fridge until the very last moment.

If you knock over a glass or spill something on the carpet, don't go on about it at length. A few words are enough and swift action to remedy the effects is more appreciated. But do send flowers with a renewed written apology to your hostess the next day.
****

Can you tell me how long one can keep wines, spirits and liqueurs after the bottle has been opened? My husband and I don't drink much and we always have some bottles left three-quarters full after Christmas. I often wrap some sticky tape round the tops to seal them before I put them away. Does this help?

Mrs K. Harvey, Langford, Essex.

Expert opinions vary so I've combined them with my own experiences: Young red wine, two to two and a half days. Old red wines (burgundy, claret and so on), from one day to the next at the most. White wine should be drunk at one sitting but if kept, cork it up again, put it in the fridge and it will last one to one and a half days. Champagne can only be kept for one day as it goes flat. Their own corks can never be put back in the bottles but there are one or two special gadgets in chrome or gilt made in France and Germany and available at most big department stores. With these you can re-cork an unfinished bottle of champagne to keep it airtight in the fridge for up to two days. Port, some say three to four weeks, others as little as two days. Vintage port is certainly better decanted through fine gauze and nicer drunk sooner than later. Sherry, three to five weeks – but the richer

sherries keep longer. Spirits and liqueurs will keep indefinitely. Sticky tape round the cork will not re-seal the bottles, but it is a good idea to keep a selection of new different-sized corks to replace the originals.

I am a widow in my mid-50s and I'm getting married in the Winter. I'd like your advice on what would be suitable to wear and your opinion of my plan to have my grand-daughters as bridesmaids. We are having a church wedding and I just don't know the procedure.

Mrs J.O., Gloucester.

Yes, it's fine for your grandchildren to be bridesmaids. Put your mind at rest about the details by going along to have a word with the vicar of the church at which you plan to marry. As for what you wear – well, without knowing your colouring or height, I can only remind you of a few facts. Soft salmon pink and coral shades give a glow to dullish complexions – but steer well clear of seaside-rock pinks. Blue-greys tone in beautifully with pretty pink and white skins, but in the cold

****
Never leave good wine standing in your glass when you leave your host's table. Not only is this rather rude – but an expensive waste.

Even when you have been invited by the man of the house to dinner and you are meeting his wife for the first time, it is always to her that you should address your thank-you letter. And don't tell me that such a courtesy is out of date – it will always be appreciated far more than a quick telephone call which is just plain lazy. I also find it hard to believe that there are people who say no thank you of any kind when someone has gone to the trouble of entertaining them.
****

light of Winter, blue can be very hard. Pat-terned chiffon is attractive but be careful of the colour of the lining – find one to suit your skin shade as that will influence the overall look. There's always the chic and faithful standby of a lightweight worsted dress and coat or jacket. And youngsters can look very smart in suits which will come in useful for lots of other occasions.

Could you please help me with the problem of what to buy my parents for their Ruby Wedding anniversary? My mother doesn't like jewellery and my father doesn't wear cuff-links or tie-pins so I am at a complete loss as to what to buy as a present.

Mrs P. Swinson, Leek, Staffs.

Why not stick to the colour and forget the jewel? Give a beautiful red plant, or if they have a garden a red rose bush, or else fill their window box with red flowers. Red glass is attractive or how about a small painting with a predominance of red in it? If their colour scheme allows, red scatter cushions would look nice. Wrap your gift in red paper and use red ribbon to tie it. I hope you have a happy day together.

I would very much like to send my mother, who lives in Jersey and whom I have not seen for many years, some fruit by mail. I was told that this can be done, but after making in-quiries, have still had no success. I would much rather send fruit than the usual flowers.

Mrs A. Taylor, Radford, Coventry.

What a good idea, and luckily there is a nationwide scheme called Sendfruit, run by Fruit Relay Service Ltd, 238 Green Lanes, London N13 5TU (01 882 1074). This works in the same way as Interflora or Teleflower. They have several agents in Coventry and in

***

Guests used to be told to keep an eye open to see that the hostess was seated before they sat down – although the host should wait until his guests are all in their places. But these days many a cooking hostess would be enraged if you let the high rise of her soufflé sink because she had darted out for the sauce! Manners remain but modes have changed a lot!

***

the Channel Islands so you should have no trouble. Look for the sign in a greengrocer's window.

I am a widow aged 27 with a three-year-old son. In the summer I am to marry again and would be glad of some advice, firstly on what to wear. I would like something long and romantic but don't want to look like an 'overdone bridesmaid'. It will be a church wedding and my fiancé's first, so I would like to make an effort to look really special, but a traditional outfit would be out of the ques-tion. I am 5ft. 1in. tall with a tendency to be plump (though I hope to have shed several pounds on my latest diet). I also have several problems of etiquette. Should I pay for the reception? (I could not ask my parents to pay a second time, and though my fiancé's parents have offered to pay, I feel it's really my place to do so.) Should I send my present in-laws an invitation? They have indicated that they wish us happiness, but do not wish to attend the wedding. Would it be in order to have my little son as page-boy?

Margaret Donegan, Highworth, Wilts.

I'd aim for the soft, feminine look of the Thirties which is always very flattering anyway. Either a multi-coloured small-patterned chiffon, or a pastel shade in silk crêpe would make up beautifully into a slightly bloused-top long dress. Have the shirt cut on the cross, lying smoothly over the hips and flared towards the hemline – this is very slimming and will camouflage the odd inch you haven't managed to shed. You could have either a V-shaped neckline edged with a soft, stand-up frill, or a high-at-the-back collar which shapes into a large floppy bow in the front (in this case have the ends left loose so you can tie your bow). Long, narrow set-in sleeves which fall into a loose frill at the wrist are attractive and also slimming. A medium-sized floppy hat swept up at the front to give you extra height and sashed round with the material of the dress should complete the picture. As far as the reception is concerned, you could either share the expenses with your fiancé, or gratefully accept his parents' offer to foot the bill (especially if you know they can afford it) then bring them back a nice present from your honeymoon. Your present in-laws will probably change their minds about attending the wedding when the time comes – meantime, I'd show them the invitation as a matter of interest to let them 'in on things'. Life's so much easier with friendly in-laws. Of course, have your young son as a page-boy – no eyebrows need be raised and it's so important that he should feel an intimately active member of your new family from the start. I hope it will be a lovely day and wish

you every happiness for the years to come. P.S. Although I wrote this advice originally in 1972, it's curious to see that the same essential thoughts on fashion would apply today – except perhaps for the hat, which now would not even be necessary. I still think making friends of in-laws from the start is the best way to set out on a new set of family relationships.

I am getting married for the second time and am unsure what colour I should wear. Two recent weddings I attended were second marriages and both the brides wore blue. Is this etiquette or a coincidence? Also, should I send my future mother-in-law a wedding invitation? It seems rather formal but when her other son got married she didn't attend because she wasn't asked. Of course we want her to be there but are not sure of what is the right way to ask her.

Mrs M.L.C., Maidstone, Kent.

It's surprising, but the white wedding dress, symbolising virginity, only goes back to the later part of Queen Victoria's reign. Before that, brides went in for all colours and this trend is back with us, especially for second marriages. Pick any shade that suits you – rich, jewel colours are very effective in the Winter, trimmed perhaps with white fun-fur, while pastels and patterns are flowingly flattering under a warmer sun. Don't send your future mother-in-law an invitation through the post, but drop by, have a friendly talk about wedding arrangements, or if she lives far away, give her a ring and say something on the lines of: 'Of course the groom's mother doesn't need a formal invitation but I'd love you to see this – would you like to keep one?' Then you can write the name you call her by on it there and then.

I have always heard that it is bad form to arrive absolutely on the dot when you are invited to a party. So if the invitation reads 7.30 for 8 p.m. aim for 7.40. On the other hand, make sure you arrive as the clock strikes for all professional and daytime appointments (except for social luncheons, which you would treat as an evening occasion). Just as a personal warning, if Greeks or Spaniards are on your guest list, may I suggest that you don't start off your menu with a soufflé or some other crucially-timed dish. I have never known many people of those nationalities to arrive within an hour of being invited! In fact in South America, if visitors are supposed to arrive at the time stated, the hostess will say, 'Hora inglesa' (English time) to let her guests know that the usual delay is not to be observed.

Can you please give me any ideas which would be a little different or unusual for a son's 21st birthday party? He's having two parties – one in his flat for his own friends (which he can manage) and one the parents are giving for their friends in his honour, which will include a few of his friends. So it will be a mixed-age group of about 30 people, with a buffet supper, not too difficult to prepare.

Mrs Joan Packwood, Cheam, Surrey.

I immediately thought of an enormous rice salad, but decided to ask TVTimes Cookery Editor Kathie Webber for her opinion. She agreed – and her recipe is completely different from mine. To her cold cooked rice she adds cucumber, mandarin oranges, chicken pieces, onion, sweetcorn kernels, peas and perhaps bacon pieces – then moistens with either mayonnaise or vinaigrette. My ingredients are (for six people) 10oz long-grain rice, 2oz Gruyère cheese (cut in small squares), five hard-boiled eggs (sliced), 1 large tin of red peppers (strained and chopped), 2 large tins of tuna fish (strained and shredded) and 2 teaspoons of fresh or dried basil. Cook the rice, pour cold water through it, strain and cool. When rice is cold add all the ingredients, folding in each in turn. Finally, toss with salt and pepper to taste, three to four tablespoons of olive or corn oil and one or two tablespoons of vinegar. You can either put this salad into a mould and let it stay for an hour or so in the fridge before turning it out, or serve it loose in a large glass bowl. But don't forget to make lots of home-made mayonnaise to serve with it.

Do you know of any books which would give me a guide to complete table etiquette: which knife to use for what, the purpose of the

★★★★★★★★★★★★★★★★★★★★★★★★★★★★★★
If you are leaving a large party it is not neces-
sary to say goodbye to everyone you have met
or talked to. But do make the effort to take
formal leave of your host and hostess. How-
ever difficult it is to locate them both, this
courtesy, to my mind, is a must.
★★★★★★★★★★★★★★★★★★★★★★★★★★★★★★

mysterious mini spoon and so on? Please help.
My ignorance is infuriating!

Mrs Ann Heath, Belfast.

Expensive but comprehensive is Table Setting, Entertaining and Etiquette *by Patricia
Easterbrook Roberts, published by Thames
and Hudson.*
*P.S. You may still find this book in a library
but it is now out of print. The most comprehensive recent publication is* Etiquette and
Modern Manners *by Debretts.*

I am getting married soon and plan a sit-down
reception. Are there any rules about the plac-
ing of people at the top table? My mother says
the chief bridesmaid sits next to me, but I
thought it would be my fiancé's father. Would
you please settle this argument?

Miss P. R. Shorten, Norwich.

*Until I sat down and used a pencil and paper
I didn't realise how tricky this sit-down plac-
ing could be. Here are two alternatives, both
correct as far as etiquette goes. In the first, the
best man will be most strategically placed for*

*toasting the bride. In the second he can take
his place next to his 'partner for the day', the
chief bridesmaid, but in this plan, one parent
will sit next to his or her offspring, whichever
way you permutate them. Don't worry too
much, have a lovely time, and I hope that for
you and your fiancé it'll be the first day of a
very happy marriage.*

Our two daughters are having a double wedding. Do we send out a double invitation to
our relatives and separate invitations to each
of the two grooms' families?

Mrs H. Henderson, Waltham, Kent.

*The same double invitation will do for every-
one. The following layout is simple and correct: but remember to send a personal note
with the cards you send out to the grooms'
families.*

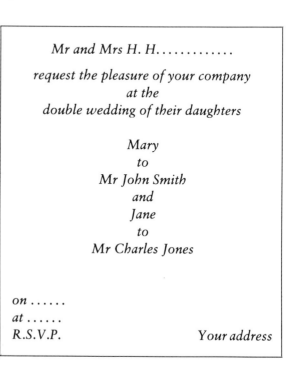

Mr and Mrs H. H. . . . .

*request the pleasure of your company
at the
double wedding of their daughters*

Mary
to
Mr John Smith
and
Jane
to
Mr Charles Jones

on . . . . . .
at . . . . . .
R.S.V.P.   *Your address*

Bride's Father	Groom's Mother	Best Man	Bride	Groom	Bride's Mother	Groom's Father	Chief Brides-maid

Bride's Mother	Groom's Father	Bride	Groom	Groom's Mother	Bride's Father	Chief Brides-maid	Best Man

While strict formalities about entertaining can be a bore, quite a useful rule to go by when you are planning a fairly organised dinner party is that the host and hostess should sit opposite each other at the table, with the 'most important' (eldest or first time) male guest on the right of the hostess, and his partner on the right of the host. Then it is easy to slot the other guests in the remaining spaces alternating a man and a woman.

An ideal plan for six people, here's how to amend it for eight – a good number conversationally, but more difficult to place. Host and hostess cannot sit opposite each other but you will be fine if you pick two 'priority' couples and then place the wife of the first on the host's right, and the husband of the second couple to the right of the hostess, and then the others can be arranged so that no wives sit next to their own husbands, and each person has a place of 'importance'.

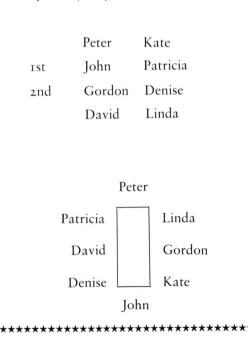

	Peter	Kate
1st	John	Patricia
2nd	Gordon	Denise
	David	Linda

I have just moved into a new flat and am now penniless, but I would still like a house-warming party. I am not very familiar with parties so please could you give me some ideas for very inexpensive drinks and food?

Miss A. G., Crouch Hill, London.

You can take the old bottle party a step further and call it a picnic party. Then ask your guests (who must know you haven't many pennies) to bring something to swell the menu. Ask the men to bring enough wine for two. The menu could be basically hot French bread (which you could provide) while guests bring various spreads, cheese, savoury flans and biscuits. For dessert have fruit salad. Start it off with a few supermarket bargain tins and add whatever fresh fruit is in season. Guests will add more and maybe you can add a jug of cream. The wine will go further laced with lots of ice or even diluted with soda. It's only good red wine that has to be served at room temperature. With everybody chipping in I have the feeling that your house-warming party will establish you as the hostess of the year and consolidate your friendships.

I am to be married soon and have asked my younger brother to be best man. He is 17 and rather self-conscious. Perhaps you could give me some ideas of his duties at the ceremony and reception so I may brief him. I want him to make a success of it because I feel it would help bring him out of his shell.

N. G., Dundee.

This important 'supporting role' of best man need not be too scaring, but he must keep his cool when those around him may be flapping. He must ensure that there will be enough buttonholes and hand them out on the day. If there are ushers he must be sure they either know or will ask which are the groom's

It is still good manners (and kind to the flowers) when a guest arrives with a bouquet to put it in water at once even though you obviously haven't time to arrange the flowers, there and then. The same goes for a gift – open it at once to give your visitor the pleasure of your accepting it.

Strike a match when you've been to the loo and nobody will ever know! This a godsend in others peoples' houses, when you have children, or just share a bathroom with your loved one!

friends, who sit on the right side of the aisle, and which are bride's, who sit on the left. He must drive to the church with the groom, making sure he has the ring and enough money to meet any fees. He must also check with the minister at which moment he hands over the ring. At the reception he reads out all the telegrams and messages, and by tradition, should make a speech. If this proves too awesome, he may cut it to merely introducing the bride's father. If there are still questions you want answered, buy one of the paperbacks on the subject.

For months my fiancé and I could not decide where to marry. I couldn't bring myself to go through a church wedding as this seemed so hypocritical when neither of us is a member of a church. He would not agree to getting married in our local register office. This deadlock almost brought me to the point of wanting to live in sin. That is until we saw the film of *Love Story*. We were both so impressed by the simple moving wedding in the film that we are now keen to recreate a similar (non-religious) ceremony at home. Could you tell me whether this is legally possible in England?

Miss J. Dursley, W. Bromwich, Staffs.

In this country, only on compelling compassionate grounds (such as physical disability) can a couple be married in a place other than that set aside for the solemnisation of matrimony; that is, church or register office. The American tradition of getting married at home is a hangover from the days of frontier life and the wandering preachers of the Wild West. Your nearest alternative would be a quiet register office marriage with just two witnesses. I'm afraid our registrars have to stick to the normal marriage vows, but if you know of a particularly attractive register office where you would like to be married – provided you or your fiancé stay locally for 15 days – you can qualify to marry there. Why not find a register office in a pleasant setting, say somewhere in our own West Country, and get married there? At least it will be a memorable episode in your own Love Story.

My daughter was recently married in Australia. She will be home in March and is having her marriage blessed in church followed by a reception for family and friends. Firstly, I should like to know what type of invitation card should be sent. Secondly, she has written to say she would like the men to wear morning dress. Would this be in order?

D. Kerrigan, Epsom, Surrey.

You could send out a formal invitation in your name on the lines of that shown below (top), but I would have thought it more friendly and suitable to have a small card from your son-in-law and daughter simply stating their intention as in the sample below (bottom). I'm sure dark suits for the men would be more appropriate (not to mention comfortable), unless your daughter really wants to re-stage a full white wedding.

Mrs D. Kerrigan
requests the pleasure of your
company at the Blessing of
the Marriage (which took
place earlier in Australia)
of her daughter and her
husband.
At .... [place]
On ... [date] ... At ... [time]
and afterwards at a reception
to be held at .... [place]
R.S.V.P.
[Your address]
Morning coats for gentlemen.

Mr and Mrs N.N.
invite you to attend the
Blessing of their Marriage,
(which took place earlier in
Australia)
at ...... [place]
on ...... [date] at ...... [time]
and afterwards a reception
at .... [place]
R.S.V.P.
c/o Mrs D. Kerrigan

When dining out, I always thought it correct to tell my escort what food I had chosen from the menu, and he would tell the waiter. On television, I have noticed that ladies often order direct from the waiter. Which is correct, please?

Helen Douglas, Dorset.

Officially, your escort should order, but etiquette is based on good manners, not hard and fast formal rules. I usually turn to the waiter for his advice on a dish I fancy, say it sounds lovely, then leave it to my escort to settle the order.

If you want candles to burn more evenly and drip less, chill them overnight in the freezer section of your fridge.

Mrs Adams, Morecambe, Lancs.

If your family and friends are likely to smoke over the festive season, clear the atmosphere with some Kandelles Smokers' Candles. They burn for 25 hours, and are available from gift shops and good department stores.

Formal rules state that while host and hostess get up automatically when a new guest comes into a room, be it a man or a woman, an invited female guest remains seated when introductions are being made except when she is being introduced to a cleric or a person of high rank. Unless a female guest is elderly herself I do not agree: as an invited guest I still stand up to be introduced to anyone older, male or female, out of respect for the dignity of age and sometimes out of instinctive friendliness. I never feel that extra good manners are demeaning – quite the opposite. In my opinion they stimulate the friendliness of any occasion.

I would like to get a book on how to fold napkins in different designs, such as water lilies. Can you suggest a good one?

Mrs V. Tallett, London.

I suggest you try the following book, available through W.H. Smith, and recommended as the most complete coverage of the subject – which can transform a simply-laid table into a party centrepiece. A Guide to Napkin Folding by James Ginders, from Northwood Publications.

I wish I could think of something different to send an elderly relative who has everything. Her birthday is at the beginning of the year and I always end up giving her something she already has or doesn't need. I would love to send an original gift this year, particularly as she has been rather ill recently. I'd be grateful for any suggestions.

D. Green, Edinburgh.

With St Valentine's Day (14 February) and Mothering Sunday (movable) around this time, I'm sure my suggestion will be wel-

comed by many people. Why not send her an orchid? *They are particularly lovely and long-lasting flowers, and there's a marvellous service called 'Send an Orchid' which operates all over the world. It costs a few pounds to send a bloom with a message by first-class post and it is also possible to send one overseas. Write to Send an Orchid, Monks Eleigh, Ipswich, Suffolk, or telephone Bildeston (0449) 740 780. I think such an exotic present will bring a bloom to the palest cheek.*

For my daughter's christening gift, my husband and I gave her a charm bracelet with the idea that for each of her birthdays we would buy her a charm. When she reaches 18 it

I rather like the idea that according to old world etiquette it is always the woman's prerogative to greet a male acquaintance in the street or to offer him her hand, and not the reverse. This is because, had he been her lover and she were now out with either her husband or current beau, she might wish to conceal her knowledge of him!

should be quite a present for her. However, we now have a son and would like to do something similar for him, but the problem is we cannot think of anything to collect for him. Friends have suggested a stamp collection but I don't fancy that. Could you give us some practical ideas?

Mrs J. Kerslake, Ipswich, Suffolk.

You and your husband could become numismatists. Coin collecting can be fascinating. There are so many to choose from, in different metals, from different ages and countries and to suit all pockets – not just gold sovereigns and krugerrands (South African gold pieces)! Write to, or visit Spink and Sons Ltd., 5 King Street, London SW1, who will tell or show you what is available. Coins look most impressive when laid out in velvet-lined boxes, so you could build up over the years a handsome and increasingly valuable collection.
P.S. Another suggestion might be beautifully-bound editions of classic books, which will become heirlooms for the family in time.

Each summer I have a foreign student to stay for a month to study English and to see a British family's way of life. I often receive gifts from these students – something special from their own countries such as French perfume, wooden horse figures from Sweden and pottery from Germany. When they return I always try to send their parents something typical of Wales: Welsh dolls, 'brass' Welsh ladies, or Welsh cakes, but there must be lots of other typical British souvenirs.

Phyllis Buss, Swansea, S. Wales.

I find lots of friends from across the Channel are thrilled by gifts such as Oxford Marmalade, tea in illustrated tins and kippers – but don't do as I did and send kippers to Italy

Table manners do vary from one country to another but if a lettuce isn't trimmed into small mouthfuls I have found the European way of 'folding' the leaves more practical than cutting them up, especially when they're lavishly dressed.

When you have meat on your plate cut it up and eat it as you go along – do not reduce your plate to rubble before you start! Incidentally, a funny and true story came my way about a young executive's childbound wife who had to attend a business dinner to be vetted by the board of her husband's prospective employers. Determined to make a good impression she bought a new dress, read up the newspapers and held forth with great charm and wit at the table, where she was seated next to the boss. Suddenly, on noticing midstream that she held everyone's attention with awe, she glanced sideways to find she had just cut up the man's steak for him, into child-size bites!

during a postal strike! For something more permanent, a shop near the British Museum named Best of British, 25 Museum Street, London WC1 (01 580 6285), has a wide selection of gifts: glove puppets of policemen, Beefeaters and guardsmen, ashtrays with a well-polished old penny set in the middle, and brass rubbings, which can be posted in a special cardboard roll for a little extra cost. You can write or telephone with orders, but when you are in London this shop is well worth a visit.
P.S. The Tate Gallery and the National Gallery also have a great variety of good quality prints of British painters, which also make a rather special souvenir.

How does one eat snails? I have always wanted to try them, and at a recent business dinner we had such a helpful, friendly waiter that I took the plunge. He was just the chap you could ask without making yourself look foolish before colleagues. Unfortunately, he vanished and I was served by a man who spoke no English! Faced with something like sugar tongs, I thought; 'Oh well, I expect you grip the shell in these and extract the flesh with this fork thing.' But when I squeezed the tongs together, they opened! With dexterity and (outward) aplomb, I coped, and my friends never knew. But I'm sure I should have consumed that lovely sauce-cum-gravy as well, somehow. Spare my blushes ... conceal my name, and with your aid I'll try them again at the first opportunity.

D.W.D., Whitchurch, Cardiff.

I'm sure you convinced you friends you were a veteran snail eater ... no mean feat when those tricky tongs hold tight only when you stop squeezing *them! I've mastered snails at last, and I just crumble bread or grissini (Italian breadsticks) into the sauce and when it has been absorbed, I eat the gooey mixture with a fork. Delicious!*
P.S. When you eat mussels, eat the meat out of the shell with your fork, but it is perfectly all right to pick up the half-open shell with your fingers to sip the delicious juice.

Useful Addresses

Fruit Relay Service, Ltd (for Sendfruit service, presents by post),
238 Green Lanes, London N13 5TU.
(01 882 1074)

Send an Orchid,
Monks Eleigh, Ipswich, Suffolk.
(0449 740 780)

Best of British (for interesting traditional present ideas),
25 Museum Street, London WC1.
(01 580 6285)

Flying Flowers (carnations from Jersey),
PO Box 373, Jersey, C.I. (0534 54657)

Useful Reading

The Blender and Juice Book, Maurice Hanssen (Dietmart Books)
How to Mix 100 Cocktails (Foulsham Ltd).
Table Setting, Entertaining and Etiquette, Patricia Easterbrook Roberts (Thames and Hudson).
Etiquette and Modern Manners (Debretts).
The Bride's Book, Drusilla Beyfus (Allen Lane).
Good Housekeeping Cookery Book (Ebury Press) (Has a special section on weddings and parties.)
Guide to Napkin Folding, James Ginders (Northwood Publications).

4
Activities and Hobbies

Total recall is great fun, though it can give you all kinds of twinges at times. I do not hanker after being young again, but it is good to feel that I can still remember quite clearly what it was like. I know all the doom and gloom spreaders say that this is a dreadful time to be starting out in life – but I doubt if there ever was an ideal world where everything was laid on for the youngsters. Starting out in life is always a daunting experience, whatever the current social or economic climate. Youth is equipped with health, energy and the enthusiasm to explore – and as a bonus in these trying times there has never been such a wealth of help in the form of associations and clubs orientated towards the younger generation and ready to give help in any number of ways, from the serious issues of careers to the pursuit of pleasure in pastimes. People are *there* to give information and advice. But of course it takes the initiative of each and every individual to go out and find what is available. The people who will get the most from these resources will always be those who never ask passively, 'What have they got to offer me?' but rather, 'Where can I go to find out how we can get together, and when we can set off?' – and are therefore willing to take the first step.

I maintain that those who expect the good things in life to be handed them on a platter are going to turn into embittered losers – and through every age it will be the positive thinkers and doers who will be the ones to turn minuses into pluses. I always remember the looks of 'Poor love, you'll be bored' and the expressions of sympathy that came my way when my late husband became madly enthusiastic about buying a minute plot of land on a tropical island because the pressures of civilisation were getting him down. But the 'poor darling' expressions were all lost on me because I had decided that conchology was the one thing I had always wanted to study and I had already bought books on the subject. I still look at them nostalgically and wonder whether I ever *will* get the chance to dip into them. For a sideline, I had also discovered a vet on the island, whose help I intended to enlist, besides that of a local carpenter, with my plan to build kennels. This would help the vet realise his long-standing plan to provide a residence for pets while their owners were away, and a home for bitches who needed spaying, as well as the large colony of unwanted animals that existed on this 'dream island'! Needless to say my husband abandoned his plans, but I did decide then that even on a desert island I would never have had enough hours in the day to do all that could be done.

Even now while I am still, luckily, extremely active I make plans for what I imagine might be a slightly more sedentary old age (though somehow I doubt it!). I find myself stockpiling very special books I want to read, making a note of art galleries and exhibitions I intend to visit, and inquiring about lectures and courses I will attend on subjects which spread from antiques to ants. And I know that I will reach the end of my life not having gone half way down the list. It is my sincere intention to be too busy to fulfil all my plans anyway, for I hope always to be distracted by someone or other who will need my time and attention. As I get older, I enjoy being a 'talking block' for younger people, not just in my family but outside it too – hearing their stories, helping them to gauge their progress through the world, and trying always to keep that memory alive in my own head, of what it was like, what it *really* felt like to face that selfsame situation when I was young. This is the best method I have devised for preventing the gloom that sets in when someone becomes too wrapped up in his or her own life.

On the following pages, you will find information on all aspects of being active, whatever your age, from teens to 80s. Readers have supplied some wonderful tips and hints on holidaying, hobbies, and special problems. No address list on such a vast range of material can be absolutely infallible, but at least it will point you in some of the right directions. Nor can I give answers on a plate – but there are many, many willing, helping hands.

I am writing a biography of my grandmother and her family. Unfortunately, my book has come to a halt through lack of information on Gog and Magog, those two giants whose statues once stood at Cheapside, London. As they are vital to the story I hoped you would be able to give me some information on where they now stand and their story.

Linda Ayres, Hornchurch, Essex.

References to Gog and Magog appear in the Bible – in the books of Revelation and Ezekiel. Gog was leader of an evil army which God prophesied the Israelites would destroy. Two large statues in Guildhall, London, are called Gog and Magog.

According to legend, Gog and Magog were survivors of a race of giants descended from the 33 wicked daughters of Diocletian. After their brethren were slain they were brought to London and compelled to officiate as porters at the gate of the royal palace.

The original figures were burned in the Great Fire and were replaced in 1708. These were subsequently destroyed in an air raid in 1940 and the new figures were installed in 1953.

Can you tell me anything about a ring on which two hands are holding a heart, with a crown above? My mother says it is an Irish wedding ring.

Miss K. Evans, Leics.

This is a Claddagh ring, which derives its name from the ancient village of Claddagh in County Galway. Originally betrothal and wedding rings, they are now more popular as tokens of friendship. The hands signify friendship, the crown loyalty, and the heart love. They are made in either gold or silver. For further details contact the Irish Shop, 11 Duke Street, London W1 (01 935 1366).

I am 16, have a well-paid Saturday job and a generous allowance from my parents. This sounds perfect, but I am worried what to do with my money. Until recently I was happy to put it in a bank account. Lately, however, I have become worried about devaluation. I feel that money I save now will be worth less when I really need it. Do you think it would be a better idea to spend it on items such as household requirements, ready for my home, or buy antiques which are likely to appreciate in value? If I don't take precautions I see myself paying exorbitant prices in the future with my money being of less real value than it is now.

Nicola Bulbeck, Alton, Hants.

Such far-sightedness in one so young staggers me. Make an appointment with a bank manager. I think he will agree you should invest in short-dated, index-linked gilt-edged stock. You can always add to these investments which will give you a guaranteed interest as well as useful capital appreciation. A well-stocked bottom drawer will prove a boon, but concentrate on things that you will always need and which are least likely to change over the years, such as household linen. Somethings we find invaluable now may look 'out of the ark' in a few years; for instance jewellery designs do date, but single good stones will always increase in value. And, to get your eye trained and to learn about articles which should prove to be a good investment, go to a library and read up on china, silver, furniture, and oriental carpets. Visit museums and auction sales, then you'll be able to start collecting things which will prove to be not only an investment but also enjoyable to have around.

Most people know what a music score looks like, but what does a ballet score look like? Is it all written out in long hand – *frappé, pas de chat* and so on, and if so what do choreographers write when some athletic or acrobatic steps are included, as so often happens in modern ballet? Also, why is the terminology in French – didn't ballet originate in St Petersburg in Russia?

Joan Stanesby, Petworth, Sussex.

I had great fun in discovering the answers from the Ballet Rambert. Choreography is the marking of ballet steps on a normal musical stave. There are six signs and their meaning depends on their position on the stave. The Laban notations are used in America, but British companies and those in Canada and Germany use Banesh, invented by Rudolph Banesh and first adopted by the Royal Ballet in 1956. Until then, ballet steps were passed on verbally, or demonstrated by the ballet master. But dancers develop a memory and don't necessarily use the Banesh scores for every movement. Though these are used by the man who writes the ballet and the ballet master who teaches it, many modern ballets have points on the stave which indicate when the dancer may improvise. As to why French and not Russian, the Russian Ballet was a Royal Ballet and the language of the Russian Court was French.

I read with interest your explanation of how the Continentals came to cross the figure 7. The reason given was simply that it avoids mistaking the 7 for the 1. This is not the whole reason. In fact, this custom stems from the original Arabic numbering system, where the mathematical Arab race invented figures with as many angles as the number itself. The figures were as follows (with the angles shown by dots).

In usage most of these symbols became

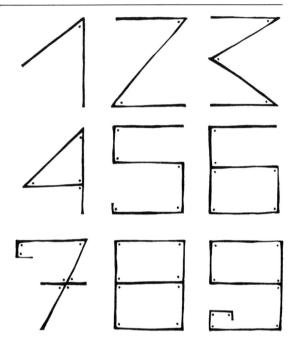

rounded-off in curves and the 7 lost its cross, the Arabic origins becoming generally forgotten. The Continentals kept the cross, however, and the custom has stayed.

Geoffrey Whiley (aged 11), Eaton, Norfolk.

I have a lot of old music, dating back to the 1800s. Is it worth anything?

H.H., Birmingham.

I suggest you write to Travis and Emery, 17 Cecil Court, Charing Cross Road, London WC2 (01 240 2129). They will be able to give you an evaluation.

I have in my possession a copy of the Silver Jubilee *Daily Mail* dated Monday 6 May, 1935. I feel it is worth more than a few pence to a collector, and the proceeds could go to our fund here at the Cheshire Home.

Sister J. Davies, St Michael's Cheshire Home, Axbridge, Somerset.

If it is in good condition, freshen it up with a warm iron, then put it in a plastic bag – folded so that the headlines and date show temptingly. The Manager of Goldie Oldies, 339 Old Kent Road, London SE1, deals in second-hand items of the Twenties and Thirties and he says that it might fetch £3 or £4. On the other hand, with an able auctioneer or raffle tickets at 20p you might raise £20 or so for your good cause.
P.S. This shop is no longer in business, so I checked again with The Vintage Magazine Shop, 39/41 Brewer Street, London W1 (01 439 8525) who said the value would still be around that figure, and added that they would welcome all enquiries about newspapers, magazines, comics, or old photographs.

Recently I saw an interesting programme on polishing pebbles. Housewives were doing this work at home. The pebbles were made into ear-clips, necklaces and rings. Where can one purchase chains and ring shanks, etc?

M. Whitaker, Curbridge, Oxon.

I can understand anyone getting hooked on lapidary work. Write to Kernowcraft Rocks and Gems Ltd, 21A Pydar Street, Truro, Cornwall TR1 2AY, enclosing a sae for their comprehensive catalogue. It includes, as well as coloured pictures and prices of stones and tools, a list of periodicals which will guide your first steps.
P.S. Dryad have a shop at 178 Kensington High Street, London W8 7RG, which can supply similar equipment by mail. The firm produce a comprehensive art supplies catalogue which you can obtain for a low sum from Dryad, Leicester, PO Box 38, Northgates, Leicester LE1 9BU.

This sounds a bit crazy, since I'm 50 years old and have grown-up children, but I want to find out about parachuting. My family think I'm a nut-case but is there anywhere I can go to see first-hand what goes on and if there's a chance for a granny to have a go?

Barbara Morrison, N. London.

I don't know about being a nut but you are certainly very brave. You will have to have a medical and if you pass that there's nothing to stop you jumping. Apply to the British Parachute Association, Kimberley House, 47 Vaughan Way, Leicester (0533 59778) for a list of clubs and a medical form to take along to your doctor.

I'm trying to teach myself to play the acoustic guitar, but have grown dissatisfied with just strumming chords. I have tried to find books with the finger-picking method, but to no avail. Every book I find has the same monotonous rhythm throughout the tune. I want a method of folk guitar using finger-picking and incorporating the melody with the chord such as that used by Don McLean and Labi Siffre. Can you help me?

Miss C. Blanche, Kidsgrove, Staffs.

I do hope one of these books will be what you are looking for. Stefan Grossman's Contemporary Ragtime Guitar (*this one is printed with tablature music for guitar players who do not read keyboard*); Mairants *Folk Music Accompaniment for the Guitar or* F. Noad's *Solo Guitar Playing. These were recommended to me by Ivor Mairants and are available by post from his shop: Ivor Mairants Musicentre, 56 Rathbone Place, London W1P 1AB (01 636 1481).*

Where can I buy the old-type steel gramophone needles? My son has an old wind-up gramophone and some 78 r.p.m. records, but we cannot find the needles anywhere here.

Mrs M.A. Stone, Keyham, Devon.

I didn't believe they still existed, but you can indeed get these needles from Imhof's Ltd, 112 New Oxford Street, London WC1A 1HJ (01 636 7878).

I am almost 90 and hard of hearing. I have an aid, but although I get plenty of volume, clarity is missing. Please can you tell me if it is possible to learn to lip-read? I can't converse with family or friends and television is very frustrating. I have to rely on imagination to make a story fit the pictures, which is often very wide of the mark.

Mrs J.A. Garnsey, Fulwood, Preston.

Lip-reading classes are run all over Britain and you can get details of your local classes from your education office whose address will be in your telephone directory. The Royal Institute for the Deaf issues a lip-reading booklet which I hope will be of help to you, too. *Write to The RNID, 105 Gower Street, London WC1E 6AH.*
P.S. *The RNID will also help refer you to a local social worker or appropriate contact, to find you a class, if you contact them directly.*

I live in a large council estate and a year ago we started a community association which resulted in us now having a temporary centre for our use. Our problem is raising funds, mainly for a play-group and an Over-60s Club. We have coffee mornings and raffles, but the profit from these is small and we would welcome new ideas for raising money. I have been told that it is possible to get a leaflet or book on fund-raising ideas – is this true?

Mrs M. Hill, Farnham, Surrey.

It sounds as though you need Chistine Figg's book, Raise Cash, Have Fun. *It is published by Elek Books in their Life and Leisure Series.*
P.S. *You may still find this book in your library, although it is now out of print. A new title on the subject is* Fundraising: A Comprehensive Handbook, *by Hilary Blume, published by Routledge & Kegan Paul.*

I am often asked by people who work in fund-raising, or who have illegible hand-writing, for a way to speed up or improve their systems for labelling parcels or addressing letters. I find the very best method is to buy a long roll of Butterfly self-adhesive address labels, which you can find in any large stationers. I thread these into the typewriter (taking care to put a large sheet of backing paper behind the roll so that I do not get paper jammed in my machine) and type away, one address after another. At least you do not waste so many expensive envelopes.

My friends and I are intrigued by the idea of people having a 'cosmic number' like the well-known singer on a recent television show who said her luck had changed when she added another letter to her name, thus altering her 'cosmic number'. Can you tell me anything about the 'cosmic game'?

Mrs M.S. Willington, Hyde, Ches.

Funnily enough I know a girl who changed her name on the advice of a numerologist, and swears she owes much of her success and happiness to this. It sounds like changing your birthday to get a better star; all the same, there's lots of fun to be had from numerology! This is basically an Indian fortune-telling game in which the letters of the alphabet represent numbers. The sum total of your name indicates your character and fate. Books that will tell you more are: The Numbers Book *by Sepharial, published by Foulsham and Co, or a more expensive book, but one of the best,* Romance in Your Name *by Juno Jordan, published by De Vorss. These are available from a speciality bookshop for numerology, Watkins, 19/21 Cecil Court, London WC2N 4HB (01 836 2182).*
P.S. *The Atlantis Bookshop, 49A Museum Street, London WC1A 1LY, also stocks books on numerology and have an expensive but definitive imported two-volume edition,* Numerology: The Complete Guide *by M.O. Goodwin, for devotees of the subject.*

When I was in Halifax recently I was interested to notice that people there seem to practise the hobby of growing miniature trees. I'd love to try my hand at it. Can you recommend a book on the subject?

S. Gibb, Basingstoke, Hants.

The art of bonsai or growing miniature trees in pots and trays has been practised since about 2,000 BC in China where they regard it as a kind of living sculpture. It is popular in Japan too and now, by applying the same techniques to specimens of our local trees, the British Bonsai Society is growing fast, especially in the North of England. If you want to become a bonsai expert yourself, contact The National Bonsai Society of Great Britain, c/o Miss Brenda Marshall, 61 Halsall Road, Birkdale, Southport, Lancs.
P.S. *The Society now publishes a magazine for members, four times a year.*

Some time ago you gave advice to people who want to trace their family history. I know from experience that this can become an absorbing hobby. I think you mentioned some kind of federation of people who like to do this. Could you give me the address?

Tom Wetherby, Hereford.

I'm glad you wrote because the federation has changed its address since I last gave it. It is now The Federation of Family History Societies, c/o The Honorary Secretary, 96 Beaumont Street, Mile House, Plymouth PL2 3AQ, but please remember they can't send you a reply without a sae.

My friend and I are interested in spending an archaeological holiday. Could you please give the address of an organisation which deals with these?

C. Leese, Rudyard, Staffs.

You don't say where you'd like to dig but I would guess you haven't any archaeological experience yet, so write, enclosing a sae to The Council for British Archaeology, 112 Kennington Road, London SE11 6RE (01 582 0494) for information about digs you could join for your holiday. Before you can join a dig abroad you need experience in this coun-

try, so when you've dug up a few bits of ancient Britain you can contact *Archaeology Abroad, c/o The Institute of Archaeology, 31-14 Gordon Square, London WC1H 0PY (01 387 6052).*
P.S. The Council would like to add that it's very hard work, five to six hours a day, often humping wheelbarrows and the like! Sometimes specially qualified helpers, doctors, nurses, cooks, for example, may be exempted from the requirement for experience to go abroad.

I'm an American living in England for a year because of my husband's work and I want to take the opportunity to enjoy my hobby of brass rubbing. But I can't travel to churches far afield as I have two young children with me here. Where can one find the best brasses in London?

Mrs I. Schoor, London W2.

Original brasses have in some cases been loosened or spoiled by the attention of too many dedicated brass-rubbers, but facsimiles have been made of the originals carefully that every detail is just as clear as the original. These facsimiles can be used at The Brass Rubbing Centre, St James' Church Hall, Piccadilly, London W1, from 10 am to 6 pm Mondays to Saturdays, or 12 pm to 6 pm on Sundays. There is a similar centre at Christ Church, Lancaster Gate, on the Bayswater Road. The cost of making a rubbing, which includes the necessary materials, varies depending on size, from a little group of 15th-century children to a medieval knight seven feet tall.

I would be grateful if you could give me some information on whether I can take flying lessons, and if so, where. Is there a barrier in age? I am 19 and wonder if I am old enough.

Craig Scothern, Southwell, Notts.

Your first step should be to ask your local public librarian for addresses of nearby flying schools, a flying club, local airfield or the town's airport. Write to any one of these places and ask for information on flying lessons. You can begin learning as soon as your feet reach pedals, but you can't go solo until you are 17. You don't need any educational qualifications and there is no upper age limit. One Chief Flying Instructor I spoke to had taught several healthy grandfathers and one grandmother to fly. But the snag is the price, around £50 an hour and probably rising because of fuel costs. How about gliding? If you are interested, make inquiries at the nearest Air Training Corps (address again from the public library).

I understand that there are people who can tell a person's character from his or her handwriting. I would like to have a friend's handwriting analysed, but don't know how.

Miss C.K., Middx.

Alan Bishop is a graphologist who will give you a personal assessment of a handwriting sample. His main work is concerned with industry, offering analyses of employees' potential as a career aid. If you write to him at 232 Priests Lane, Shenfield, Brentwood, Essex CM15 8LE he will be able to tell you his scale of fees for his services, which vary according to the depth of analysis required.

I passed my driving test a year ago but did not drive regularly until three months ago when I bought an oldish car for work. I have always enjoyed driving, and felt I would like to brush up my technique after a long gap between my test and car ownership. So I rang around local driving schools for some 'further education' in driving. Unfortunately I got no further than being offered advanced driving lessons, which I did not want. When I passed my nursing finals, a sage old staff-nurse warned me that now I would really start learning. That was true, but please, where are the courses for driver novices?

Miss Josephine Fox SRN, Lowestoft, Suffolk.

You're a woman after my own heart. If each of us tries to improve our driving, I feel we're doing our bit to increase safety on the roads. Get in touch with the League of Safe Drivers, Apex House, Grand Arcade, Tally Ho Corner, London N12 0EH. They only recommend schools which are run by ex-police officers who have been trained at a police driving school – or driving instructors who have attended one of their diploma courses on the special techniques of teaching advanced driving. But don't be put off by the word 'advanced' because common sense and practice will bring it into perspective.
P.S. When you feel a little more 'advanced' you might like to consider taking two other tests and becoming a Member of the Institute of Advanced Motorists and going on the High

Performance Course – you have to approach them in that order – I show off both those badges on my car and like to think I'm a much safer driver because of them.

I am greatly fascinated by antique silver, china, and so on, Could you suggest a book identifying silver and china marks?

Derek Mein, Edinburgh.

A paperback entitled British and Irish Silver Assay Marks, *compiled by Frederick Bradbury and published by J.W. Northend Ltd, Sheffield, should give you lots of information. Your local newsagent or bookseller should be able to get it for you.*
P.S. This book has been updated and is now known as Bradbury's Book of Hallmarks, *from J. W. Northend Ltd, 49 West Street, Sheffield S1 3SH. (Sheffield 730341).*

I would like to embark on a profitable hobby. I have considered various ideas, such as jewellery making, but haven't the faintest idea how to start or even if jewellery would be saleable once made.

Gareth White, Goring-by-Sea, Sussex.

Edna M. Tarr, 8 Pinetree Avenue, Scotter, Near Gainsborough, Lincs BN21 3TY (0724 762513), supplies the materials you need to start you off on your hobby.

I make all my own clothes and am becoming quite good at it. I would like to learn all about pattern drafting, tailoring and so on, but I do not know where to go. Can you help me please?

Miss June Carr, Pontefract, Yorks.

Your local education authority can give you the answer to this sort of question. If you get nowhere with them, try the Jacob Kramer

College, Vernon Street, Leeds LS2 8PH (Leeds 39931) where City and Guilds evening courses in tailoring and pattern drafting are available. P.S. For people elsewhere in the country, write, giving your area of interest, to the publications department for addresses of nearby colleges offering City and Guilds courses: City and Guilds of London Institute, 46 Britannia Street, London WC1X 9RG (01 278 2468).

My Mum started to make soft toys from odd bits of wool and material and then found a pattern for rag dolls, making matching boy and girl toys. Friends and neighbours began to ask if they could buy them, and also gave her bits of material, wool and trimmings. Not knowing how much to charge, Mum gave people an envelope and asked them for a donation to the Imperial Cancer Research Fund. Now, 18 months and £500 later, business is booming and orders are pouring in. Mum gets so much pleasure from her work that I wondered if other pensioners might like to start a similar scheme in their area.

Mrs E. Nicholls, Beds.

My husband would like to build an old-fashioned dolls house for our small daughter. He's looking for the sort of design with a front that opens up. Can you tell me where we might find a pattern or instructions to build such a house?

Mrs D. White, Essex.

I think the book that might help you most is Make Your Own Dolls House *by Christopher Cole, and published by Shepheard-Walwyn. It gives complete instructions for making a three-storey London terrace house called The Dickens House and it does have a front that opens up. For the sort of house that children can build in paper cut out on their own with their parents' guidance, there's* Make Your

Own Victorian House by Rosemary Lowndes and Claude Kailer, published by Angus and Robertson.
P.S. The mecca for dolls house enthusiasts is a wonderful shop called The Dolls House, 29 The Market, Covent Garden, London WC2E 8RE (01 379 7243), which sells antique houses, period furniture, kits, books and will give you valuable advice.

My grand-daughter has a favourite doll whose eyes need renewing. Where I live there is no dolls' hospital. What do you advise?

Mrs S. Hoare, Poole, Dorset.

If you send your grand-daughter's doll to the Dolls' Hospital, 16 Dawes Road, London SW6 (01 385 2081), I feel sure her eyesight will be restored. Enclose a sae, so that they can let you know how much the operation is likely to cost and how long she'll have to stay in hospital.

Are there any books about collecting old postcards? I am in the Girl Guides and trying to pass my Collector's Badge and would be grateful if you could tell me.

Denise Evans (13), Ystrad Mevrig, Dyfed.

My grandmother has an album of old postcards which she shows me. I would like to collect modern cards so that in 50 years time I could show my grandchildren, but I do not know how to begin.

Jean Lawson (14), Lowestoft, Suffolk.

Collecting old cards is called deltiology. Complete lists of all current books on the subject are available direct from Ken Lawson, 12 Suffolk Road, Cheltenham, Glos GL50 2AQ, or Vera Trinder Ltd, 38 Bedford Street, Strand, London WC2E 9EU. Information on modern cards is available from Ron Griffiths, 47 Long

Arrotts, Hemel Hempstead, Herts HP1 3EX or Drene Brennan, Postcard Club of Great Britain, 34 Harper House, St James' Crescent, London SW9. Please enclose sae.

I am 15 years old and very interested in gymnastics. I'd like to join a club where they train people to become gymnasts. Could you tell me where I might find such a club?

Miss Murray, London W5.

For a list of clubs in your area, I suggest you write to the Development Director of the British Amateur Gymnasts Association, 95 High Street, Slough, Berks SL1 1DH (Slough 32763). I'm afraid you would, according to them, be too old to take up gymnastics with the idea of serious international competition. Children usually begin training for this at about the age of seven. But you may well be eligible for club competitions. The Association can supply you with more details if you write to them at the above address enclosing a sae.

Years ago I learned to play the piano, but like most children I hated having to practise. Now I regret not carrying on with my lessons. I still have my piano and play a little from time to time. Is there a book I can buy which will help me play again? With two small children I can't afford lessons. I know there are Teach Yourself Books, but is there one for the piano? Also can you tell me where I can buy sheet music of the old 'pop' tunes like *My Old Man, White Cliffs of Dover*, and so on?

Mrs Lesley J. Slobbs, Kenilworth, Warwks.

The answer to the first part of your question should be one of the following: Smallwood's Piano Tutor or Amateur Pianist's Companion by James Ching, both published by EMI and both available from W. and G. Foyle Ltd, 119-125 Charing Cross Road, London WC2. *I should think a music retail shop – selling records and instruments in your own area – would stock the kind of sheet music you're after, or could order it for you. Failing this, Francis Music Supply, of 12 Gerrard Street, London W1V 7LJ (01 437 2532) should be able to help.*

P.S. Chappell of Bond Street, 50 New Bond Street, London W1 (01 491 2777), are the largest stockists of all kinds of sheet music from classical to simple folk songs and also keep basic music books and dictionaries too.

Can a person with no birth certificate go abroad on holiday? My husband's parents did not register him at birth and are now dead. How can we get a passport?

Mrs H.G.P., Colwyn Bay.

Your husband can get a British Visitor's Passport from the Post Office by applying in person and taking his National Health Medical Card. To obtain a full passport he would need some evidence of the place and date of his birth, like a baptismal certificate, a letter from the authorities, from his first school, or just a letter from an older relative. Then he can apply as normal.

I would dearly like to invite two orphans to spend a week's holiday with us in the summer. Could you tell me if children's homes allow this and if you think it is a good idea. We are a young couple with a son of two and a young baby. Unfortunately my house is too small for us to adopt or even foster a child.

Mrs E.R. Davies, Dyfed.

This is a kind thought, but the National Children's Homes say that one-off visits have never been allowed, as the children would be staying with complete strangers. However, you could become a social aunt to one child in particular. After visiting the child regularly and building up a relationship, it might be possible to look after that child for a weekend. The NCH point out that they have very few orphans in their care, but if you or any other interested readers contact Child Care Department, National Children's Homes, 85 Highbury Park, London N5 1UD, they will put you in touch with your nearest branch and send a social worker to check your credentials and assess your reliability. I am sure you will think carefully about whether you feel it is good or disturbing for children to leave homes for short periods. It is not an easy decision.

In reply to Mrs E.R. Davies of Dyfed, who wanted to offer orphans a holiday, she should contact The Children's Country Holidays Fund, 1 York Street, Baker Street, London W1H 1PZ. This registered charity provides holidays for disadvantaged children during the school holiday period. She will be put in touch with her local representative in her area. The Fund has been in operation since 1884.

E. Batchelor, Sussex.

The Women's Royal Voluntary Service runs a scheme to arrange holidays for underprivileged children to stay with caring people. My husband and I were hosts to two lovely little girls last year and we have kept in touch and welcome them again this summer. Perhaps Mrs Davies could contact her local WRVS office for details.

Mrs A.B. Downing, Dyfed.

I am thinking of taking a week's holiday walking along one of this country's long-distance footpaths – either the Ridgeway Path or the South Downs Way. I have read

If you reach a hotel room and are plagued by mosquitoes, then there is an easy remedy before you spend money on expensive sprays. Try cutting a couple of oranges in half, and sticking whole cloves in the surface. Place a section at the foot of the bed, and one on each side, and you will sleep without a buzz or bite.

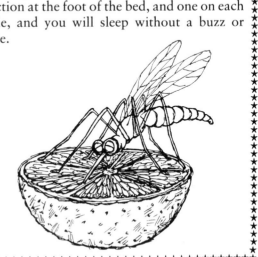

about these historical routes but have only been given directions for taking short walks on them. I need maps for the whole distance, historical notes and the names of suitable inns or hotels near the route to break the journey.

Mrs R.S., Reading, Berks.

You can get free information about long-distance walking routes in England and Wales from the Countryside Commission, John Dower House, Crescent Place, Cheltenham, Glos. GL50 3RA (0242 21381). These have excellent maps and directions but do not tell you about historic monuments you pass along the way. Books about these have been prepared by H.M. Stationery Office. These are called The Long Distance Footpath Guides and are obtainable from any HMSO bookshop. A full list is given at the end of this chapter.

I do not belong to the stoic 'I haven't had a holiday in years' brigade. To my mind a regular holiday is a necessity and not a luxury. I enjoy the pressure of work but when a whole year has gone by, my batteries are virtually flat and only a 'get up and away from it all' break recharges them. I have had this self-protective attitude for a very long time, and I am more than willing to forego some other luxuries in order to save for the special break that will revive me. I know from experience that many insoluble problems or deep-seated worries can be sorted out when I have had time to relax and to get a little more perspective on the situation.

It is because my life is so multi-faceted that I have devised some routine tricks which may sound over-methodical, but are in fact a safeguard against my innate forgetfulness. For instance I make lists and stick to two holiday rules whatever happens: while I am away I jot down the things I really needed and didn't have, and tick the ones I took and was glad to have by me from the year before. My list includes basic first aids, cosmetics, books, embroidery, games, jewellery, or whatever.

When I get home, I make out a new list immediately and tape it into the lid of my suitcase – and leave that open until all my special holidaying clothes have been washed, ironed, aired and then packed away. All traces of sea and sand are washed off sandals, and they are nourished, polished, or simply thrown out if I have worn them to death. The ones I keep are stored in cotton shoe-bags, so they are not left lying about to get scuffed in the bottom of a wardrobe. Then the holiday suitcase is stored away, complete with scented herb bags while I start my stockpiling drawer again for the following year.

It is because I am lazy as well as forgetful that I need to do this kind of groundwork!

For your accommodation there are Youth Hostels on all these walks (you must first become a member by writing to Youth Hostels Association, 14 Southampton Street, London WC2E 7HY (01 836 8541).

I wonder if you could advise my husband and me about the need for taking a holiday? We are pensioners, and manage to save a small amount to enable us to have a week annually by the sea, but our home is now getting shabby, and needs things like new curtains. Do you think, in view of this, that we are justified in spending our savings on a holiday?

Mrs J. W. Keynsham, Bristol.

I most certainly do – the lift you get from new curtains cannot possibly replace the tonic effect of a holiday. If you want some advice on where to go, write to The Elderly Invalids' Fund. In some cases they will also give financial assistance.

P.S. This organisation now goes by the name of Counsel and Care for the Elderly, at 131 Middlesex Street, London E1 7JF. They offer advice not only on holidaying but on all problems, from accommodation to medical care, financial and pension difficulties, etc. They do make grants, most often for people needing full nursing care. (See book list.)

My 19-year-old son and 16-year-old daughter have reached the age when they want to do something without us during the summer holidays. My son is thinking of getting a summer job, which his father and I wholeheartedly support. We would feel happier though if our daughter was with a youth group so that someone was keeping an eye on her without her being too restricted. How can I find out what sort of things are available?

Mrs Eileen Chapman, Barnet, Herts.

Vacation Work of 9 Park End Street, Oxford, OX1 1HJ (0865 41978) publish some very helpful guides for all kinds of teenage holidays – including a Directory of Summer Jobs Abroad *which I'm sure your son would find useful. I suggest you invest in two handy books –* Adventure Holiday Guide to Britain *and* Adventure Holiday Guide Abroad *– so that you can help your daughter choose a suitable holiday. These books list an enormous variety of holidays for all age groups. P.S. These two books have been combined into a single big volume now called* Adventure Holidays. *Vacation Work publish many other titles, listed at the end of this chapter and available by mail order.*

I am 20 and have just finished a three-year course at college. I would like to travel abroad for about a year before actually finding a permanent job. Where can I get details of working abroad? I am particularly interested in working on a kibbutz and I seem to remember that you recommended a book on the subject.

Mrs K. Stoltman, Alness, Highland.

The book to tell you all you need to know is Kibbutz Volunteer, *a Vacation Work publication available by mail order or from branches of W.H. Smith and large bookshops. Another handy book for holidays and working abroad is the* Travellers' Survival Kit *which gives information on local customs and how to deal with any emergency. If you have difficulty obtaining either book you can get them direct from Vacation Work (see above and in address list at the end of this chapter).*

★★★★★★★★★★★★★★★★★★★★★★★★★★★★★★★★★
If you cross paths with a jelly fish or man-of-war on your holiday beach, spread wet sand all over your lashed skin, just like butter. If the stings are extra severe, spend a penny into a container and use that instead – fresh urine is a disinfectant and very relieving. Do not be squeamish about this – we are all made up of natural products.
★★★★★★★★★★★★★★★★★★★★★★★★★★★★★★★★★

My recent marriage has meant that my widowed mother lives on her own. In the past she has enjoyed holidays abroad but is reluctant to travel on her own. How can she find companions?

Mrs V. Chester, Mill Hill.

Most of the tour-operated 'package deal' holidays not only give excellent value for money but also offer instant companionship. Your local travel agent could advise which is best for you. I'm afraid accommodation for one tends to be more expensive because it is obviously more profitable for hotels to put two people into a room. Some tour operators arrange tours for people who share interests: The Holiday Fellowship Ltd, 142 Great North Way, London NW4 1E (01 203 3381), runs houseparties in Britain only; these are specially for lone holidaymakers and social events are laid on. P.S. Your mother should also contact Cruse, The National Organisation for the Widowed and their Children, 126 Sheen Road, Richmond, Surrey TW9 1UR, who produce a truly comprehensive Holiday List, giving not only many tour operators, but wonderfully varied ideas for special holidays such as staying with a French family, walking tours or painting courses.

After visiting Spain several times my husband and I have decided we would like to retire there. We want to sell our terraced house here in England to buy an apartment there, but do not know how to go about it. Agents' brochures lack details about the inevitable difficulties in moving to another country.

Mrs W. Repnaar, Maidstone, Kent.

Your British passport entitles you to stay in Spain for three months and at the end of that time you apply to the local police for an extension, which is almost always granted. Similarly, you may apply for residents' permits which may take some months to come through but are rarely refused. You may buy property in Spain at any time and should go to your bank for details of how to transfer your money over there. There is a new law, operational from this April which will enable you to receive the rises in state pensions that are granted in Britain. At present retired people living abroad receive only the pension that was paid when they left the country. For information about financial and tax matters write to: The Spanish Consulate, 3 Hans Crescent, London SW1, and ask for their booklets C-16 and Tax Regulations for Foreigners. *When the time comes to move you must draw up a list, in Spanish, of all the items of furniture you will be taking with you and their value in Spanish currency. Moving house is always an ordeal, but uprooting to another country is especially unnerving – so I wish you both every happiness.*
P.S. For younger people considering a life abroad there's a useful book called the International Employees Tax Handbook, *published by Woodhead Faulkner Ltd, 17 Market Street, Cambridge CB2 3PA.*

Do you know of any organisation dealing with short-stay students from abroad with which I could get in touch? We are a young family and would like to have young people staying with us. We could learn something of their countries while showing them our own. The language barrier may present difficulties but the effort should be fun.

Mrs Cooper, Bromley, Kent.

What a good idea – and I have a feeling that other families might like to stretch this friendly invitation to youngsters from across the sea. Write to the Press Office, The Central Bureau for Educational Visits and Exchanges, 43 Dorset Street, London W1 (01 486 5101), and ask for their leaflet, called Young Visitors to Britain.
This includes, among many other things, a list of paying-guest agencies through which you can get in touch with students. I shouldn't think the language barrier will be big enough to cause any real bother.

Now that the cost of living has reached such a high level any ideas of going abroad for our holidays seem to be out of the question. Even the cost of hotels in this country seems to be extraordinarily high. During the last couple of weeks I have been trying to think of some way to have a pleasant, inexpensive holiday and the only idea which seems reasonable is to find someone who would like to exchange homes with us for a couple of weeks. Advertising in the press seems to be expensive, so do you know of any agency that will try and match our exchange requirements at a reasonable cost?

Mrs C. E. Eden, Chippenham, Wilts.

I don't think this is a good idea for the very houseproud, but easy-going families with similar standards of living may jump at it. Home Interchange Ltd, 8 Hillside, Farningham, Kent (0322 864527), do just what you suggest for holidays in Britain, Europe,

America and Canada, so write to them for a prospectus.

I am a middle-aged housewife and love painting. I would like to go on a painting holiday where there were other beginners like myself and we could have instruction.

Mrs J.M., Cromarty, Highland.

The Holiday Fellowship (see address list at end of chapter) organise several painting holidays. One is on Arran, another in the Lake District, and one in Wales. They also offer painting holidays abroad. Prices vary according to accommodation. You don't need tremendous ambition or even great talent to get pleasure from painting, so you are bound to have a very happy holiday.

Have you any suggestions for a holiday for a man on his own? I think I've coped pretty adequately with most of the problems of my solitary life but I need a holiday that will give me a change of outlook. Where do you suggest I go?

Mr A. Morris, London NW3.

How well I understand this. Singles Holidays of 23 Abingdon Road, London W8, could have the right solution. Their monthly magazine, Singles *is on sale at all branches of W.H. Smith and Sons.*

★★★★★★★★★★★★★★★★★★★★★★★★★★★★★★★★★★
★ All sporting managers take into consideration ★
★ that we lose one pint of liquid in one hour's ★
★ flying time – easily counteracted if you keep ★
★ up a similar intake of non-alcoholic liquid ★
★ during the flight, and a bonus is that those ★
★ deep lines that appear, especially round the ★
★ eyes, just won't! (Drinking alcohol on a flight ★
★ only speeds up the process of dehydration.) ★
★★★★★★★★★★★★★★★★★★★★★★★★★★★★★★★★★★

There are an enticing number of holiday possibilities for single people. For instance, you could join a Houseparty, run by Countrywide Holidays of Birch Heys, Cromwell Range, Manchester M14 6HU (061 225 1000). If you are active and adventurous you could have the excitement of a voyage, without losing sight of land, touring the canals of England on a hotel boat. Particulars from Boat Enquiries, 7 Walton Well Road, Oxford. Or if you have any special hobby get Activity and Hobby Holidays In England *from any branch of W.H. Smith and Sons or by post from The English Tourist Board, 4 Grosvenor Gardens, London SW1W 0DU.* England Holidays *can be seen at any travel agency and is full of varied suggestions.*
P.S. For older people, a most supportive and helpful organisation is Saga, who specialise in holidays for the over-60s and also operate a club so that people who meet while away can keep in touch on their return home. They offer special holidays to cater for your hobbies or interests too. Write for full details to Saga Holidays Ltd, PO Box 60, Folkestone, Kent (0303 30000).

We are 23-year-olds interested in becoming beauty consultants. For the past four years we have worked as hotel receptionists and we want to try something new. It appears there are two ways to go about this – take a college course or apply direct to one of the private beauty schools. Which course of action do you advise?

Angela and Mary, Edgbaston, W. Midlands.

First if you even thought of this as a glamorous career, think again. Believe me there is more hard work than glamour and it is mentally and emotionally demanding because you will often be working with temperamental *people. The college course is very thorough and includes art, biology, chemistry, physical exercise and business management. The entrance requirement is three GCE O-levels, preferably in English and two sciences. With private school the situation is more confusing. When you look at a school it is important to check that the training includes make-up and skin care, electrolysis, anatomy and body-massage, nutrition and control of weight problems. Some schools belong to the Confederation of Beauty Therapy and Cosmetology and a list of both these and the Technical College courses can be obtained if you send a sae to the Training Secretary, Mrs Eve Taylor, 22 Bromley Road, Catford, London SE6 (01 690 2149). Alternatively, contact the International Health and Beauty Council, The Thatched House, Littleheath Road, Fontwell, Near Arundel, Sussex BN18 0SR. Since you have been working for over three years you might qualify for a technical opportunities grant. These, claimed from local Job Centres, are earnings-related. But the 16-year-old should stay on for O-levels or if she has them already, work on a beauty counter until she is $17\frac{1}{2}$ and old enough for a beauticians course. Do bear in mind that training at beauty schools is very expensive and, despite the best will in the world, they cannot guarantee you a job at the end of your course.*

I am interested in becoming a nanny and looking through *The Lady* magazine at the situations vacant, I came across an NNEB qualification. I wondered if you could tell me what these initials stand for, and where I could obtain it? I will be 16 in November.

Miss V. Solman, Exmouth, Devon.

NNEB stands for Nursery Nursing Examinations Board. If you write to them at 29–31 Euston Road, London NW1 2SD, enclosing a sae, they will send you particulars of how to train. There are five fee-paying residential colleges where you may train, but it is no longer easy to get a grant for the two-year course because many local authorities now run their own – job-based and college-based. The first involves working in a council children's home where you are paid for your work. You also go part-time for college instruction. With college-based training you do a two-year course mainly in college, though going part-time to help in a home. For this you might get an education grant. You can begin the training at 16. Most local authorities prefer students to have two or three 'O' levels when applying for a place.
P.S. For other nursing career inquiries there is a special service at the Nursing and Hospital Careers Information Centre, 121 Edgware Road, London W2 2HX (01 402 5296); write to them with any problems.

I have been asked to take a keep-fit class for our local Farm Women's Club. I was trained as a part-time physical education instructor in the ATS 30 years ago and badly need some revision. Do you know where I could receive this?

Mrs Margaret Nobbs, Ventnor, Isle of Wight.

All readers with the same urge should contact The General Secretary, Keep Fit Association, 16 Upper Woburn Place, London WC1 0QG (01 387 4349).

My son, aged 15, is interested in becoming an osteopath. How should he go about training for this profession? He is very interested in body-building and is a member of the National Amateur Bodybuilders' Association. I have multiple sclerosis and find great relief when I am able to visit an osteopath privately – the National Health hospitals don't seem to provide this valuable service.

Mrs P. Mescall, Balham, London.

The British School of Osteopathy gives training but the student has to enrol for a full-time four-year course. To be accepted, he must have passed five subjects in GCE, including two A-level passes, preferably in chemistry, biology or zoology. Some local authorities may give grants for osteopathic training. Further details can be obtained from The Secretary, The British School of Osteopathy, 16 Buckingham Gate, London SW1. Alternatively, your son may prefer to get medical qualifications before training as an osteopath. If so the London College of Osteopathy, 8 Boston Place, London NW1 6QH (01 262 5250), trains qualified medical practitioners.

I am aged 58 and was made redundant six months ago. There seems little chance of further employment around this area, and as a lady friend of mine has had to go to Devon to look after her ailing mother, I want to find a home in that area. I am a tenant of a good council house here. The Newton Abbot council do not operate an exchange scheme, so I'm left in the position of remaining here and unemployed, yet I would willingly move near my lady friend as I know I love her.

Mr R. L., Uttoxeter, Staffs.

I do not know what work you have done, but how about applying for a job with accommodation in Devon? I'm sure your friend would help you by looking through the local newspapers for vacancies for a school caretaker, caretaker of a block of flats, or something similar. Most councils will only put you on their housing lists if you have lived in the area for three years, but you could put your name down the moment you got there. If you are in love, time flies and at your age you have many years to look forward to. So go!

I am working towards my GCE A-level examinations in the summer of 1974 but I have no idea of what I want to do afterwards. I don't want to pick the wrong occupation and find out I am unhappy in my work.

'Frustrated student', Birmingham.

You are wise to be thinking of your career now but even if you are undecided next year, you can always spend a year working abroad and getting invaluable experience of life, until you have a concrete idea of what you want to do. The Careers Research and Advisory Centre produce some excellent publications: Your choice at 13+, 15+, 17+ and Your Choice of A-levels. Write for these to CRAC, Bateman Street, Cambridge CB2 1LZ. If you feel that you want to pay for advice, the Vocational Guidance Association, Upper Harley Street, London NW1 (01 935 2600), should be able to point you in the right direction. They charge full-time students a fee for tests and questioning followed by a guidance interview. (They do also offer advice to people of all age groups, not just students.) At least you've made up your mind about one thing – you don't intend to be a failure of any kind – so the odds are that you won't be.
P.S. CRAC publish another very useful series of Degree Course Guides, and a book called Careers Without A-levels.

I have always been interested in teaching deaf children, but do not know how to go about this, or what qualifications are needed. I am 21 and would very much like to take up this worthwhile work.

Cheryl Hargreaves, Ashton-under-Lyne, Lancs.

It's so easy when faced by someone with a physical shortcoming to appear rude or indifferent out of embarrassment or shyness. But, remember, they live with their problem and so develop an extra understanding towards people's reactions to them. If you write to the Royal National Institute for the Deaf, 105 Gower Street, London WC1E 6AH (01 387 3033), they will send you free a card with the Manual Alphabet, and they will post you a booklet called Sign and Say. Some colleges and universities run one-year training courses on teaching deaf children, but only for qualified teachers. Information about these courses can be obtained by writing to the National Deaf Children's Society, 45 Hereford Road, London W2 (01 229 9272).

Here's a chance to learn the manual alphabet, enabling you to converse with deaf people.

My son is at college, my daughter is married and although I have many hobbies I get lonely when my husband is at work. I have always wanted to train as a switchboard operator, but it is difficult to find out where and how. Apparently there is no evening-class course.

Mrs Joyce Davies, Pontypridd, Glamorgan.

The Post Office gives excellent switchboard training (for outsiders as well as Post Office staff) so ring your local supervisor or go to your nearest post office for details of where you should apply. After your switchboard training you can be given help with locating a job by Marketing and Sales Service, 15 Poland Street, London W1V 4PB (01 734 1011).

I'm happily married with three children. However, since we moved house and I have not had the daily social life I had before, I feel the need for mental stimulation. Housework bores me and I find myself becoming constantly depressed. I have 12 months to plan or train, as my youngest child starts at school after that. My interests are mainly artistic and I had thought of something to do with cosmetics – perhaps selling them in a large store. I need pointing in a definite direction! Have you any suggestions?

J.E. Whitehead, Bourne End, Bucks.

Many young wives and mothers feel as you do. I think your best plan would be to write to The National Advisory Centre on Careers for Women, Drayton House, Gordon Street, London WC1H 0AX (01 380 0117). They give a practical service, assessing what you could do from your education, interests, experience and present home situation. They charge a small fee for postal information or for a career interview and follow-up advice. P.S. The NACCW also publish several books and leaflets; one of their most popular titles is

Returners, for women considering going back to work. Write for their complete booklist; it is very helpful.

What began as fun to amuse my 'coffee morning' guests has now snowballed into something more. Since I was a child I constantly have been able to foretell things – which did in fact happen. I would forecast what colour dresses women would wear and then tell their fortunes for fun. Now I am invited, under my assumed name, to galas and bazaars through which I raise money for charities. Many people have been delighted with my forecasts, and I am being asked to do private readings and be paid for them. My problem is, that if I decide to take this up 'professionally' what steps must I take to register, and how much duty and tax would I have to pay? I hope you can help. I enjoy predicting, but don't want to run foul of the law.

S.H., Stafford.

You don't have to have a licence to practise as a clairvoyant or mind reader, but in theory if you call yourself a 'fortune teller' you could be prosecuted under the Vagrancy Act – so avoid that tag if you advertise professionally. You can use your address for private consultations, but don't put a board up outside your house saying Samantha – Clairvoyant *because your house is probably not listed as a business address by the local town planning department. The only person you must notify when you start any kind of business is the tax man! Keep a book showing on one page your takings, and on the opposite one all your business expenses. The balance is your earned income which you must show on your annual tax assessment form (or your husband's if you are taxed as a couple). What a fascinating gift. But does it really foretell whether it will bring you fame and fortune?*

Useful Addresses

The Vintage Magazine Shop,
39–41 Brewer Street, London W1. (01 439 8525)

Kernowcraft Rocks and Gems Ltd,
21A Pydar Street, Truro, Cornwall TR1 2AY. (0872 2695)

Dryad (art supplies),
178 Kensington High Street, London W8 7RG.

Dryad Leicester (for complete catalogue),
PO Box 38, Northgates, Leicester LE1 9BU.

British Parachute Association,
Kimberley House, 47 Vaughan Way, Leicester (0533 59778)

Ivor Mairants Musicentre,
56 Rathbone Place, London W1P 1AB. (01 636 1481)

Imhof's Ltd,
112 New Oxford Street, London WC1A 1HJ. (01 636 7878)

Royal Institute for the Deaf,
105 Gower Street, London WC1E 6AH. (01 387 8033)

Watkins (specialist books, numerology etc),
19/21 Cecil Court, London WC2N 4HB. (01 836 2182)

The Atlantis Bookshop (specialist books, magic, occult, numerology, etc),
49A Museum Street, London WC1A 1LY. (01 405 2120)

The Federation of Family History Societies,
c/o The Honorary Secretry, 96 Beaumont Street, Mile House, Plymouth PL2 3AQ.

The National Bonsai Society of Great Britain,
c/o The Secretary, Miss Brenda Marshall, 61 Halsall Road, Birkdale, Southport, Lancs.

The Council for British Archaeology,
112 Kennington Road, London SE11 6RE. (01 582 0494)

Archaeology Abroad,
The Institute of Archaeology, 31–34 Gordon Square, London WC1H 0PY. (01 387 6052)

The Brass Rubbing Centre,
St James's Church Hall, Piccadilly, London W1.

J.W. Northend Ltd (specialist publishers),
49 West Street, Sheffield S1 3SH. (0742 730341)

Edna M. Tarr (jewellery craft supplier),
8 Pinetree Avenue, Scotter, Near Gainsborough, Lincs BN21 3TY. (0724 762513)

City and Guilds of London Institute,
46 Britannia Street, London WC1X 9RG. (01 278 2468)

The Dolls House,
29 The Market, Covent Garden, London WC2E 8RE. (01 379 7243)

Ken Lawson (deltiology books),
12 Suffolk Road, Cheltenham, Glos GL50 2AQ.

Vera Trinder Ltd (deltiology books),
38 Bedford Street, Strand, London WC2E 9EU.

Ron Griffiths (deltiology dealer),
47 Long Arrotts, Hemel Hempstead, Herts HP1 3EX.

Drene Brennan, Postcard Club of Great Britain,
34 Harper House, St James' Crescent, London SW9.

British Amateur Gymnasts Association,
95 High Street, Slough, Berks SL1 1DH. (75 32763)

Francis Music Supply (sheet music),
12 Gerrard Street, London W1V 7LJ. (01 437 2532)

Chappell of Bond Street (sheet music and books),
50 New Bond Street, London W1. (01 491 2777)

National Children's Homes (holidays for children in care),
Child Care Department, 85 Highbury Park, London N5 1UD.

The Children's Country Holidays Fund,
1 York Street, Baker Street, London W1H 1PZ.

Youth Hostels Association,
14 Southampton Street, London WC2E 7HY. (01 836 8451)

Counsel and Care for the Elderly,
131 Middlesex Street, London E1 7JF. (01 621 1624)

Vacation Work International Club,
9 Park End Street, Oxford OX1 1HJ. (0865 41978)

Cruse, The National Organisation for the Widowed and their Children,
126 Sheen Road, Richmond, Surrey TW9 1UR.

The Central Bureau for Educational Visits and Exchanges,
43 Dorset Street, London W1. (01 486 5101)

Home Interchange Ltd,
8 Hillside, Farningham, Kent. (0322 864527)

The Holiday Fellowship,
142-144 Great North Way, London NW4 1EG. (01 203 0433)

Single Holidays,
23 Abingdon Road, London W8. (01 937 6503)

Countrywide Holidays,
Birch Heys, Cromwell Range, Manchester M14 6HU. (061 225 1000)

Boat Enquiries (canal holidays),
7 Walton Well Road, Oxford.

The English Tourist Board,
4 Grosvenor Gardens, London SW1W 0DU. (01 730 3145)

Saga Holidays Ltd,
PO Box 60, Folkestone, Kent. (0303 30000)

Beauty Therapy Courses,
Mrs Eve Taylor, 22 Bromley Road, Catford, London SE6. (01 690 2149)

International Health and Beauty Council,
The Thatched House, Littleheath Road, Fontwell, Near Arundel, Sussex BN18 0SR. (024 368 3868)

Nursery Nurses Examinations Board,
29-31 Euston Road, London NW1 2SD.

Nursing and Hospital Careers Information Centre,
121 Edgware Road, London W2 2HX. (01 402 5296)

The Keep Fit Association,
16 Upper Woburn Place, London WC1H 0QG. (01 387 4349)

The British School of Osteopathy,
16 Buckingham Gate, London SW1. (01 828 9479)

London College of Osteopathy,
8 Boston Place, London NW1 6QH. (01 262 5250)

The Careers Research and Advisory Centre,
Bateman Street, Cambridge CB2 1LZ. (0223 354551)

Vocational Guidance Association,
7 Upper Harley Street, London NW1 4RP. (01 935 2600)

Royal National Institute for the Deaf,
105 Gower Street, London WC1E 6AH. (01 387 8033)

National Deaf Children's Society,
45 Hereford Road, London W2 5AH. (01 229 9272)

Marketing and Sales Service,
Telephone and Office Personnel, 15 Poland Street, London W1V 4PB. (01 734 1011)

The National Advisory Centre on Careers for Women,
Drayton House, Gordon Street, London WC1H 0AX. (01 380 0117)

Further Useful Addresses

Holidays:

Project 67 Expeditions (kibbutz holidaying),
21 Little Rusell Street, London WC1A 2NH.

Colony Holidays (for unaccompanied children),
Linden Manor, Upper Colwall, Malvern, Worcs WR13 6PP. (0684 40501)

The Lake District Adventure Centre
(unaccompanied children),
Fallbarrow Hall, Windermere, Cumbria LA23 3DX. (096 62 5454)

Galleon Painting Holidays,
Galleon World Travel Association Ltd, 77-87 King Street, Maidstone, Kent ME14 1EG.

West Dean College (residential courses in arts and crafts),
West Dean, Chichester, Sussex PO18 0QZ.

Swans Art Treasure Tours,
237 Tottenham Court Road, London W1P 0AL. (01 636 8070)

The London Tourist Board (publishes many useful guides),
25 Grosvenor Gardens, London SW1W 0DU. (01 730 3450)

Transalpino (cheap holidaying in Europe for people under 26, by rail at up to 50 per cent of normal second-class rates),
71-75 Buckingham Palace Road, London SW1W 0QL. (01 836 6283/9656)

Jobs and Careers:

National Extension College (especially for women re-training),
131 Hills Road, Cambridge CB2 1PD. (0223 63465)

Social Work Advisory Service,
26 Bloomsbury Way, London WC1A 2SR. (01 242 5654)

Reach: Retired Executives Action Clearing House (helps with information about activity with low pay or no pay in charity work),
Victoria House, Southampton Row, London WC1. (01 404 0940)

Success After Sixty (Employment Agency, London area only),
40-41 Old Bond Street, London W1X 3AF. (01 629 0672)

Employment Fellowship (employment for over-60s),
Drayton House, Gordon Street, London WC1H 0BE. (01 387 1828)

Useful Reading

Contemporary Ragtime Guitar, Stefan Grossman (Ivor Mairants Musicentre).

Folk Music Accompaniment for the Guitar (Ivor Mairants Musicentre).

Solo Guitar Playing, F. Noad (Ivor Mairants Musicentre).

Fundraising: A Comprehensive Handbook, Hilary Blume (Routledge & Kegan Paul).

The Numbers Book, Sepharial (Foulsham and Co).

Romance In Your Name, Juno Jordan (De Vorss).

Numerology: The Complete Guide, M.O. Goodwin (available from Atlantic Bookshop).

Bradbury's Book of Hallmarks, Frederick Bradley (J.W. Northend).

Make Your Own Dolls' House, Christopher Cole (Shepheard-Walwyn).

Make Your Own Victorian House, Rosemary Lowndes and Claude Kailer (Angus and Robertson).

Smallwood's Piano Tutor (EMI).

Amateur Pianist's Companion, James Ching (EMI).

Long-distance Footpath Guides: all available from Her Majesty's Stationery Office:
1 Pennine Way
2 Cleveland Way
3 Pembrokeshire Coast Path
4 Offa's Dyke
5 Cornwall Coast Path
6 Ridgeway Path
7 South Down Way
8 Dorset Coast Path
9 South Devon Coast Path
10 Somerset and North Devon Coast Path

Where to Live After Retirement (Consumers Association).

Accommodation for the Elderly (Outside London); Sheltered Housing Schemes (Age Concern).

Claiming a Supplementary Pension towards the Fees of a Private Home (Counsel and Care for the Elderly).

The Directory of Jobs and Careers Abroad, Philip Dodd (Vacation Work).

The International Directory of Voluntary Work, Gillian Nineham and David Woodworth (Vacation Work)

Kibbutz Volunteer, John Bedford (Vacation Work).

Travellers' Survival Kit Europe, Roger Brown (Vacation Work).

Travellers' Survival Kit to the East, Susan Griffith (Vacation Work).

International Employees Tax Handbook (Woodhead Faulkner Ltd).

Activity and Hobby Holidays in England (English Tourist Board).

Your Choice at 13 +, Michael Smith (CRAC).

Your Choice at 15 +, Michael Smith (CRAC).

Your Choice at 17 +, Michael Smith and Peter March (CRAC).

Degree Course Guides (CRAC).

Careers and Jobs Without 'O' levels, Thelma Barber (CRAC).

Time Between, Philip Hall and Martin Murphy (CRAC).

Careers – A Guide for Parents, Hugh Ramsbotham (CRAC).

Into the Professions, Alan Jamieson (Daily Telegraph/CRAC Careers Guide).

Into Industry, Alan Jamieson (Daily Telegraph/CRAC Careers Guide).

Returners – A Career Guide (National Advisory Centre on Careers for Women).

5
Cookery

My attitude to food is simple: I love it. I'm not what the French would call a *gourmet*, I am a straightforward *gourmande*. In English that would translate as just plain greedy, though the foreign language turns it into something slightly more attractive.

It is a blessing that I seldom have the time to spend with my nose in a cookery book, because I would be quite happy hovering between hob and oven, but above all I am lucky to have a husband who would far rather settle for a pill called 'lunch' and another labelled 'dinner' than face any fancy meal. He has virtually no interest in food and I hate to think what would happen if he had, because I have a definite tendency to put on weight and at the slightest encouragement I start whipping up concoctions which do waistlines no good at all.

However, I have learned to prepare food that satisfies my desire to eat in an enthusiastic way, without doing too much damage to my figure. What I would call a 'working lunch' is a delicious, health-giving, sustaining salad: avocado, apples, tomatoes, celery, nuts, and raisins (or similar raw mixture) generously laced with cottage cheese *and* yoghurt (both low fat, as a gesture in the right direction!) but I confess to spicing up my sparse repast with an Italian speciality called Mostarda di Cremona, which truthfully translated is candied fruit matured contentedly in a sharp mustard-based syrup. And on the days when I succumb to a rule-breaking dessert and settle for a banana fritter or a buttered crumpet lightly coated with Bulgarian jam, I remember the words of a pencil-slim acquaintance: 'One moment on your lips, forever on your hips!' but this does little to restrain me.

After that glossary of greed it comes as no surprise to confess that I do full credit to my native Italy. I am a considerable expert at spaghetti variations with sauces of all kinds. I still think the Neapolitan way of preventing pasta becoming glue-like is the best. After it is cooked just place an empty saucepan under the colander, so that when it is drained you have some of the cooking water saved. Then, after turning the pasta into a deep bowl, on to a big knob of butter, stir gently as you ladle, a little at a time, some of this left-over cooking water. Keep doing this until the pasta stops lapping it up and you can see a little liquid gathering. Having satisfied its thirst, whatever shape or size the pasta is, it will never become the consistency of wallpapering glue and each piece or strand will remain separate.

The emphasis of this chapter is to give you kitchen lore, not recipes, some suggestions for effortless cooking, rather than carefully planned reminders of what really can be achieved by super cooking in the kitchen. This is a reflection of the attitude I have expressed in other pages of this book – to try to make life easier, more enjoyable, and your activities less of a chore. Take pasta as an example: the most economical and successful party food can be created if you prepare vast bowls of cheap spaghetti, but then add fun and choice for your guests by making three or four different sauces, so that people can choose one or two as they prefer. In my experience the women do exactly as planned while the men ladle every variety on to their plates – one after another if they are elegant about it!

I firmly believe that good cooking should also be simple. Guests are often slightly intimidated by over-elaboration in the presentation or ingredients of dishes, which is a style of cookery I find out of keeping with modern notions of healthy eating anyway. The best cooks are always those who can turn something mundane into something delicious, without slaving over a hot stove so that they cannot share your enjoyment of the final dish. You can build up experience in this style of cooking by learning to savour the simplest combinations of flavours. Transform a boring old supermarket chicken by popping a peeled onion, or half an apple or half a lemon or orange inside the bird. If you use a citrus fruit, squeeze the juice all over the bird first, then push the half-shell inside the breast. Add a few sage leaves, a sprig of rosemary, or a dusting of paprika if it is at hand. Experiment with these herbs and spices one at a time, so that you develop a good memory for their taste, and can then try combining them with other dishes you often prepare. If your family likes the crunchy skin of a chicken, rub it with oil and salt (incidentally the best trick for pork crackling, too) and then try smearing a little Dijon mustard (French and very aromatic!) over the breast before putting the bird to roast in the oven.

Incidentally, any joint of meat tastes even more delicious if you smear it with mustard about two hours before cooking: a very basic 'marinade'. If you prefer to grill chicken or other meat on a grill, try sprinkling some salt in the bottom of the drip tray underneath before you start cooking. When the fats drip down, the salt prevents it from catching alight or spitting furiously.

In spite of my advice, I consider myself an emotional vegetarian. Put my imagination to work for a while and I would turn away every kind of meat. But I enjoy fish and eat free-range chickens if they are genuinely free-range and have had a good life and a quick out at the end of it. However, I could never be a vegan (eating only vegetables and beans and no animal products) because I am sure chickens were born to lay eggs and it would be such a waste to throw them away. I attribute my pragmatic views to frequent travel abroad: we eat so well at home with little thought for people in other lands who would be glad to have one-tenth of our choice, that I find it difficult to be so hard and fast in my rules. Besides, travel abroad has offered me the delights of other styles of cooking, more modest in ingredients perhaps, but a delight to the eye and exceedingly easy on the digestion – such as the Japanese way of preparing fish in lemon juice, or the subtle peanut sauces for tiny slivers of vegetable or meat in Indonesian dishes. These are ideas that can so readily be adapted to our own kitchens, and I have suggested suitable books for beginners at the end of this chapter.

My own enjoyment of food is made complete when I see other people enjoy the meal as much as I do. My condition was best summed up once by a waiter in Paris who brushed aside my doubts on facing yet another succulent dish: 'Si on mange avec plaisir, on assimile.' Of course we assimilate more if we love our food and I sincerely hope that he meant 'burn up' rather than 'store up' so that I can go on taking pleasure in eating my favourite dishes, and in passing them on for others, too.

Smells and how to deal with them

Do you like cabbage but dislike the smell while it's cooking? Put the end of a loaf on top of the cabbage (cooking in only a little water), and there will be no nasty smell. The crust can be removed before serving.

Mrs I. McMinn, Belfast, N. Ireland.

While I was visiting my sister in Germany, she gave me this tip to keep bread fresh and prevent it from getting mildew. Wash the bread bin with vinegar and wipe dry. Place a small container of salt in the bin (I use the top from a jar). After a few days the salt turns to water and needs replacing. I find this keeps the bread beautifully fresh.

Mrs L. Wakely, Swansea, W. Glamorgan.

A spoonful of sugar may make the medicine go down, but did you know that a white sugar lump absorbs stale smells and moisture? I pop one in my empty vacuum flask to keep it fresh, and another into my teapot and kettle when I go on holiday.

Mrs M. Heath, Mid Glamorgan.

Just a quick handy hint – mustard completely removes the smell of onions from hands and from knives. Use it dry, rub in well and then rinse off. Wash the hands in the usual way – and they will smell clean.

Mrs Val Carroll, Wallasey, Merseyside.

A less messy, but equally effective way to banish strong smells from cutlery and fingers is to rub them with the skin of a lemon or lime – but thank you for the 'hot' tip – I shall certainly add it to my list of smell-banishers. Another remedy you might like to try is a cream just for this purpose called Handjoy, obtainable from Fulford Williams (International) Ltd, Cornwall Road, Hatch End, Pinner, Middlesex HA5 4JY.

Butter tips

Everyone knows that if you keep butter for too long it is likely to go rancid or at least taste 'tinny' when you use it. But you can 'rehabilitate' it if you're feeling economical by sticking a peeled carrot into the dish. Leave it to do its work for about four hours, and to your (and my own) amazement you will find the butter dairy fresh again.

You can keep butter quite fresh, even when the fridge is out of action, if you wrap it in a clean linen cloth which has been soaked in vinegar and then wrung out. (Worth remembering for picnics.)

There's always some butter wasted when you take a block out of its wrapping. You can either save these up to butter your cake or pastry pans for cooking, or run the block under the cold tap before you open it – the butter comes out clean.

An excellent tip to prevent your frying pan from spitting at you! Before you cook with butter, or any other fatty substance for that matter, throw a pinch of salt into the pan. It stops the grease from crackling and splattering.

Frying oil smell

A good way to stop the smell of frying oil from penetrating the entire house is to drop a stalk of parsley into it as it begins to warm up.

I am sure there are many housewives like myself who hate peeling onions, but if you put a piece of bread on your knife and push it up to the handle this will absorb whatever it is in the onion that makes your eyes water.

Mrs E. Rousse Woodthorpe, Notts.

I find a pad of foam rubber lasts longer than bread on the knife handle. And may I suggest a way of peeling onions which is absolutely tearproof? Just leave the tufts on each end as you slice, and you can keep your eyes wide open.

Kitchen tips and hints from readers

I'd been married about a week and my cooking was not exactly Cordon Bleu, so I thought I'd make life easier and bought a tinned steak and kidney pie. I was putting the pie in the oven when the insurance man came to the door, so I left the kitchen to help my husband fill in his policy. He had just signed on the dotted line when there was a terrific explosion from the kitchen. We rushed in to find the oven hissing and steaming like a volcano. Our intrepid insurance man opened the oven to reveal our pie (or what was left of it) splattered all over the inside. The oven shelves were twisted beyond repair. What I had forgotten to do was remove the lid from the tin, which may seem funny, but has taught me to read all labels fully before cooking anything. It was bread and cheese for us that day, but I hope my story serves as a warning to others.

Mrs C. Hatton, Stirchley, Birmingham.

I would like to tell you about my latest brainwave. When mincing meat or anything juicy I fasten a clean plastic bag with no holes in it on to the cutter of the mincer with a rubber band. Mince away with no splashes, and everything is ready to pop into the freezer with a clip round the bag, or to pour into the

An economy tip: if you are mixing minced meat into a meat loaf, add a tablespoon of oil instead of an egg to bind it. It is cheaper and stops the meat from going too hard during the cooking.

pan for cooking. This is particularly useful for mincing citrus fruit for marmalade.

Mrs H.G. Brown, Winchester, Hants.

The other day I spent an infuriating half-hour wrestling with a jar of pickles, but the lid just wouldn't come off. I was about to resort to smashing it when I had a brain-wave. In desperation I put on my rubber gloves, hoping this manoeuvre would improve my grip, and tried again. Sure enough I then unscrewed the lid with ease. What a 'glovely' feeling of power. What was that about the weaker sex?

Miss Claire Gordon, Altrincham, Ches.

Next time the milk is burnt, take the saucepan off the stove and put it in a bowl of cold water. Ensure there is enough to cool the milk, but not so that the water slops over the side of the pan. Then add a pinch of salt to the milk, and the burnt taste will disappear.

Miss G. Rayner (aged 14), Ilford, Essex.

Prevention being better than cure, use a chunky glass circle that rattles when the milk boils so you catch it before it burns. Solidex is made from a special heat-proof glass and is available from hardware stores, and branches of Timothy Whites.

Boiling milk

To stop milk from forming a thick crust inside your saucepan when you boil it up, rinse out the pan with cold water first (do not wipe dry) and then boil the milk. It really works.

★★★★★★★★★★★★★★★★★★★★★★★★★★★★★★★★

Soft cheese from old milk

Have you ever tried saving a bottle of milk that has gone off, and making your own soft cheese? It is very easy: buy a packet of fine coffee filter papers, stand in a filter over a jug, and pour the soured milk into this. Allow the liquid to drip slowly (in the fridge of course) and you will find the results very tasty: add sugar or salt to the cheese according to taste.

Hard ham

No doubt you have come across hard, dark slices of ham, left too long in your refrigerator. You can bring them back to a tasty and supple existence once more by soaking them in a dish of milk for a few moments.

★★★★★★★★★★★★★★★★★★★★★★★★★★★★★★★★

With plenty of fresh herbs available now, I've been making sure I am stocked up for winter by packing ice-cube trays with chopped mint, parsley and other varieties. I top each with a little water, freeze, then transfer the cubes to polythene bags or containers and keep in the freezer.

Mrs M. Caffrey, Devon.

Lemons are expensive and often one needs only a little of the juice for a recipe or a drink and much of the fruit is wasted. When lemons are cheap buy four or five, squeeze the juice into an ice tray and freeze. When the cubes are solid, remove them from the tray, place in a plastic freezer bag and keep them in the freezer compartment of the fridge. The cubes will keep indefinitely. During a recent spell of sore throats in the family this was the simplest way to make honey and lemon drinks.

Mrs H. Turnbull, Uxbridge, Middx.

A friend of mine has brought me a great many lemons from her orchard abroad. Can you tell me how to use them up and how best to keep them from drying out?

Mrs N. Wilkinson, Glasgow.

You may find you'll use up this gift more quickly than you expect – lemons are so versatile. You can make marmalade, lemon curd, lemon mousse, lemon sauces (sweet for puds, tangy for fish) and squeeze the juice for cordials and general cooking. You can also freeze lemons in slices for drinks, or whole, though the peel is not firm when thawed. Alternatively, keep some in the bottom of the fridge, or in a bowl of cold water in a cool place. Change the water daily and they'll keep for weeks. If you want the juice of a whole lemon,

★★★★★★★★★★★★★★★★★★★★★★★★★★★★★★★★

Garlic is one of the best flavourings to use in the kitchen, especially in sauces, but it is not entirely wonderful to find lumps of it on your plate when eating. If you spike a clove on a toothpick before dropping it into your cooking, you do not have to fish endlessly for it to take it out just before serving up your dish. (Crush the clove slightly so that its full flavour is released.)

★★★★★★★★★★★★★★★★★★★★★★★★★★★★★★★★

dip it into boiling water for a few seconds before squeezing it, but if you need only a few drops, pierce the skin in one place and then stick in either a toothpick or a strong match to act as a plug until the next time.

P.S. *Lemon juice makes a lovely dressing for raw shredded carrot: so much better than vinegar.*

If you just want to have the slightest trace of garlic in your food, a good way is to peel a couple of cloves of garlic, cut them in two, place them in a screw-topped jar and cover with corn oil. Use this oil in salads and stews where you want just a delicate trace of garlic. You can top up the oil each time you use some and the garlic keeps fresh for a long time.

Rosa Margolis, London NW11.

Helpful onion hints. Place onions cut-side up in saucers on the floor to absorb paint smells.

If you overdo garlic or onions nibble a spray of parsley – also good for fresh breath!

Washing the face in water in which onions have been boiled is said to be good for spots, pimples, blackheads and skin problems.

Hot onion soup with garlic toast and peppermint tea is very good for colds and flu, while sore throats can be eased by wearing a stocking rubbed along the inside with a cut onion.

Onions and garlic disperse blood clots and lower high blood pressure in humans and in horses.

Lady Viedor, London SE20.

As the 'salad season' is practically upon us, I simply must know how only three people can be expected to eat a whole lettuce between them in just one go! At the moment I keep the remains in a plastic bag in the fridge, but it still seems to go brown. Unfortunately, I am a terribly economical person, and when I marry, I shall eat margarine instead of butter,

Salty soups

If you have made a soup or for that matter any stewy dish which turns out to be too salty, there are various ways to save the day.

Try adding a teaspoon of sugar. This only works if the taste is just mildly disgusting. If this fails, drop in a few slices of peeled potato. For some reason they draw all the salt and the dish returns to something edible.

An altogether incredible trick, which actually does work, is to add a glass of milk to the liquid and then drop in a silver *teaspoon. Leave this lot to bubble up for about 10 minutes. And of course do your best to remember to remove the spoon before you serve your rescued masterpiece!*

even though I can tell the difference. Therefore I feel it is a waste of money to buy a lettuce and throw half of it away.

Carolyn Hill, Stratford-upon-Avon.

As I find it only too easy to eat a whole lettuce, medium-sized and French-dressed, on my own and at one sitting, let alone with two friends, your letter surprises me! But maybe I have a few rabbits in my ancestry.

To keep a lettuce crisp and bright wash it in very cold water as soon as you get it home, shake the water out, and dry one leaf at a time with a clean cloth. Enclose the dissected lettuce tightly in a airtight plastic box and put it in the fridge. The drier the lettuce the longer it keeps – but don't stretch it beyond four or five days. 'Dressed' salad will never stay fresh for longer than an hour or so.

P.S. *Limp lettuce leaves can be revived by washing in* warm *water, rather than cold, first. You'd be surprised by the effect. And salad dressing can be made more piquant if you add a tiny pinch of curry powder: try it for a change. If the idea appeals, try chopped mint, a herb often neglected for dressing a salad.*

You might be interested in a method of preserving eggs I have been using since the war. Buy eggs fresh from a farm when they're at their cheapest. Put a knob of lard or cooking fat on the palm of the hand and roll each egg in it, completely, thus sealing the shell. The eggs can then be stored in egg boxes or racks and numbered, so that they are used in the correct sequence of freshness when prices are high in winter. I am still using last year's preserved eggs in all my cooking. Visitors given the test can't tell which are fresh hard-boiled eggs in a salad and which are a year old.

Mrs T. Sanders, Lyme Regis, Dorset.

Save yourself the trouble of melting chocolate to decorate cakes and buns. Simply place a few chocolate drops on your buns or cakes and return them to the oven for a short time.

Mrs Hurst, Halifax Road, Rochdale.

I was making jam the other day and I accidentally spilt some over my hand, but luckily I had a bowl of cold water in the sink next to me so I was able to swill my hand in the water at once to get the jam off before putting it under the tap. I really think this action, quickly taken, stopped me from getting a severe scald mark.

Mrs Joan Crouch, Bridgend, Glos.

The paper from a cornflake packet is excellent for lining cake tins and making jam pot discs for home-made jam.

Mrs H. Naylor, Caterham, Surrey.

Eggs

Your egg custard will not turn out runny if you add a teaspoon of flour to the eggs before beating them up. This helps the eggs to stay fluffy and dry. Try it for creme caramels, too.

Eggs: are they fresh?

The old trick to test the freshness of eggs is to float them in a glass or bowl of salted water. If they fall to the bottom and remain there, they are fresh, good enough to eat soft-boiled. If they hover half-way in the water, they are all right to eat cooked hard. If they float, throw them out!

Perfect boiled eggs

Fresh eggs can be kept for at least a week out of the refrigerator, and three weeks inside. But a cracked egg should be eaten within 48 hours at least. You can prevent boiling cracked eggs from losing their innards by adding a dash of vinegar – or throwing one or two spent matches into the boiling water. To get a perfectly boiled, soft egg, put it in cold water, bring to the boil and take out at once. If you use an egg cosy, cut down your cooking time by a further half minute.

I make sure my sponge cake does not crumble when fresh by putting it away on the lid of the tin and lowering the base over it.

Mrs L. Jackson, Cirencester.

A well-scrubbed dry potato in your bread bin keeps bread fresher longer if you have no fridge. A new loaf also cuts more easily if you dip your knife in boiling water.

Mrs M. Whalley, Macclesfield, Ches.

Jams

Whenever you are making jam with hard-stoned fruit, crack the stone and put the little 'almond' you find inside into your jam mixture while cooking. It improves the flavour enormously, adds a nutty surprise to the finished pot, and helps to improve the setting consistency.

Whatever jam you are making, always add the 'zest' of an orange or lemon, or even a pinch of cinnamon.

If you are making jellies, as opposed to jams, add a few unripe fruits to the ripe ones – it helps the jelly to have a better consistency without spoiling the full flavour of the mature fruit in any way.

To avoid the alarming boiling-over of jam in the making throw in a nut of butter. It stops that foam forming on the surface of the boiling fruit, and you do not have to watch like a hawk for accidents.

If you own one of those glass discs which are so good at stopping milk from bubbling over, try putting it in your pan of boiling jam: it will stop the sugar-fruit mix from catching on the base of the pan.

If your jams tend to crystallise while in store, it is usually because you have added too much sugar, or because you boiled the mixture too vigorously. Save the day by adding a few drops of boiling water to the pot when you unseal it, and give the jam a stir to mix the melted sugar back in. Crystallised jam also comes from using fruit which is over-ripe, not sufficiently acid. If you think this is the reason, tip all the jam back into a pan and re-boil it, adding the juice of a lemon or the juice from a handful of gooseberries.

Like many other readers I'm always keen to try out new recipes. Recently I discovered I had an enormous collection of cuttings from magazines and scraps of paper from friends. I finally came up with a way of keeping all these bits together. I bought an inexpensive photograph album – the type with sticky pages covered with clear plastic sheets. The recipes can easily be placed under the plastic, which can be wiped clean without spoiling the recipe. When indexed, there's no more searching for that recipe you need in a hurry.

Mrs P. Broomham, Rollesby, Norfolk.

Coffee: once you have ground it, store the left-over grains in a jar in the refrigerator, so that the fresh flavour lasts longer.

Coffee boiled is coffee spoiled, they always say. If, like me, you economise by keeping left-over fresh coffee for re-heating, you needn't despair. If you have let it bubble up, add a few drops of very cold water to the pot before serving. It takes away that bitter taste at once.

I am getting married this summer and a friend is making the wedding cake. I have always wanted a heart-shaped wedding cake (preferably a three-tier). However, there is one problem. Where can we buy or hire, three heart-shaped tins?

M.B., Bristol

You have certainly got the right kind of friend. Divertimenti of 68-70 Marylebone Lane, London W1M 5FF (01 935 0689), make just the heart-shaped tins you need. They also do a mail-order catalogue full of things they call 'small tools'. If you send a sae for this and their price list, you will probably find a number of useful ideas for the first kitchen of your married life.

In our house we don't just use ice cubes in summer drinks. When draining off fat before making gravy from meat juices, I pop a few ice cubes in the roasting dish. The fat congeals in a moment and can be scooped out, leaving the juices behind.

Mrs Bridget Clee, London.

Your ice cube tip for gravy reminds me of other culinary dodges. If you've made a stew and there is an unattractive layer of grease floating on the top of it, you can get rid of it (and improve the flavour and texture of your dish enormously). Gently lower a piece of blotting or kitchen paper on to the surface, wait until it has absorbed the fat, and lift off. Repeat until the meaty juice in the dish looks light and less shiny. Another very useful trick is to try the coarse leaves of a lettuce. (A handy way to make them serve a purpose if you don't have rabbits!) If you have a little forethought, you can adapt the ice-cube idea, by soaking a small clean cloth in water, wringing it out and sticking it in the freezer while you cook. If you lower that on the dish at the end of the cooking time, the fat will immediately congeal and come out of the pan without wasting any of the juices in the process. To prevent ice cubes sticking together in a bowl, squirt them with water and spray

with soda water before storing in a plastic freezer bag. I sometimes freeze a lemon sliver in some of mine to cut down time when serving drinks.

Here is a fuel-saving and trouble-saving recipe. Take 1½lb stewing beef and any vegetables you like, all cut small and flavoured with salt and pepper. Add water, bring to the boil and put into a food-storage vacuum flask which has been warmed by letting it stand with boiling water in it. Screw the top on, leave all day and in the evening you have a perfectly cooked meal for one. Variations are endless – steak and kidney, chicken casseroles, tripe and onions, or just meat for pies. No cooking smells, no dirty pans. I find this invaluable on holiday, or prepared the previous evening, as a stew-snack to take to work.

Mrs Betty Shepherd, Taunton, Somerset.

I'm not the world's best cook but the other day I carried out an experiment. I used up an old bit of cheese by grating it and using it instead of suet in some very nice, tasty dumplings. I'm going vegetarian – but I do like the odd dumpling.

Christine Jewell, Coulsdon, Surrey.

There are so many recipes using egg whites (meringues, syllabubs, etc) and I wonder if you can suggest any recipes for using the yolks?

Mrs Sheila Poulton, Newport, Salop.

****
* *If you have bread rolls that have gone a bit* *
* *dry, wrap them up in tissue paper, soaked in* *
* *water and squeezed out a little. Place in a* *
* *medium hot oven for a few seconds, and they* *
* *will come out bakery-fresh again.* *
****

Here are three of many uses for those leftover yolks. 1) To your yolks add a little milk, pepper and salt, plus another whole egg and scramble. Served on toast for breakfast it is impossible to tell the difference from 'real' eggs. 2) Use them as a base for home-made mayonnaise. With a wooden spoon stir in drop by drop, very slowly, some olive oil until the mixture thickens, then add a little vinegar (also drop by drop) until quite thin again. Then thicken further with more drops of olive oil. Continue alternately with this method until you've got the amount and consistency you want – add a pinch of mustard, pepper and salt and a touch of crushed garlic if you like. 3) Boil some rice, rinse it through with hot water, then throw in your fresh egg yolks (as many or as few as you have), a lump of butter and some grated Parmesan cheese. Toss well and serve. The yolks cook as they're stirred with the hot rice, making a delicious supper dish.

May I pass on a useful hint for cooking rice? I put the rice I require in a vacuum flask, add salt and then top up with boiling water. Screw on the lid and leave for at least an hour. The rice will then be found to be cooked.

Mr W. Simians, Northwich, Ches.

If you used savoury rice, which you can buy in one-meal-sized packets and which will absorb all the water, this would make a very easy warm meal when travelling with children.

I thought you might like to know how I get full value out of a 6p orange. I always wash my oranges, then, when I have peeled them, I cut the peel into one-inch squares and put it to soak with enough water to cover it overnight. Then I put the peel with the same water into a saucepan and simmer until the water has evaporated. Add 2 oz. of granulated sugar and one tablespoonful of water and simmer again, stirring with a wooden spoon until all the liquid has gone. When cold, store in a jar. I use this in cakes or put it in a little dish and offer it to visitors who always want to know how I make it. Then, if there is a pip in the orange, I put that into a flower pot and with care and watering grow a little green plant from which I get a lot of pleasure during the long Winter – and I've also enjoyed the orange itself. How's that for a few pence?

Mrs H.B. Smith, Sittingbourne, Kent.

You may also like to know that Mrs D.T. Waino of Formby, Merseyside, can double the amount of juice she gets out of a lemon or orange by warming the fruit first and then squeezing it gently in the hands before putting

---

If you have trouble with damp in a salt cellar, try adding a few grains of rice. It will absorb the moisture.

Salt, by the way, does not dissolve in oil. If you want a smooth and tasty vinaigrette, add the salt to the vinegar before you pour in the oil.

it in the lemon-squeezer. And a last word on oranges which will please the garden-proud when they have trouble with neighbouring cats. Mrs Garret from Margate, Kent, says that finely chopped orange and lemon peel sprinkled over the garden will keep cats away. If you think this looks unsightly you can dry the peel in the oven first and then crush it with a rolling pin. It is just as effective dried.

Cooking for children

When I ice plain cakes or buns I add half to one teaspoonful of blancmange powder to the icing sugar. This not only flavours and colours, but also stops the icing from running,

If you cook your own beetroot (better than buying them overdone and soggy from some market stall) remember when you tip out the boiling water to plunge them immediately into cold, and then you will find them even easier to peel.

Never bother to peel small mushrooms – it is not necessary, and their flavour can be improved by giving them a quick wash only in cold water, to which you add a dash of vinegar. They will emerge with more aroma, and you will save time.

Chestnuts are always difficult to peel – but here is the answer. Put them in the freezer overnight, and on the day you wish to use them, plunge them in boiling water. Once they are soft, rinse them at once under a very cold running tap. These hot and cold treatments loosen the skin and save you painful fingernails! (Other people swear that soaking overnight in salt water, then roasting dry, does the trick.)

Vanilla sugar seems like a luxurious ingredient in so many recipes, but it is easy to keep a store at home. Simply buy a stick of vanilla from a health-food shop or good delicatessen, slice it into thick one-inch pieces, and pop into a jar, into which you pour a bag of castor sugar. Shake or stir it so that the vanilla pieces are evenly distributed. If you can find one, a whole fresh vanilla pod can be stored in a sugar jar for ages, and will give a delicious flavour to your cake- and biscuit-making.

making it taste more like fondant. If you buy a packet of mixed flavours the children can choose their own favourites at very little cost.

Mrs E.M. Day, N. Yorks.

It also saves the need for bottles of colourings and flavourings, and doesn't set and crack like glacé icing but stays soft. I suggest you add one teaspoon of blancmange powder to 2 oz icing sugar and mix in warm water to a soft consistency.

I have found a very easy way of making delicious icing. Instead of mixing the icing sugar with water, use a little warmed milk. This keeps the icing soft for two or three days until the family has devoured the whole cake!

Mrs A.A.B. Little, Witcombe, Glos.

With a toddler and a young baby to feed, mealtimes can be a bit hectic. I've found a way to save both time and money by making my own baby food. When cooking a meal, I prepare extra meat, vegetables and a few potatoes. I liquidise the surplus with gravy made from meat stock and then put the mixture into ice-cube trays and freeze, finally storing the cubes in labelled bags in the freezer. There are endless varieties of food to do. Today I cooked a batch of stewed apples and custard and froze it. When needed I take out the required amount of cubes, thaw and cook them. The food tastes good and baby loves it.

Mrs F. Shooter, Notts.

Our doctor, however, warns readers that young babies under eight months should not have salt in their food, so small amounts of the family's meals may be liquidised for baby then salt added to the main portion for the rest of the family.

Having three always-hungry young children, I find that a packet of chocolate biscuits these days is not an economical buy. I have a cheaper alternative. Buy a packet of the cheapest supermarket biscuits – better still, make your own – then melt some cooking chocolate and dip one side of each biscuit into it. Place the plain side down on a cooling tray until set. If you're feeling extravagant, both sides may be covered.

Mrs J. Robson, Nottingham.

Here is an economical tip for Easter which children will enjoy, too. Take an egg and make a small hole (gently) at one end with a skewer – about a quarter of an inch in diameter. Pierce the other end with a pin and gently blow through this tiny hole until the yolk and the white of the egg drop into a cup. Put this on one side for cake-making or an omelette. Melt a bar of chocolate, either plain or milk, in a double boiler, or oven-proof dish over a pan of boiling water, allowing 2oz of chocolate per egg. Pour the melted chocolate into the egg shell through the larger hole and put it in the fridge to set. You can either break the shell and have a solid chocolate egg which can be decorated with icing sugar, or decorate the shell of the egg, or even just leave them as plain 'eggs'. What a lovely Easter surprise.

Mrs F. Quinton, Enfield, Middx.

Katie's advice on special foods

The revulsion I feel when I pass a butcher's shop forces me to find other kinds of food, so I think I must be vegetarian by instinct. Can you suggest any books which give vegetarian recipes and tell you how to work out a balanced diet?

Mrs Ann Walker, Durham.

Write to the Vegetarian Society, 53 Marloes Road, London W8, enclosing a sae for details which include recipe books. Your local information bureau should be able to tell you of any vegetarian restaurants in your area, so that you could get an idea of their menus – they are far more varied than you might think. But watch the calories if you have a tendency to put on weight.

After reading a recipe for bird's nest soup I am left confused with the thought that the nests used and those that birds actually live in are the same thing. Is this so? The recipe suggests soaking the nests in warm water and removing any protruding feathers.

'Worried Cook', Watford, Herts.

I used to wonder too, what kind of 'nests' they used. Recently I was told that they are not ordinary nests, but ones with an edible gelatinous coating produced by tiny swallows or swiftlets indigenous to the South China Sea. The nests, beige in colour, look like finely-shredded and glazed coconut. They must be soaked and cleaned before use. When cooked, they separate into shreds and have a subtle, distinctive taste. They are also high in proteins and vitamins. Bird's nest soup is considered a mark of great hospitality and the high point of formal dinners in China. Bird's nests are available in three grades: the rarest and most expensive grades are the whole nests which look like small, transparent egg-cups. The best of these are nearly white, with few twigs or feathers. Next are the curved chips of broken nests or 'dragon's teeth'. Last are ground-up birds' nests made into porous, brittle cakes. For information on Chinese cooking consult Step by Step Guide to Chinese Cooking, or Regional Chinese Cookbook, both written by Kenneth Lo, and both published by Hamlyn. For Eastern cookery try Spicy and Delicious or Oriental Cookbook, both by Priya Wickramasingh and published by Dent.

All our family like Italian food, especially my young son and my daughter who will eat spaghetti bolognese until it comes out of her ears! But I would like to vary this diet and try some other pasta dishes and simple Italian meals. The trouble is, I do not have any recipes. I enjoy cooking, but I live in a village, so I need recipes with ingredients I can get in the local supermarket. Can you give me a few ideas?

Mrs C.M. Spalding, Totton, Hants.

Elizabeth David has written just the book for you, Italian Cooking (Penguin). There's also a very beautiful book called Mediterranean Cookbook by Arabella Boxer, published by Dent, with sumptuous photographs by Tessa Traeger which will certainly give you a flavour of Italy!
P.S. An extra tip if you have left-over pasta. You can use it again if you plunge the pasta in boiling water for a minute or two, then rinse in a colander with boiling water again. It comes out as if freshly-cooked. But also, try it cold!

A fish dish, hot or cold

A delicious alternative to a vinaigrette sauce for shellfish, and particularly easy to make for a party buffet: mix together mayonnaise, whisky or sherry and tomato concentrate – half a pint of the first, a teaspoon or so of the last, and whatever you prefer of the alcoholic middle! If you wish to make a hot version of this dish, try warming up half a pint of thick cream, an egg yolk, the whisky or sherry and tomato concentrate as before, taking great care not to overheat or overcook the sauce as the egg will turn to tiny bits of scrambled egg otherwise.

To continue the festive air, a cold potato salad can be transformed if you add a glass of cold white wine to the bowl, turning the salad round until it is evenly absorbed, and then adding seasoning.

Fried fish revisited

A delicious alternative to battered and fried fish is easy: try rolling the pieces in instant potato mash, or potato flakes. The fillets come out crustier, and are lighter on the digestion. If you want to try something that turns fried fish into a galactic feast, dip the pieces in fresh cream before rolling in seasoned flour. The taste is unbelievable!

Could you tell me how to make sourdough bread? I have tried Mrs Beeton's cookbook and various other sources without success. It is, as you know, the bread eaten by a section of the Russian population who live to 100-plus, and is supposed to be better than wholemeal bread. On the evergreen topic of food I would like to offer the following wholesome meal. Cook a marrow bone (which costs a few pence) and then remove the bone and fat. The resulting broth can then be cooked with vegetables.

Edmund Sowter, Melton Mowbray.

The recipe for sourdough, known as Balabushky in Russia, is found, surprisingly, in an American cookbook and is as follows. Mix 4 oz of flour with 8 fl oz of water and 1 tablespoon of sugar, leave in a warm place for three days until fermented. Then sprinkle $\frac{1}{2}$ oz of active dried yeast over 12 fl oz of warm water to dissolve, and stir into the dough. Add to this mixture 1 lb of flour, two teaspoons of salt and two of sugar and stir vigorously. Place in a greased bowl and cover with a tea towel. Leave for two hours to rise. After it has risen, add $\frac{1}{2}$ teaspoon of baking powder, two teaspoons of salt and 4 oz of flour and stir. Knead this dough on a board, shape it and put in a greased tin. Then leave until it rises again to double its size. Brush the top with water and score. Pre-heat your oven to 400° F or gas Mark 6 and bake for 20 minutes. Then reduce the heat to 350° F or Mark 4 and bake for a further 20-25 minutes. Place a shallow pan of water in the bottom of the oven to prevent the dough from becoming too dry. I don't know whether man can live by bread alone to be 100 but here's wishing you many happy returns as you tackle your Balabushky!

Here's my own and many times proven method of cooking a 14 lb turkey in approximately one and a half hours.

Preheat the oven for approximately 30 minutes to 450° F, gas Mark 8, and do not change this temperature at all throughout the cooking. It is vital to keep the same temperature, so watch for fluctuations (especially during the Christmas morning 'cooking rush') and remember that small ovens are more likely to overheat.

Stuff the bird in the neck end only and leave the other end empty. (I make and serve my chestnut stuffing separately.) Pour hot melted lard over the bird and place in the oven.

Baste often and cook until, when the baking dish is tilted, the juices inside the turkey run out clear and water-like. This is the most reliable gauge for the cooking time of no matter how large a bird. I found a 14 lb bird took approximately one and a half hours. The great benefit is that there is no drying out or stringiness – especially noticeable when cold.

Calorie and Cholesterol chart

Abbreviations used in table

aver = average
ckd = cooked
gran = granulated
lg = large
med = medium
oz = ounce
sl = slice
sm = small
sq = square
t = tablespoon

Cholesterol content

H = high	L = low
M = medium	O = none

VEGETABLES

Artichoke	1 lg	95 O		Cauliflower	8 oz	30 O
Aubergine	8 oz	50 O		Celery	1 stalk	15 O
Asparagus	12	25 O		Corn	1 ear	100 O
Beans, Baked	8 oz	200 O		Courgette	8 oz	45 O
Beans, Kidney	8 oz	225 O		Cucumber	1 aver	20 O
Beans, Green	8 oz	25 O		Leek	8 oz	40 O
Beetroot	8 oz	70 O		Lentils	8 oz	110 O
Broccoli	8 oz	45 O		Lettuce	1 head	50 O
Brussels Sprouts	8 oz	60 O		Marrow	8 oz	35 O
Cabbage, Raw	8 oz	35 O		Mushrooms	8 oz	30 O
Cabbage, Cooked	8 oz	45 O		Onion, Cooked	1 lg	50 O
Carrots	1 med	25 O		Peas, Cooked	8 oz	110 O
Carrots, Cooked	8 oz	50 O		Pepper, Green	1 lg	25 O
				Potato, Boiled	1 med	125 O

Potato, Crisps	10 med	100 O
Potato, Fr. fried	6	100 M
Sauerkraut	8 oz	50 O
Soybeans	8 oz	200 O
Spinach, Boiled	8 oz	100 O
Tomato	1 med	25 O
Turnip	8 oz	45 O
Watercress	8 oz	10 O

SOUPS

Beef Bouillon	8 oz	25 L
Beef Broth	8 oz	35 L
Bean Soup	8 oz	225 L
Celery, Creamed	8 oz	200 M
Chicken	8 oz	100 L
Chicken Rice	8 oz	125 L
Chili with Beans	4 oz	175 M
Noodle	8 oz	125 O
Onion	8 oz	100 L
Pea	8 oz	140 O
Tomato, Plain	8 oz	100 O
Vegetable	8 oz	100 O

FRUITS

Fresh fruits

Apple	1 sm	75 O
Apricot	5 med	100 O
Avocado	1 sm	425 M
Banana	1 med	100 M
Blueberries	8 oz	80 O
Cherries, Unpitted	8 oz	95 O
Dates, Pitted	4 oz	250 O
Figs	1 aver	30 O
Fruit Cocktail	4 oz	65 O
Grapefruit	½ sm	50 O
Grapes, Concord	8 oz	85 O
Grapes, Gr. seedless	8 oz	90 O
Lemon Juice	1 t	4 O
Orange	1 med	75 O
Peach	1 aver	45 O
Pear	1 aver	95 O
Persimmon	1 aver	95 O
Pineapple	8 oz	75 O
Strawberries	8 oz	55 O
Watermelon, sl	1 med	100 O

Dried fruits

Apricot, halves	3	50 O
Coconut, Grated	2 t	50 M
Figs	1 aver	50 O
Prunes	4	100 O
Raisins	8 oz	430 O

Frozen fruits
(one third of 9-10 oz package)

Apricots		100 O
Blueberries		105 O
Cherries		110 O
Peaches, Sliced		90 O
Raspberries		100 O
Strawberries		115 O

POTPOURRI

Brown Sugar	1 t	15 O
Capers	1 t	3 O
Cranberry Sauce	1 t	100 O
Dill Pickle	1 aver	15 O
French Dressing	1 t	100 L
Golden Syrup	1 t	60 O
Granulated Sugar	1 t	18 O
Honey	1 t	65 O
Jams	1 t	50 O
Ketchup	1 t	25 O
Mayonnaise	1 t	100 M
Molasses	1 t	50 O
Mustard	1 t	10 O
Olives	6 sm	50 O
Olive Oil	1 t	125 O
Peanut Butter	1 t	100 O
Tomato Sauce	2 oz	50 O
White Sauce, Med	1 t	25 H

SWEETS AND NUTS

Boiled Sweets	1 oz	110 O
Caramel	1 med	75 M
Chocolate Bar	1 sm	300 H
Chocolate Creams	1 med	75 H
Fudge	1 sq	110 L
Marshmallows	1 lg	25 O
Almonds	12	100 O
Chestnuts	8	50 O
Peanuts	10	100 O
Popcorn, Butter	8 oz	150 M
Walnuts	4	100 O

BEVERAGES

Ale	8 oz	100 O
Beer, Lager	8 oz	110 O
Brandy	1½ oz	75 O
Cider	8 oz	100 O
Chocolate Milk	8 oz	225 H
Cocoa, Milk	8 oz	235 H
Coffee, Black	8 oz	0 O
Fruit Punch	6 oz	150 O
Grapefruit Juice	6 oz	75 O
Liqueurs	1 oz	80 O
Martini, Dry	3½ oz	125 O
Orange Juice	6 oz	75 O
Pineapple Juice	8 oz	125 O
Soda Drinks	6 oz	75 O
Tea, Black	8 oz	0 O
Tomato Juice	6 oz	50 O
Vegetable Juice	6 oz	75 O
Whisky	1½ oz	100 O
Wine, Dry	3½ oz	70 O
Wine, Sweet	3½ oz	125 O

DAIRY PRODUCTS AND EGGS

American Cheese	1 oz	105 H
Blue Cheese	1 oz	95 H
Butter	1 t	100 H
Camembert	1½ oz	125 M
Cheddar	1 oz	105 H
Cottage Cheese	4 oz	105 L
Cream Cheese	1 oz	105 H
Cream, Single	1 t	30 H
Cream, Double	1 t	50 H
Milk, Evaporated	8 oz	200 H
Milk, Dried Skim	1 t	25 O
Parmesan, Grated	1 t	25 M
Sour Cream	1 t	50 H
Swiss Cheese	1 oz	100 M
Whipped Cream	1 t	50 H
Yogurt, Skim	8 oz	115 L

Eggs

Boiled	1 med	70 H
Fried	1 med	100 H
Omelette, Butter	2 eggs	185 H
Scrambled	aver	150 O
White	1 med	15 O
Yolk	1 med	55 H

POULTRY

Chicken

A La King	4 oz	375 H

Chicken Pie	4 oz	350 M	Kidney	4 oz	150 H	
Creamed	4 oz	150 H	Liver	4 oz	155 H	
Fat	1 t	45 L	Roast	4 oz	200 H	
Fried	½ med	325 M	Stew	8 oz	250 H	
Fricasse	4 oz	225 L	Tongue	3 sl	150 H	
Giblets	4 oz	150 H				

Pork

Grilled	½ med	200 L	Bacon, Rashers	3	100 L	
Livers	4 oz	150 H	Bacon Fat	1 t	50 M	
Roast	4 oz	200 L	Chop, Fried	1 aver	250 H	
Salad	4 oz	225 L	Chop, Grilled	1 aver	225 H	
Stew	½ med	225 L	Ham, Boiled	4 oz	350 H	
Tinned	4 oz	200 L	Ham	1 sl	100 H	
			Ham, Smoked	4 oz	450 H	

Others

Capon, Roast	4 oz	225 L	Kidney	4 oz	130 H
Duck, Roast	4 oz	300 M	Liver	4 oz	150 H
Goose Fat	1 t	145 L	Loin Roast	1 sl	100 H
Goose Liver	4 oz	150 H	Sausages	2	150 H
Goose, Roast	4 oz	325 L	Spareribs	6	250 H
Pheasant	4 oz	175 L			

Others

Quail, Grilled	4 oz	175 M	Frankfurter	1 aver	125 H
Turkey, Tinned	4 oz	330 L	Rabbit	4 oz	175 L
Turkey, Roast	4 oz	250 L	Salami	1 oz	125 H

LAMB, BEEF, PORK

Beef

Brains	6 oz	200 H
Corned	4 oz	250 H
Heart	3 oz	100 L
Liver, Beef	4 oz	150 H
Liver, Calf	4 oz	160 H
Minced	3 oz	310 H
Pot Roast	4 oz	250 H
Roast	4 oz	200 H
Steak	4 oz	200 H
Tongue, Fresh	2 sl	100 H
Tongue, Tinned	8 oz	250 H
Tripe	4 oz	175 M

Veal

Chop	1 med	150 L
Cutlet	4 oz	125 L
Minced	4 oz	250 M
Roast	4 oz	150 M
Steak	4 oz	250 L
Stew	4 oz	250 L
Sweetbread	4 oz	125 L

Lamb

Chop, Fried	1 aver	325 H
Chop, Grilled	1 aver	250 H

BREADS, CEREALS, FLOUR, PASTA

Rolls

Bagel	1	110 L
Bkg Powder	1 lg	55 O
Buttermilk	1 lg	110 M
Plain	1	100 O
Shortcake	aver	175 M
Yeast	1 lg	100 M

Breads

Bran	1 sl	75 L
Cinnamon	1 sl	200 L
Date, Nut	1 sl	90 M
Egg	1 sl	75 H
French	1 sl	50 L
Gluten	1 sl	75 L
Graham	1 sl	75 O
Protein	1 sl	40 O
Raisin	1 sl	75 O
Rye	1 sl	75 O
White	1 sl	65 O
Whole Wheat	1 sl	65 O

Cereals

Bran Flakes	6 oz	100 O
Corn Flakes	8 oz	100 O
Oatmeal	8 oz	150 O
Rice Flakes	8 oz	120 O

Flours

All Purpose	8 oz	400 O
Corn Flour	1 t	30 O
Wheat Germ	8 oz	400 O
Whole Wheat	8 oz	400 O

Pasta

Egg Noodles	8 oz	105 O
Macaroni	8 oz	200 O
Noodles	8 oz	150 O
Spaghetti	8 oz	220 O

Rice

Brown	8 oz	130 O
Polished	8 oz	130 O
White	8 oz	200 O
Wild	8 oz	110 O

Others

Muffin	1	125 M
Pancakes	1 sm	100 M
Waffles	1	225 M

SEAFOOD

Fish

Bass	4 oz	100 L
Cod	4 oz	100 L
Flounder	4 oz	150 L
Haddock	4 oz	180 L
Hake	4 oz	125 L
Halibut	4 oz	200 L
Herring	4 oz	225 L
Herring, Pickled	4 oz	150 L
Mackerel	4 oz	150 L
Perch	4 oz	100 L
Salmon, Grilled	4 oz	140 L
Salmon, Tinned	4 oz	200 L
Sardines, Tinned	4	100 L
Sole	4 oz	125 L
Trout	8 oz	225 L
Tuna, Tinned	4 oz	125 L

Others

Caviar	1 t	50 H
Crab	4 oz	65 L
Crab Cocktail	4 oz	90 L
Lobster	4 oz	65 L
Lobster Newburg	aver	350 H
Mussels	12	125 L

Oysters	6 med	50 H	Oatmeal	2 sm	50 M	Eclair	1 aver	275 H
Oysters, Fried	6 med	250 H	Vanilla Wafers	3 sm	50 L	Fruitcake	1 sm	250 L
Scallops	4 oz	90 O				Sponge Cake	1 sl	125 M
Shrimps	10 aver	100 L	**Cakes**			Sponge Finger	1	25 L
Shrimps, Fried	6 med	250 M	Angel Food	aver	100 O			
Shrimps, Tinned	4 oz	145 L	Brownies	1 sq	50 H	**Others**		
			Cheese Cake	1 sl	350 H	Ice Cream, Scoop	1	150 M
DESSERTS			Chocolate Cake	aver	250 H	Jelly, Sweet	aver	100 O
			Coffee Cake	aver	150 M	Pie Crust	aver	250 M
Biscuits			Custard	4 oz	125 H	Sherbet, Scoop	1	100 O
Butter	6 sm	100 H	Danish Pastry	1 aver	200 H	Sundae, Fancy	aver	400 H
Chocolate Drop	3 sm	65 M	Doughnut	1 aver	150 H			

Food for positive health

Vitamin	What it is needed for	Foods in which it is found
Vitamin A	Proper growth in children. Good eyesight; ability to see in the dark. Healthy teeth and gums, hair and skin. Repair of body tissues.	Margarine, butter, whole milk, eggs, chicken, liver, kidneys, fruit, carrots, leafy green and other vegetables.
Vitamin B1 (Thiamine)	Proper functioning of heart, muscles and nervous system. Converts carbohydrates to energy.	Milk, poultry, liver, lean meat, pork, fish, peanuts, brazil nuts, wheatgerm, flour, cereals, bread, brown rice.
Vitamin B2 (Riboflavin)	Good eyes and eyesight, mouth and hair. Releases energy, and helps body to use fats, proteins and carbohydrates.	Milk, yogurt, eggs, cottage cheese, liver, lean meat, yeast, wholegrain bread, cereals, leafy vegetables.
Vitamin B3 (Niacin)	Healthy central nervous system. Breakdown and use of fats, proteins and carbohydrates.	Milk, eggs, chicken, liver, kidneys, mackerel, sardines, wholegrains, bread, leafy vegetables.
Vitamin B5 (Pantothenic Acid)	Healthy central nervous system, and forming of hormones. Healthy skin and hair. Use of fats, proteins and carbohydrates.	Most foods, especially eggs, liver, kidneys, wholegrains, peanuts, potatoes, tomatoes, leafy vegetables.
Vitamin B6 (Pyridoxine)	Correct chemical balance in tissues and blood. Healthy central nervous system.	Lean meats, yeast, wholegrains, walnuts, bananas, leafy vegetables.

Vitamin	What it is needed for	Foods in which it is found
Vitamin B12 (Cyanocobalamin)	Correct functioning of body cells. Manufacture of red blood cells.	Milk, soya beans, foods from animals (eg offal, fish).
Biotin (B10)	Conversion of food into energy.	Dried milk, raw egg yolks, liver, kidneys, pulses, nuts, cauliflower, leafy vegetables.
Folic Acid (FA)	Formation of red blood cells. Correct functioning of intestines.	Milk, meat, yeast, walnuts, almonds, vegetables, fruit.
Vitamin C (Ascorbic Acid)	Healthy bones, teeth and gums. Healing processes of the body. (Some believe it prevents the common cold).	Potatoes, tomatoes, leafy vegetables, fruits (especially citrus and strawberries).
Vitamin D (Calciferol)	Use of calcium and phosphorus. Strong teeth and bones.	Cod liver oil, egg yolks, tuna fish, herrings, salmon, bananas. Sunshine.
Vitamin E (Tocopherol)	Protects fatty acids. Helps manufacture and function of red blood cells.	Eggs, wholegrains, wheatgerm, peanuts, sunflower seeds, lettuce, carrots, cabbage, apples.
Vitamin K	Healthy blood clotting.	Eggs, wheatgerm, oats, potatoes, leafy vegetables.
Calcium (C)	Healthy blood clotting, muscles, nerves, tissues, plasma. With phosphorus, builds and maintains teeth and blood.	Milk, cheese, bread.
Potassium (P)	Healthy muscles, body growth and skin.	Milk, fruit, green vegetables, tomatoes.
Iron (Fe)	Production of haemoglobin.	Eggs, bread, liver, lean meat, leafy vegetables.
Copper (Cu)	Storage of iron in the body. Production of red blood cells.	Green vegetables.
Iodine (I)	Proper growth and manufacture of hormones.	Common salt, kelp (seaweed).

Useful Addresses

Fulford Williams (International) Ltd (makers of Handjoy cream), Cornwall Road, Hatch End, Pinner, Middx HA5 4JY.

Divertimenti (special shaped tins and other kitchen accessories), 68-70 Marylebone Lane, London W1M 5FF. (01 935 0689)

Tante Marie School of Cookery, Woodham House, Carlton Road, Woking, Surrey GU21 4HF. (04862 4050)

Lakeland Plastics (home freezing equipment), Alexandra Buildings, Station Precinct, Windermere, Cumbria LA23 1BQ. (09662 2255)

Home and Freezer Digest Magazine, Subscriptions Dept, 106 Hammersmith Grove, London W6 7HB. (01 748 8783)

Anything Left-Handed, PO Box 4SL, 65 Beak Street, London W1A 4SL. (01 437 3910)

Useful Reading

Step by step Guide to Chinese Cooking, Kenneth Lo (Hamlyn).

Regional Chinese Cookbook, Kenneth Lo (Hamlyn).

Spicy and Delicious, Priya Wickramasingh (Dent).

Oriental Cookbook, Priya Wickramasingh (Dent).

Mediterranean Cookbook, Arabella Boxer (Dent).

Italian Cooking, Elizabeth David (Penguin paperback).

Pasta Cookbook, Myra Street (Hamlyn).

French Cooking, Helge Rubinstein (Good Housekeeping/Ebury Press).

Vegetarian Cooking for You, Marguerite Patten (Hamlyn).

Wholefood Cookery, Gail Duff (Good Housekeeping/Ebury Press).

Japanese Cooking, Peter and Joan Martin (Penguin paperback).

South East Asian Food, Rosemary Brissenden (Penguin paperback).

Rose Elliot's Cookbox (Fontana paperbacks). **Not Just a Load of Old Lentils** **Simply Delicious** **The Bean Book**

Traditional Scottish Cookery, Theodora Fitz-gibbon (Fontana paperback).

Caribbean Cooking, Elizabeth Lambert Ortiz (Penguin paperback).

Cooking for Special Diets, Bee Nilson (Penguin paperback).

The Arthritic's Cookbook, Dr Colin H. Dong and Jane Banks (Granada).

The Diabetic Cookbook, Elisabeth Russell Taylor (Newman Turner).

Hedgerow Cookery, Rosamund Richardson (Penguin paperback).

Cooking in a Bedsitter, Katharine Whitehorn (Penguin paperback).

Kentish Kitchen (written in aid of the Mental Health Foundation), available from Kent County Committee, Old Vicarage, Bodsham, Ashford, Kent.

6
Clothes and
Home Maintenance

One of the most interesting aspects and difficulties of putting this book together is how methods, remedies and even reactions to the same subjects have changed. Perhaps 'evolved' would be a better word. I would not say that the old laws were wrong, because I still believe in grandmother's teachings, but there can be quicker ways of tackling household problems, and sometimes the earlier solutions had side effects which the more modern approaches eliminate.

Take carpet cleaning, for instance – a squirt of soda-water on a puppy puddle left untouched to dry will still work, but the acid of white vinegar, slightly diluted for young dogs' errors, or used neat for older ones, will deal more scientifically with the alkali of urine. At the same time it will remove all leftover sniffing value which could lead to a repeat performance. Then again, I know now that to rub a carpet is a sin, and the verb is 'to dab'. Speed is essential when it comes to drying out the area where a spill has occurred, so either keep treading on it with many pads of clean tissues, or blow a hairdryer over it (taking care not to scorch the pile). Leave a final pad of clean tissues under a heavy object overnight and that should ensure no trace of the incident by morning.

This is just one example, but over the years I have built up an incredible repertoire of cleaning facts – and there are still going to be gaps in that. This chapter gives the problems and answers which seem to have cropped up most over the years – plus a few decidedly original slants on the same subjects.

Clothes care and maintenance have altered a lot simply because 'easy care' is the keynote of modern living – but the understandably cautious manufacturer, who must protect himself from the whirlwind approach of the over-enthusiastic, does insist on a 'dry-clean only' label in garments which, with care, could be tackled by hand. I think common sense is the gauge in this case. If you are going to be wearing something every day to the office, play safe and choose an outfit that is machine-washable, or drip-dry, otherwise your cleaning bills will be vast. But if it's a beautiful crêpe silk blend in stunning white, it might be less of a burden to pay the cost of maintenance only a few times a year. One other note of caution about clothes and cleaning: I am sorry to say that I would seldom trust a sales assistant in a shop to tell me if something is machine-washable. After all, she probably works for a percentage! Some shops take a great deal of care to keep their staff well-informed, but in all honesty, it saves you annoyance and heartache if you check the garment for a manufacturer's label before you walk out with your purchase. It is surprising how easy it is to make this mistake about fabrics and clothes and end up with something unsuited to your needs just over this one vital issue.

I start off this chapter with your letters on those precious possessions – your costly fur, the family christening robe. In the more day-to-day clothes-care section I am sometimes simply passing on some of the invaluable tips and tricks *TVTimes* readers have sent to me, and that includes knitting and dressmaking skills aimed at saving tears, time and money.

When it comes to the home, dealt with in the latter part of this chapter, I doubt if anyone is more houseproud than I am – but although I enjoy not only the smell of wax polish but the actual polishing, and do admit to keeping a duster in a drawing-room drawer, I would never go as far as the lady who wrote and asked me how she could persuade her guests to exchange their shoes for slippers, wash their hands before touching her upholstery and preferably to slip into white overalls before sitting down! One could shroud the entire lot in clear plastic of course (the furniture, not the guests) but however beautifully cared for, a house is just a husk to me if it fails to be a *home*.

I have dispensed with clutter, but any china shines as a result of frequent washing, and although I resisted it for as long as I could, I have settled, for some objects, on a less gleaming glow from brass and silver, under a coating of lacquer. Although I love and enjoy my special possessions, I refuse to be a slave to my standards when I could be occupied with other interesting things.

From experience I try to beware of overstrong colours because I find these difficult to live with through all my moods and pressures. So I chose a ripe, rich apricot rather than a bright red apple when it came to curtains and sofa-covers for my living room, and for both dining-room and bedroom discovered some reasonably-priced chintzes which look somewhat garish on the right side. Made up on the *wrong* side, however, I have the benefit of good-quality fabric and the colours come through in beautifully subtle shades. Then again, even though my choice of a stippled grey wall to offset the apricot curtains may sound dull to many, I would still suggest that in the long run most of us should stay away from a room with a deep purple and/or bright green wall unless you have a strong 'Jekyll and Hyde' personality to match: it will be seductive and cool in the midsummer sun, but could turn into a combined morgue and refrigerator in the cold snowy light of winter. In the same way, a tartan ceiling certainly would be a talking point at any party, but could kill conversation when you are alone together and the guests have gone.

Not only the colours we choose, but the source of light in a room makes the atmosphere warm and relaxing, or flat and inhibiting. I would not try to dictate specific colours to anyone, because tastes vary as much as rooms do, but I would suggest that you should take a long-term view, having hindsight with foresight as it were, in confronting that colour chart. The size of a room, the amount of light, the blend with other colours in carpets and furniture, can alter the way a colour 'reflects' on walls, and create an entirely different atmosphere from the one you imagined when you chose from a square of colour on a white page.

We all groan inwardly when making decisions and spending money; a house is, after all, for most of us, the major investment of our lives. What delights me, reading so many letters, is not just the care but also the originality that goes into so much day-to-day running of homes, as well as the long-term decorating plans. That is what I hope you will find here – the most bizarre uses for ordinary objects, the most unorthodox cleaning notions, the most charming ideas for enlivening domestic chores, plus a wealth of useful, tried and tested household hints.

Clothes: the precious things

Your most treasured garment may be an ancient lace shawl, or it could be your little daughter's brand new party dress. If it is important to you, it deserves the finest treatment – and even the strangest remedies are worth trying if you think they might work. Here are some less usual clothes care inquiries . . . and some seemingly unlikely solutions.

I have recently acquired a Canadian squirrel fur jacket which is in very good condition although it is about 25 years old. I would be very grateful if you could give me any tips you may have about its care and storage. I particularly need to know what to do after it has been worn in the rain and whether I can brush it.

Miss Elizabeth Townsend, Oxford.

Personally I am against wearing real fur – but your squirrels have been dead a long time. The jacket must be treated with great care because squirrel fur is far from hard-wearing. Any fur worn in wet weather needs only a good shake and then should be left to dry out naturally in a warm room – but well away from direct heat. A gentle brush will bring up the sheen. As for storage, I suggest you first get it cleaned, then simply hang it on a padded hanger and cover it with an old sheet or pillow-case. Give it a good shake once a month. It's not necessary to put it into cold storage – if it has lasted this long it must be pretty adaptable. If the fur is dyed you won't need mothballs.
P.S. If you place a small lump of charcoal inside a paper tissue, and put that in an open plastic bag it will take away the smell of mothballs left in a pocket or tucked in a storage cupboard or drawer.

I am sending you a tried and tested tip for washing black lace. Simply soak it in cold tea, black coffee or vinegar and water. If it is very soiled and greasy, use a few drops of ammonia in warm water and sponge before washing. Don't use soap on the lace. Stiffen it with sugar dissolved in water, roll up to dry in a cloth or spread out on linen and iron between paper. Guipure lace should be ironed on the wrong side, with a piece of flannel underneath.

John Trewick, Co. Durham.

I delved into a fascinating book printed in 1899 called Enquire Within About Everything *and this advises those who want to wash white lace to put it in a strong lather of white soap and simmer it slowly for a quarter of an hour. Rinse it twice in cold water to which a drop of 'liquid blue' has been added. They, too, suggest sugared water to stiffen it – the more sugar you add the stiffer it will be – but insist that it should be laid out to dry on a linen cloth. Iron when dry using muslin over the wrong side of the lace.*

How can I bring back a 30-year-old, yellowing, Nottingham lace christening robe to its former whiteness?

Mrs E. Dawson, Norfolk.

This isn't easy, but you may be able to brighten it a few shades. Lay the robe out flat and tack it on to a piece of sheeting with long stitches. Slip it carefully into a white pillow-case and dunk the lot in water foaming with pure soap flakes, not too hot. Leave it for 15 minutes or more, but don't use any form of bleach. While it is still in the pillow-case, rinse thoroughly, then take it out carefully and while it is still tacked to the sheeting, lay it flat on a rough towel to dry naturally away from any direct heat.

I once read that to keep a wedding dress white you can wrap it in black tissue paper. I have tried numerous shops and stores for some, but no one seems to stock it. Can you help please or suggest alternative methods of preserving the whiteness of the dress?

Sheila Hodgson, Rainham, Kent.

This is a good method: most branches of W.H. Smith and Son Ltd sell black tissue paper, or can order it for you.

I've just been reading one of your letters on wrapping white articles in black tissue. Although this won't do any harm, I think you will find it is royal blue for white and black for silver things. If I'm wrong, I've been selling the wrong colour tissue for the last 22 years to my customers.

Mrs Sheila Sampson, Torquay.

Fur-trimmed coats are so fashionable; could you please tell me the correct way to cut an old full-length musquash fur coat to trim a coat I am making? I would also like to make a fur muff for my little grandchild. The coat is worn down the front but is otherwise in good condition.

Mrs Pearl Harris, Hereford.

Here, straight from the furrier, are some dos and dont's.
1. Lay the fur horizontally across the coat then cut the strip. 2. The fur should flow towards the centre back of the coat, i.e., the 'heads' of the animals to the front, the 'rumps' to the back. 3. Use only a razor blade and cut along the skin side, then you won't snip the hair. 4. Sew by hand a half-inch tape along the cut edge of the skin, then turn in a fraction of an inch before sewing to the coat. You can get bag frames specially made to be covered either with fabric or fur. If your local store

doesn't stock them, try writing to John Lewis, Oxford Street, London W1.

Could you please advise me how to remove shiny iron marks on velvet? I was making a party dress for my daughter and used a damp cloth to iron it on the wrong side. When I saw what was happening I finished with a cool, dry iron and it seemed much better. Can you recommend anything to remove the marks? It's very disappointing as I put such careful work into the dress.

Miss H. Collins, Lisburne, Co. Antrim.

If the velvet fibres have been snapped there's nothing you can do to repair them, but if they're just laid low you could revive them. Lay a damp cloth on the velvet, pile side up, then skim it with a really hot iron – but whatever you do don't actually rest it on the cloth or press down with the iron at all. The pile should perk up towards the heat. In future, press velvet pile down on a terry towel, but again, never lean heavily on the iron. By the way, velvet brushes up beautifully if you rub it over with a piece of stiff dressmaking canvas.

As you have written a book on home hints I thought you would like to hear about a book my grandmother bought in Chicago in 1895. It has recipes for soap, ice-cream, toothpowder and dynamite. Under '*to wash silk*' it has the following: *The dress must be ripped apart from the band at the waist and the lining removed as the bustle will not lie flat otherwise. If the dress is old and rusty a pint of gin or whisky should be mixed with each gallon of water.* No wonder Granny spent so long at the wash-tub.

Mrs L. Brumby, Hayling Island, Hants.

My son's fiancée wishes to wear my large Brussels lace veil for her wedding in early October if it can be restored to its former whiteness. Is there a safe way to do this?

Mrs M. O'Neill, Bristol.

Part of the beauty of Brussels lace is its creamy colour and if your son's fiancée chooses for her wedding dress a similar tone of silk or satin she'll look particularly feminine. Unless the lace is patchy or discoloured, or unless it disintegrates at the edges when you pull it gently, you should be able to wash it in pure soap flakes in hand-hot water. Plunge the lace in and squeeze it gently without rubbing. Rinse thoroughly under softly running water, then dip in a bowl of clear water laced with a spoonful of fabric conditioner. Spread a sheet on the floor and spread the veil on this to dry. I would hesitate to put such a delicate veil in the hands of a dry-cleaner but a top-class one may help by the very careful use of modern chemicals on it (at your own risk) if you're not pleased with your washing efforts.

I have recently become the proud owner of a gorgeous mink jacket. Please would you give me some tips on how to take care of it as I want it to last a lifetime?

Rosamund Hope, Beckenham, Kent.

You couldn't have a hardier fur than mink. It seems to thrive and shine on being worn. If you get caught in the rain just shake it well when you get home and leave it to dry on a hanger – never by a fire. If you pack it, turn the lining outwards so that suitcase straps don't cut into the fur. Watch your cuffs when wearing chunky, sharp-edged bracelets and be gentle when you do up any button-holes. Have it cleaned professionally every two years (or every year if you wear it often) and I think it's wise to have it put into a furrier's cold storage if we continue to have heatwave summers.

P.S. If you have greasy hair or skin, it's a good idea to wear a scarf so that the fur collar is protected.

I have inherited a lovely crocodile handbag complete with claws and have been told the skin should be 'fed'. I experimented on a small patch with olive oil, but it seemed to darken it. I should be most grateful if you could advise me on how to treat it.

J. Rathbone Vaughan, Bangor, Gwynedd.

Yes, olive or most other edible oils will make any skin dark and greasy. The best thing you can do is wipe the remainder off as thoroughly as you can with a soft tissue. The only kind of polish to be recommended for crocodile is a wax furniture polish – genuine, wax mind you – not the cream or aerosol variety. Crocodile has a hard, almost glazed surface and with care should last for 40 or 50 years. If the lining is torn and the handles have seen better days, The Handbag Services Co, 16 Beauchamp Place, Knightsbridge, London SW3 1NF (01 589 4975), will repair these and even re-model the entire bag if you wish.

Clothes: readers' good ideas

Here is where I bow to the ingenuity, wisdom and experience I witness daily through your letters to me. Your invention in turning quite simple objects to multiple uses, your ability to make things last and give the longest possible service and your knack of turning mistakes into successes all demonstrate that the art of positive thinking is still with us.

Washing and ironing are traditionally tedious and tiring. If you follow my advice you will find more time and energy for fun and frolic at the end of the day. You will also save on the budget. If you have a washing machine, wash linen and clothes on the coolest setting. Modern washing powders will make them clean whatever the temperature, and the result will be minimal creasing. It is the very hot water which eats up fuel and turns washing as wrinkly as a prune. Empty the machine at once and hang the clothes up, indoors or out. This means less creasing, and most clothes will be ready with very little or no ironing. Shake and fold linen and towels and place under mattresses or settee cushions. I get best results when friends plonk tubby backsides on the settee. Energy-free pressing, hooray! So please tell your readers, Katie, to cool it, hang it, and then sit on it.

Mr J. Truscott, Kent.

A headband can be made by knotting a laddered pair of tights. It can be easily stretched over the head without upsetting a new hairdo and is light enough not to give you a headachey constriction. I also cut the feet off old tights and use them inside shoes to stop chafing in hot weather – and I find old waistbands from tights make splendid garters! Long twisted strips of tights are also very useful for tying up bundles of all shapes.

Finally, I think most housewives will know that plaited nylons stitched together in continuous strips make quick-drying bath-mats and welcome kneeling pads.

Joan T. Hickey, Clevedon, Avon.

P.S. Another very useful tip with old tights is to stuff a stocking tightly with other laddered ones, and use it to tie round difficult corners or walls in the garage, to prevent your car getting the odd scratch as you manœuvre it out.

I was given a lovely pair of boots for Christmas, but to my dismay found they became water-marked after I wore them in wet weather. My mother suggested the following tip, which really does work. Stuff the boot or shoe with paper, then, away from direct heat, smear petroleum jelly over the whole surface. Leave it to sink in for the next 24 hours then polish and wax the surface. You should find the marks have disappeared.

Miss J. Clarke, Essex.

Here's a tip for washing nylon tights. Make a bag in nylon or other non-iron material pretty enough to hang in the bedroom or bathroom. Drop soiled tights in as you discard them, then draw the string of the bag tightly and put into the washing machine with other man-made fibres. Hang the bag out or pop in the dryer. This stops dripping tights hanging around the bathroom, or getting entangled with other clothes in the washing machine.

Audrey Palmer, Usk, Gwent.

Children's coat hangers are expensive to buy and are easily broken by a tug from an enthusiastic toddler. If you squeeze a wire one into a square shape they're just the right size and are virtually unbreakable. I hope this helps other mums.

Mrs E. A. Hardy, Plymouth, Devon.

P.S. As I hate the feel of wire hangers, I would stitch or stick a layer of foam rubber to pad them, picking a colour to tone with the bedroom decor. That way you'll encourage your child to be colour as well as clothes conscious!

I have discovered a way to dry jumpers without them creasing or being left with peg marks. Put the legs of a pair of tights through the sleeves of the jumper and the waist of the tights through the neck, then peg the waist and the feet of the tights to the line. The jumper is secured and it will dry in shape.

Miss Margaret Porter, South Shields, Tyne and Wear.

When spinning baby clothes, wrap them in cotton or linen and they keep their shapes much better.

Mrs T. Nicholls, Bristol.

Instead of hand-washing tights, put them inside your husband's socks, and then they can be machine-washed without snagging.

Mrs S. Marshall, Ashby-de-la-Zouch, Leics.

Fold net curtains and wash and spin dry in a pillow-case. They hardly crease and can be re-hung immediately.

Mrs D. Evans, Stockport, Ches.

If you put hosiery and delicate fabrics in a drawstring bag made from an old net curtain, they can be safely washed and spun dry in a machine.

Nancy Tomkins, Surbiton, Surrey.

My husband bought me a Moulinex salad spinner for my birthday, which I have found most useful, not only for spinning salad. If I wrap dried fruit in a muslin after washing I can spin it dry for baking. But for the best of uses, I have found that if my two-year-old daughter's smalls and cardigans need a quick wash by hand it also spins these to a near dryness!

Mrs June Pownall, Congleton, Ches.

Nowadays sweaters seem to be sold without that invaluable swatch of matching wool. This can present mending problems but to get over it I buy cards of natural wool and a range of felt-tip pens. After I've mended the garment, I go over the natural wool carefully with a pen whose colour matches the garment. The colour remains fast after washing and has solved what appeared to be an insoluble problem.

Sheila White, Isle of Wight.

P.S. Not all felt-tip pens are waterproof so try one out before using this tip.

My clothes seem to attract more than their fair share of fluff. Is there a quick way to get rid of it?

Mrs Jean Helm, Southend, Essex.

Fluff and hair (dog or human) can be coaxed off most things by winding clear sticky tape – the wider the better – over one's hand, sticky side up, and patting it firmly over the material.

Can anyone beat this for thrift? My daughters now grown up and married, have over the past 30 years absolutely refused to let me give away the coat I wore on my honeymoon. It has been altered into various styles, but the material is as good as new. Now finally they are considering turning it into a Teddy Bear for a future grandchild, so it looks as if it will be loved and regarded with affection for many years to come.

Mrs Doris Cooke, Spalding, Lincs.

Here is a tip which I think would be useful for mothers with several small children who take similar sizes of socks, vests and panties. I have a 'colour coding' system. By inserting a stitch or two into the toes of socks, the hem of vests and the waist bands of panties – each child having his or her own colour – I have saved a lot of time over the years.

Mrs J. Clare, Burnley, Lancs.

Instead of using shoe-whitener for children's canvas shoes a solution of half water and half white emulsion makes a good job which lasts well without flaking.

Mrs S. Randerson, Marshchapel, Lincs.

I was pressing a dress and to my horror scorched the top front of it. I suppose a large brooch would have covered it, but I would have been self-conscious about it. However, I discovered a remedy which proved successful. Boil two onions together with 2 oz of Windsor soap. Put 2 oz of Fuller's Earth in a basin and mix to a paste with the juice of the onions and soap. When it is cool, spread the mixture on the scorch mark (a toothbrush is ideal for doing this) and let it dry thoroughly, then wash normally. My dress is now perfect and much admired.

Iris Baldry, Langdon Hills, Essex.

I thought I would pass on this dressmaking hint which I have used for some time now. When a dress I like is wearing out I unpick it, press the pieces and use them as a pattern for making another. There is no need for a fitting, as the dress already fits.

Mrs D. Chubb, Aston.

After having used the same dressmaking pattern a few times, and found the patterns soon tore where the tailor's tacking dots were, I hit upon the idea of using file reinforcement rings and putting one on each side of the pattern where the dots are. It stops the paper tearing when lifted off the material.

Mrs Lovell, Bedlington, Northumberland.

Where would I be when sewing without my magnet at hand? Bought for a penny years ago, it finds all my dropped pins and needles, and even drew a screw which had fallen into a most awkward place in my sewing machine.

Mrs M. Pickering, St Helens, Lancs.

To encourage prompt running repairs, I keep handy a wine cork with threaded needles in one end and tiny scissors in the other.

Mrs D. George, Paignton, Devon.

I remove spare buttons from new clothes and stitch them on a piece of cardboard with a written description of which article of clothing they belong to. Now they don't get lost in my button box.

Mrs I. McLaughlin, Harrogate, N. Yorks.

I keep my spare buttons in those tiny jars we often throw away, such as mint, horseradish or mustard pots. There's no problem locating them now, when I need one in a hurry.

Mrs K. Farndon, Nuneaton, Warwks.

When casting-off knitting, I always use a size larger than the needle specified, to prevent puckering. If the pattern says 'cast off loosely' I use a needle two sizes larger.

Mrs W. Bowes, Chichester, Essex.

I knit a lot of baby clothes. When the wool becomes tight and it is an effort to move the stitches along the needles, I sprinkle my hands with a little talcum powder.

Mrs M. Burgoyne, Bartley Green, W. Midlands.

I'm a novice knitter. Can you tell me an easy way to lengthen children's jerseys? They grow out of them so fast, and trying to add extra ribbing to the welt or cuff looks amateurish.

Mrs J. Brown, Winchester.

To lengthen garments, Patons and Baldwins suggests you unpick the ribbing and add a couple of inches on to the bodywork, then re-rib. Experienced knitters sometimes start at the top of the sleeve, reversing the pattern as they go along. So cast away, ladies, and good knitting.

I am surprised Patons and Baldwins have advised to unpick ribbing as it is not possible to do this from the bottom edge of the sleeve or body, as any knitter knows. The most successful method I know is to unpick the side seams from the bottom of the sleeves, past the rib. Pull a strand of wool from side to side which will separate the rib from the garment. Pick up the stitches at the end of the sleeve, and continue to re-knit the rib until the required length is reached, using the rib wool which you can unpick now, after steaming it to remove the wrinkles. If matching wool is not available you can use a contrasting colour in a band before starting the ribbing, to add the extra length.

Mrs J. Robinson, Farnham, Surrey.

With many types of knitting yarn needing different methods of washing, and having spoiled a well-loved hand-knitted woollen jacket in my washing machine, instead of hand washing, I did not want to make the same error again. I now mark my completed knitted garments by embroidering a code on the inside seam, according to the instructions on the band from the yarn. For example, MW40 (machine wash at 40 degrees) HWC (hand wash cool). This may be done using a contrast-coloured yarn or embroidery silks and cottons. However carefully you may keep the bands from the yarn – if you have several hand-knitted garments, or have knitted them for other people – these instructions go astray.

Mrs E. Rose, Bournemouth, Dorset.

When I was knitting a mohair jumper recently I was advised to keep the balls of wool in the fridge whilst I was not using them. This stops the fluffy bits from getting all over the place or up your nose and it works for any fluffy wool.

Marcia Gladwin, Sheffield.

Clothes: cleaning queries

I have had a sufficient number of clothes that are tricky to clean and plenty of stubborn stains to make me something of an expert on clothes care – even if it is often only to recognise when to leave well alone and take the problem to a specialised cleaner.

My children's clothes always seem to get covered in felt-tip pen marks and grass stains. I can't remember what I should do. Can you help?

Mrs Jane Lanton, Penzance.

It's not just youngsters' clothes that attract this problem. I'm always covering myself with felt-tip and ball-point marks, and I only have to walk across a lawn to get covered in green stains. Not to worry, methylated spirit comes to the rescue. But you must put a clean pad of cotton wool on white linen underneath the marked material (this is an essential rule when de-spotting light materials), then wet another piece of cotton wool with meths and gently dab this over the stain. Keep an eye on the bottom pad; that one absorbs the stain, so keep turning it over to a clean bit.

I know man-made fibres are a boon in many ways, but some nylon blouses droop dreadfully after a few washes. Any ideas?

Mrs Martin, S. Wales.

Two lumps of sugar dissolved in the final rinse water will usually put crispness back into nylon.

I hope you can help to prevent my baby from suffering any longer from hard nappies. I have an automatic washing machine, but I find that the nappies become harder and harder with each wash – even though I soak them in nappy-cleansing solution before washing, and add fabric conditioner to the final rinse. I was advised to soak them in Calgon solution to counteract the hard water in my area, but I tried this to no avail. I then used Calgon in my machine instead of washing powder but this was also unsuccessful. I consulted the manufacturers of the machine who told me I needed a chemist, not an engineer! My nap-

pies are now almost rigid, so if you have any tips for returning them to their former softness, I will be grateful.

Mrs P.V. Wheeler, Royston, Herts.

After all that hard work you're defeating your own object by putting the softener into the soaking water instead of the rinsing water. Calgon is a very reliable softener but a small quantity should be put only into the second and final rinses. If your baby gets a slight rash from the alkali, reduce the quantity even more. The routine should go like this: (1) soak in nappy-cleansing solution; (2) wash in soap flakes or powder suds; (3) plain rinse; (4) second rinse with a small quantity of Calgon; (5) third rinse with a tiny amount of Calgon, plus, if you like, a dash of fabric conditioner; (6) tumble dry or hang in the open air. As the water is extra hard in your area, get advice from Permutit Boby Ltd, 632 London Road, Isleworth, JW7 4E2 (01 560 5199).

My husband is an assistant undertaker and naturally wears a lot of black clothes for work. I find his trousers seem to be getting paler – is there any way I can restore them to their former blackness?

Mrs L. Carver, Sussex.

Dip your clothes in strong black coffee and brush the material, always in the same direction of the cloth. Not only will this give back the depth of black to the stuff, but will also get rid of any accumulated grease on the fabric.

Soon after my wedding I dyed my dress with a hot-water dye. The colour took beautifully to the fabric – a mixture of silk and polyester. Despite dyeing the dress I haven't worn it again since my wedding. My sister is to be married soon and would like to wear it, but we feel it would be nicer white than beige. Can you give me any advice on dyeing it back again to white or would I risk ruining the dress?

Mrs D. B., Oxford

I have been told by most experts, including the dye manufacturers Dylon, that nothing can ever be dyed back to white. However, Guillaume, 59 Davies Street, London W1 (01 629 0868) don't say no to anything. They recommend that if you send a few samples of the material for lab testing they will advise you further. Remember to ask for an estimate for any work before you have it done.

I have a pair of gold-coloured dance shoes and I don't know how to clean them. Similar shoes I have owned have been wasted before they were worn out because it is impossible to remove scuff marks and keep that lovely shine on them. I also have several pairs of coloured leather shoes and find that after a few cleanings they lose their original colour. Finally, how can I remove a water line from leather shoes?

Mrs. A. Ashton, Bolton, Greater Manchester.

One of the cheapest and most successful dyes I have discovered is Lady Esquire, which is easy to use if you follow the instructions carefully, and also comes in a wide range of colours. It's on sale in most shoe shops and chain stores. I've found that by recolouring my shoes I can ring the changes more often than would be possible if I had to buy new shoes for every outfit.
P.S. I've always managed to remove water lines (except on suède) by wiping the surface with an impregnated shoe-shine wipe and letting this dry thoroughly before polishing the surface. Finally I spray the problem area with Bally's Impra spray – use this product on all shoes (including suède this time) before even wearing your shoes, and you can prevent that water line problem altogether.

I have a suit made from polyester fabric and it clings to my legs every time I wear it. I have tried an anti-static slip but it still clings to me. Is there any way I can stop this happening?

Mrs E. French, London W7.

I have found fabric conditioner, such as Comfort or Boots' Soft Rinse, in the final rinsing water helps to stop the unpleasant clinging of some polyester clothes – and a pure silk or cotton slip gives added help with this problem.

Several pairs of my suède shoes have become smooth on the toe-caps. How can I bring back the nap?

W. J. Wears, London N5.

Try rubbing balding suède toe-caps with a piece of 'crêpey' India rubber. Or if you have a friendly shoe mender, get him to give you a chunk of genuine crêpe soling. To prolong the life of suède, spray the brand new surface with Swade Guard. The same firm makes a small abrasive rubber called Swade Aid. Go gently, then pep up with a rubber brush.

I have been letting down dress hems, most of which were turned up with iron-on hem webbing. I have managed to unstick the hem by soaking it in water for a few minutes but when the material dries again there is still a deposit which catches on my stockings. Is there anything on the market which can take that deposit off material?

Mrs Edna Dawson, Hants.

When faced with the same problem I cover the hemline with a damp cloth, press with a hot iron, and peel off the remaining adhesive while it is still warm.

Can you please tell me how to remove a large scorch mark from the back of my coat which is 70 per cent wool and 30 per cent mixed fibres?

Mrs. L. Thornton, Yorks.

If the fibres aren't totally destroyed, mix 20 per cent undiluted lemon juice with 80 per cent cold water for woollen garments, applying the mixture to the scorch mark and sprinkle generously with salt. For 100 per cent cotton clothing apply the same mixture and put in the sun to dry but don't do this with any man-made fibres or you could make matters worse with a 'rusty' yellow stain appearing on top of the original mark.

Will bra manufacturers ever devise a practical form of underwiring in which the wires do not come out after three or four washes? I'm fed up with them sticking into me, catching clothes in my washing machine and even bringing it to a halt. I regularly sew them back but they always manage to pop out again. I pay several pounds for this type of garment. Can't something be done to make them more durable?

Mrs A. T., Kent.

The answer is in your own hands. Never put a wired bra into a washing machine. In my experience the best makes are French and you should always spend as much as you can on your underpinnings.

Having travelled some distance for a wedding, my mother found that the artificial flower on her hat had been crushed. Being resourceful, she used curling tongs to smooth and curve the petals, making the flower look as good as new. Your readers may find the tip useful.

J. F. Duffy, Essex.

I'm sure they will, and even if you are not such a dab hand with the curling tongs, I've discovered that Clairol's 'Instant' (two-minute) heated rollers do the job well, too.

Can you tell me why a maxi-cardigan I recently bought has a label in it saying *Dry Clean Only*? The cardigan is made of 100 per cent wool. I thought that wool could be washed gently by hand, using lukewarm water?

O. Bloomfield, Bury St Edmunds.

I think some manufacturers use the label to protect themselves from the results of bad washing methods – but I've found Woolite, a cold-water washing material, brings my maxi-cardigan up beautifully. It is quite expensive but a little goes a long way. It's made by E.R. Howard Ltd, Gippeswyk Avenue, Ipswich, Suffolk IP2 9AD. It is available from department stores with haberdashery sections, or larger chemists such as Boots.

Last year I bought three garments with instructions for washing given in symbols. When I bought each garment I asked the sales assistant what the symbols meant but she was no wiser than I. My husband said the last one gives me the freedom to park the car wherever I please when I am wearing that garment! Please, can you help?

Mrs A. Johnstone, St Anne's-on-Sea, Lancs.

I'm glad you asked because these hieroglyphics are quite a puzzle for lots of people. The Home Laundering Consultative Council Secretariat tell me that the signs are European Standard Symbols. They explained them as follows: (1) to be washed at temperature shown (in degrees centigrade); (2) no bleaching (any sign bearing a cross means don't do it); (3) one dot on an iron means use a cool iron (120°F), two dots mean a warm iron (160° F), and three dots a hot iron (210°F); (4) dry-cleanable – the letter in the circle tells the dry cleaners which solvents to use – let's hope they know *this!*

I am very fond of sequins and there are so many lovely dresses and jackets on television which are studded with them – but how do you clean them? Surely all these beautiful clothes aren't just discarded after they have been worn a few times?

R.O. Hughes, Merseyside.

Sequins don't mark, but they do need freshening up with a white spirit solution. Really this should be done by professionals. Make sure you go to a member of the Launderers' and Dry Cleaners' Association and get an estimate before you have anything cleaned. There are two London cleaners who also run a postal service which might be of some use. They are: Lewis and Wayne, 13 Elystan Street, London SW3 3NT (01 589 5730), and Lilliman and Cox, 34 Bruton Place, London W1X 7AA (01 629 4555).

I am an old-age pensioner and I always wear a nylon floral overall for my morning chores. Until recently, I found that when I knelt down, the lower button would burst off and the buttonhole split. Then I removed the bottom button and sewed it on, with about one inch of elastic, to the overall. Now, when I kneel or stoop down quickly, the elastic gives and saves me the bother of sewing the button back on again. It also saves the buttonhole.

Mrs Denby, Porthcawl, Glamorgan.

I used this tip on a button-through skirt I often use when driving. It made all the difference. Thank you, Mrs Denby.

Years ago, during a holiday in Paris, an assistant in an elegant store told me I would always keep my nylon blouses sparkling white if I hand-washed them in cold water with a super-fatted toilet soap, then gave them two or three cold water rinses. I bought the blouses and wore them for several years and they always kept their whiteness. I also washed my 'grey' white slips in the same way and believe it or not the greyness disappeared. They, too, were restored to a lovely new whiteness, no matter how grubby they became during wear. The secret is cold water washing with pure soap.

Miss Muriel A. Mason, Stoke-on-Trent.

Most people merely bring back romantic memories of Paris; yours is more practical· than most, and a sparkling white blouse always has a pretty charm to it!

Recently I bought about 24 oz of fawn, red and dark-brown wool from a firm which supplies direct to the customer. I knitted, very painstakingly, two Fair Isle sweaters for my younger boys. While I was pressing them, I noticed to my horror that the red wool was far from colour-fast and my pressing cloth was liberally blotched with red. Please, please can you supply me with washing instructions for the sweaters? I'd hate to lose them after only one wash.

Mrs A. Williams, Loughborough, Leics.

I hate to think of your labour of love being blurred. But I dare not take full responsibility for curbing that wayward-sounding red. However, you can try this method on a sleeve: leave in lukewarm water, well-laced with vinegar – brown or white, it still is a colour sealer – for about 10 minutes. Then wash in tepid water and the mildest of pure soap flakes, rinse in cold water with another dash of vinegar, squeeze out carefully and dry flat on something you don't mind marking. I use a sheet of foam rubber.

Help! I have an olive-green suède sleeveless coat which I have carelessly allowed to be badly marked with butter. Having tried, unsuccessfully, carbon tetrachloride, what do you suggest?

Mrs M. A. Allman, Penkridge, Staffs.

Don't tamper with it any more. Send it, with an explanation, to Suède Services, 2A Hoop Lane, Golders Green Road, London NW11 8JS (01 455 0052). They will give you advice and a free estimate. By the way, if you steer clear of butter in future, you can keep suède in good condition and give a fillip to life-worn coats, bags and shoes by rubbing them with a pad of ordinary crêpe soling.
P.S. If you get butter, grease or any oily stain on suède or other material, you can usually avoid a permanent mark by sprinkling the area at once and very generously with talcum powder – just give it a chance to absorb the fat before brushing it all off.

I have recently bought a new sheepskin coat to replace my old one. How can I ensure that it keeps in good condition, and how should I clean it if necessary?

Mrs Mitchell, Southampton.

Given normal care, your coat should not need cleaning for at least five years. When it really does require it, this should be done by a specialist. The problem usually lies with keeping the natural leather backing supple. No tanner will guarantee wool skins to be 100 per cent dye-fast, and some patchy loss of colour may be experienced. Reduce that greasy look by generously applying magnesium carbonate powder or even plain talcum powder, and leaving it for 24 hours before brushing it off. If the coat gets wet, dry in a normal temperature and never in direct heat. Rain spotting can be removed by rubbing down with foam rubber, but never while the coat is wet. And to brighten a yellow fleece at least superficially, you can apply some carpet shampoo – carefully and sparingly – but mind you don't soak the backing.

Do you know of anywhere I could have a good, solid, old-fashioned riding mackintosh cleaned? Dry cleaners say the rubber bonding would simply fall apart if they cleaned it. People at riding stables tell me to scrub it carefully on a kitchen table, but alas, I no longer have that kind of energy.

Mrs N. Findhom, London SW2.

If you can wait for 'bob-a-job' week or even contact the Scouts, you will have manpower for the job, since you don't feel up to it yourself. The only way to clean a real riding mackintosh is to scrub it as you were told. Use warm water and soap (not a detergent) and then hang it up to dry naturally in a cool place. Any hint of a fire will make the rubber deteriorate. Incidentally, this kind of mackintosh gives the best service. It is old-fashioned, but really sound and solid!

Clothes: grooming

To me, good grooming can never be out of date or old-fashioned. So I find it encouraging to be able to include in this section letters from young people who clearly take a pride in their appearance

I am 16 and still at school and have no Saturday job, so buying fashionable clothes is a problem. Still, I've solved it by looking for bargains at jumble sales. I buy huge men's shirts, cut off the collar, dye them bright colours, and wear them over jeans. Large, thick men's sweaters can be made into fantastic long scarves. Old-fashioned linen tablecloths can be dyed any colour, folded diagonally and worn with flowery skirts as a shawl. Old curtains or thick dresses can be made into cushion covers, quilts can be opened and the stuffing used for big scatter cushions which look great in a bedroom. One of my favourite bargains is a pair of massive baggy khaki shorts, which soldiers used to wear. With their large, deep pockets and braces they look

★★★★★★★★★★★★★★★★★★★★★★★★★★★★★★★★★★

Flair is having a feel for the contemporary without losing sight of your age and shape.

It is being aware of new lines, fabrics, colours, and shapes and sizes of accessories, then selecting what flatters you most as an individual. If I had to guess at the fashion accessory that dates more than any other I would choose shoes. I am always told that if you cling on to anything, it will come in useful again some time – that is true of clothes because with imagination and a skilful needle you can adapt them. But I built up a trunkful of shoes, and although heels have gone up and down, broadened and stilettoed, and toes have rounded and gone back to a point, the latest version is always balanced just that bit differently, so as to make the old shoes look completely out of date.

★★★★★★★★★★★★★★★★★★★★★★★★★★★★★★★★★★

the height of fashion with socks and sandals. With a little imagination you can have a completely new wardrobe for next to nothing.

Miss C. Thomson, Edinburgh.

As a polytechnic student with long holidays, no job and little money, I decided to beat the boredom by sorting out my clothes. I had a huge pile of them, now old-fashioned, that I decided to bring up to date. With a needle, thread and helpful Mum I quickly turned baggy trousers into smart narrow-legged pants, long-collared blouses into short-collared styles, and I've transformed other collars into mandarin ones. I also rejuvenated my old sandals by sanding them down, woodstaining and coating them with varnish. After a day's hard work I now have a wardrobe of new clothes for no extra money.

Miss K. Fear, N. Yorks.

It is a shame to discard clothes simply because they are a bit out of date. I hope your useful

tip will set others on the road to altering their own clothes. For those who are wondering where to start, it might be an investment to enrol at a local dressmaking evening or day class.

I am getting married in June and cannot get a pattern I like for my dress. I know exactly what I want and believe there is a pattern service where one can send a sketch and have a pattern cut. Do you know of such a service? Also where can I buy a hat shape? I have seen a hat I like, but it was too expensive, and I thought I might be able to buy a shape and trim it myself. I would appreciate any ideas you might have.

Miss E. Brennan, Edgbaston, Birmingham.

You are lucky you can sketch. I can hardly draw a piece of string. For the service you want, send a sketch, plus all your measurements, to Leslie Fogel, 5 South Molton Street, London W1Y 1DH. They'll make up a pattern and make your dress, too, if you wish, or even just finish off difficult bits that you're not sure how to tackle: zips, beading, and so on. Prices vary according to style and material. If you could visit London it would be easier all round. Just telephone 01 493 2541 for a personal appointment. Alternatively, why not try your local council dressmaking classes where someone might be able to help you? Perhaps after a few lessons and with some help from colleagues you will understand enough to go right ahead and cut out the dress yourself. Otherwise ask a local dressmaker to draft you a pattern and take it from there. You can get a hat shape if you explain what you want to Paul Craig, 15 D'Arblay Street, London W1 and enclose a sae for him to quote you a price.

I am going to a wedding, and would like to trim my hat with an ostrich feather, but unfortunately it is the wrong colour for my out-

fit. Would it be possible to dye it, using home dyes, and if so what would be the best type to use and how should I do it?

Mrs M. H., St Ives, Cornwall.

I can give you an answer from personal experience. Just before an appearance on a Eurovision Song Contest, I stood with wardrobe supervisor Joyce Mortlock until the small hours over a cauldron of what looked more like dark-brown ostrich-feather soup than the coral trimming for my dress on the show. If you can, start with white feathers, because even from the palest shades, you can't be quite sure of the colour on colour results. For 20 yards of ostrich feathers we used a large packet of Dylon and a two-pint saucepan, so a small packet should be plenty for your needs. Follow the instructions on the packet carefully, and make sure that all the feathers are immersed. Stir and watch carefully as the colour develops – wet feathers will be approximately four shades darker than when dry. Fish the feathers – a tatty string at this stage – out of the saucepan and shake vigorously to remove as much water as possible, then lay them on a plastic sheet slung across a clothes-horse. Now grab a hairdryer and you'll be surprised how quickly the string re-blossoms into feathers. You can even coax in an extra curl with a tail comb.
P.S. Peacock feathers which look so pretty in a vase can be freshened up by this wash and dry method too.

My brother will be getting married in late Autumn and the wedding will be formal – top hat and tails. I haven't any idea what to wear. Can you help, and can you also suggest ideas for my two little girls, aged six and four, bearing in mind that I have to keep costs to a minimum?

Mrs I. Chandler, Poulton-le-Fylde, Lancs.

The choice depends so much on your colouring, figure and age. A dress and jacket in fine wool or worsted could give you a lot of useful life afterwards – a two-piece in co-ordinating colours (the jacket a slightly different pattern from the skirt) or a patterned chiffon or fine printed wool dress would look smart under a fine wool coat, and you could choose a hat in one of the shades of the pattern and trim it with a band of the dress material. If the reception is to be held later in the day you could always consider a long dress, with a matching jacket that can be removed at the party. In this case buy one or two imitation flowers to wear instead of a hat and blend them into a dressier hairstyle than you usually have. Your little ones would look sweet in long matching dresses and their shiny hair held in place with floral bands. One very important point – mind you wear comfortable and not-too-high-heeled shoes. Nothing etches tired lines on a face more than aching feet.

★★★★★★★★★★★★★★★★★★★★★★★★★★★★★★

If you develop a certain confidence in your personal style it is extraordinary how you will find yourself unconsciously buying things in colours and lines which will interchange with your clothes.

I can generalise on one point – if you are not pencil slim and your shoulders are on the broad side, choose set-in sleeves in clothes of all kinds, because the raglan look only accentuates any hint of heaviness.

I am a firm believer in people being individual, and therefore I do not think you can be flattered by copying any look or person to the last letter. Always keep in mind your own shape, colouring and personality when you're picking up ideas from people or pictures.

★★★★★★★★★★★★★★★★★★★★★★★★★★★★★★

I have often wondered what happens to the beautiful and expensive dresses worn by showbusiness personalities and other distinguished ladies. Presumably they are worn only once, and when stars such as Shirley Bassey and Cilla Black wear three of four dresses in one show, goodness knows how many a month are required. Even with substantial incomes I can't imagine they can afford to scrap them. Is there some hire or refund service? I can think of various alternatives, probably all wrong!

Miss Eveline Cole, Selby, Yorks.

You'd be surprised how brilliant, versatile and inventive the wardrobe departments of television companies can be when it comes to running up clothes for stars and dancers appearing in series. The work that goes into many complicated shows is such that the clothes would really not be suitable for wear afterwards – even though they look incredibly glamorous on the screen. But there are times when stars do need more wardrobe space, and cast out less hard-worn objects. There is a shop in London that occasionally acquires clothes of this sort: the Frock Exchange, 450 Fulham Road, London SW6, which is run by the former Mrs Michael Crawford, Gabrielle. Here you can find everything – sweaters, shirts, evening dresses or mink-trimmed coats.

How do TV travellers always arrive looking so impeccable, considering they just throw everything into a suitcase before they dash off on some exciting mission? I always have to do my husband's packing, but this leads to a row on arrival because his suits come out of the suitcase looking as if they were wrapped round a mangle.

Mrs W. Woodhouse, Manchester.

Keep all plastic bags from the cleaners and use them as sandwich fillers when packing your own clothes. Lay a plastic bag in the bottom of the suitcase, with a generous overlay hanging outside the edge. Now put the jacket in and fold the plastic over the shoulders. Next fold the arms across the plastic, then bend up the lower part of the jacket. Now use another layer of plastic to separate the jacket from the trousers or skirt that go into the case next. Slip plastic inside the waistband, too, or inside the trouser legs to prevent deep creasing. Continue layering all your clothes in this way and you will arrive without a crumpled wardrobe: the air cushions between the plastic and the material will guarantee that 'out of the bandbox' look on arrival.

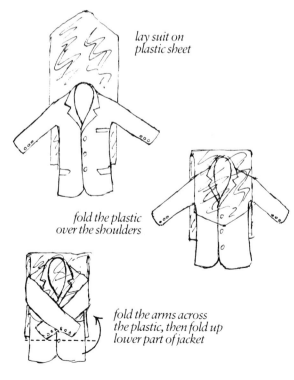

lay suit on plastic sheet

fold the plastic over the shoulders

fold the arms across the plastic, then fold up lower part of jacket

Home: the precious things

The precious things are those that make your home yours and nobody else's. They are often irreplaceable – or very costly to replace. This section deals with those special objects

I recently broke one of my little treasures, a Willow Pattern plate which was the sun spot on my kitchen wall. I used to admire it every day. There was always something new to see on it, and the two birds hovering over the bridge were really lovely. I believe there is a story behind the Willow Pattern – can you tell me it, and if it is true, please?

Angela Chadwick, Halstead, Essex.

The Encyclopedia of Chinese Symbolism and Art Motives *gives the following fable of the Willow Pattern. A rich mandarin, living in a tall house with a beautiful garden, employs a young scribe called Chang who falls in love with his daughter, Koong-see. But the mandarin dismisses Chang, betrothes Koong-see to a rich old duke, called Ta-jen, and keeps her confined to the house and garden. One day poor lonely Koong-see sees half a coconut shell floating in the stream – inside it there is a message from Chang, saying he will return to fetch her. Ta-jen comes to visit the mandarin with jewels for Koong-see. The two old men celebrate together and get drunk and Chang slips into the house unnoticed. He escapes with Koong-see and the jewels across a little bridge built over the stream, with the mandarin in hot pursuit. The couple hide and live happily for a while on an island until Ta-jen finds them. He hires soldiers who mortally wound Chang; Koong-see flees to their home, sets it on fire and perishes in the flames. In revenge, the gods curse the wicked Ta-jen with a fatal disease, and transform the two lovers into doves.*

The first Willow Pattern china was produced in 1780 by Minton, but lots of china manufacturers have made it since, and the pattern varies slightly on different pieces. Most of the designs, however, show the tall house, the bridge with three figures on it, and the two birds fluttering above.

I love this story and if your own 'treasure' isn't too badly broken, you could try contacting China Repairers Ltd, who do work for museums on special pieces, and will accept items sent by post – even giving you advice on how to pack it if you would care to contact them by phone first, or write giving details of the problem. Their address is 64 Charles Lane, London NW8 7SB (01 722 8407).

★★★★★★★★★★★★★★★★★★★★★★★★★★★★★★
Loose, non-precious stones can be re-set in a trice if you use a dab of nail polish. The best way to clean junk jewellery is with a swish in warm detergent-laced water.

Gold can be cleaned by rubbing it with a bit of bread, but if this has no effect because the piece is too tarnished, it should come out gleaming after a swirl in soapy water to which you have added a drop of bleach. Keep an old toothbrush handy for winkling dirt out of tiny crevices. Silver pieces can be brightened up with lemon juice, rather than soapy water, followed by a buff up with a chamois leather.
★★★★★★★★★★★★★★★★★★★★★★★★★★★★★★

I bought one of those copper bracelets to ease rheumatism and it seems to be helping me, but I have a dreadful time cleaning it. If I use brand cleaners the bracelet shines, but my wrist looks grubby, and if I don't use anything the bracelet looks dull and my wrist has a circle of verdigris by the end of the day. Any suggestions please?

Mrs E. Strong, London SW4.

Next time you have a gin and tonic with a slice of lemon keep enough aside in a saucer or cup to cover the bracelet and leave it, complete with the slice of lemon to soak overnight. Next morning give it a rub with the lemon. It will shine beautifully, but whether even a gold bracelet marks your skin or not depends on the varying amount of acid your skin exudes from one day to the next.

I have a number of washed and dried melon pips which I would like to make into a large necklace. However, I don't know how to set about it. I also have a number of odds and ends that I thought I could turn into saleable items for the handicraft stall our Girl Guides patrol is holding at our annual fair. These include pipe-cleaners, fir-cones, foam, felt. Any ideas?

J. Maguire, Cheadle Hulme, Ches.

Let's start with the pips. Paint these bright colours and thread them on nylon thread. Make three or four necklace lengths to use together for an important, chunky effect, and sew the threads on to ribbon. Alternatively, sew or glue pips on ribbon to make into 'jewelled' neckbands or bracelets. Pipe-cleaners can be twisted into animal shapes and given a face with a black stitch here and there. Fir-cones can be sprayed gold, silver or any other colour, and wired at the top to fix to the Christmas tree. Felt can be stuck under ornaments which would otherwise scratch furniture. Foam can be sewn into little bags for soap leftovers. Now you take over ... with a little imagination and patience, you'll surely swell those funds.

How do I clean coral? A friend of ours recently returned from a trip to the Middle East and brought back a piece of coral he had picked himself. Although we have soaked it in soda for three weeks it still has an unpleasant smell. Could you suggest a way to remove this?

J. Sandison, Tunbridge Wells, Kent.

Wash your coral in warm soap suds, rinse thoroughly and then add a dash of bleach to some water and wash it again. Just for luck, leave it to soak overnight in a bowl of bleach-laced water. Next morning rinse well, then sponge over the coral with a little eau-de-cologne.

Please could you tell me how to preserve coral shells which I collected on holiday in Thailand this summer?

Mrs V. Edser, Mitcham, Surrey.

Apparently coral is difficult to preserve. The Geological Museum in London suggest you apply a thin mist of hair spray when the surface is bone dry. Shells are self-preserving, but it is wise to keep them out of direct light, as the colour may fade, and to avoid contact with acid. Don't keep them on an oak dresser, for example, because oak has a high acid content.

I decided to strip the paint off my bedroom fireplace and was delighted to discover that it isn't wood, as I thought, but marble. What I'd like to know is how to restore it to its former beauty as it is now very dull and patchy. I really don't want to hide it under paint again.

M.E. Jones, Derby.

The only safe things to try are beeswax or liquid wax – and this may not have any effect. Cleaning and restoring marble is such a delicate and tricky job it really should be done by experts. It is too easy to ruin marble and leave it dried out and cracked, or sugary and crumbling. Far better to look in the Yellow Pages for your nearest marble yard. Ask for advice and an estimate if they are willing to help you. I agree there's something elegant about an attractive marble chimney piece and it would be a great pity to cover it over again with paint.

I have recently been given a beautiful little antique gilded wooden chair which has a badly-torn wicker seat. Could you suggest where I may either have this re-woven or replaced? The chair is very dainty, and I want the work to be well done. Also, could you tell me where I may have it professionally gilded?

Mrs V.S. Tate, Ruislip, Middx.

It seems that the demand for chair caning outstrips the service. I know of only two craftsmen: Mr K. J. Trayler of Fir Close, Frostenden, Wangford, Suffolk (Wangford 261), and Mr F. W. Groce of 104 Godley Road, London SW18, (01 870 2897). But both of them would like me to point out that there will be some delay in delivery because of the amount of work they have. Mr Louis Rich of 13 Crescent Place, London SW3 (01 589 4077) does restoration work of all kinds, including re-gilding.

I have to send a wedding present of some china or glass by post and I don't want it to arrive crushed. Can you help me?

P.A.C., Blackpool, Lancs.

Swish around a little detergent in a bowl of warm water and soak some newspaper in it. Then squeeze out most of the water and wrap the newspaper snugly around each piece of china and glass. Leave them in a warm place so that when the paper dries it will form a protective skin. Now, with the thinnest sheet

★★★★★★★★★★★★★★★★★★★★★★★★★★★★★★★

Silver

If you cannot face cleaning up prized but rarely-used sets of silver, keep a ball of camphor in the drawer and the tarnishing will be much reduced. The silver should be stored wrapped in black tissue paper, aluminium foil or polythene bags of a dark colour. If the smell of camphor offends you, and the objects are required more regularly, try wiping them once or twice a week with a cloth moistened with methylated spirits – that too will reduce the polishing job to a minimum. Silver with tiny black pockmarked stains should be washed in warm vinegar, so that all trace of the dirt lifts out.

★★★★★★★★★★★★★★★★★★★★★★★★★★★★★★★

of foam rubber to give the article extra padding, you can pack your wedding present without fear of breakages. Try to beat the Christmas rush. When the GPO is under pressure, the 'fragile' signs might be overlooked. P.S. Try saving that plastic bubbled paper that comes inside large packaged pieces: it is not yet widely available in retail outlets.

Looking ahead, I am trying to plan some interesting Christmas presents. Last year I purchased some pomanders, which hanging up make lovely decorations and provide a fragrant atmosphere, but cost several pounds each. I wondered if it would be possible to make these myself – they are, I believe, dried oranges stuck with cloves, the skins covered and decorated with ribbons and beads. Could you tell me a method to use and how to dry out the oranges?

Clare Pitloh, Leeds, Yorks.

What an excellent idea. To dry an orange, first make holes in the fruit to take the clove stems. Pierce the navel of the orange and drain it for 24 hours. Next rub the orange skin with a mixture of orris root and cinnamon and stick the clove stems into the holes you have already made. Now hang the oranges in a net bag to allow them to dry out. When the oranges are thoroughly dried out you can begin decorating them with beads and ribbons. You may also use this method for limes and lemons.

May I suggest to readers who want to transfer feathers from a mattress to a duvet to postpone the operation until early Spring? Birds will then remove every stray feather with great speed. They will be nest-building, and will snap up anything to make a warm lining for their homes. Two years ago I changed all my feather pillow covers and the birds lined up on the fence waiting for me to leave the garden. Then they swooped on the feathers.

Miss Frederica Driver, Ilfield, Sussex.

I have tried without success to find a shop where I can buy a leather to re-cover an antique desk. I would be most grateful if you would give me an address to contact so that I may put matters right.

Mrs Beane, Boughton Nonchelsea, Kent.

Philip Allen (Leathercraftsmen) Co Ltd, 132 Petherton Road, London N5 2RT (01 226 3031) run a mail order service. If you send them details of the size, colour and texture of the leather you want they will send the piece cut (tooled around the edges in classic gold floral designs should you want that) plus glue and instructions on how to fit it. If you feel the job needs an expert's touch they can arrange this too. But ask for an estimate.

I am told that in future articles made of platinum are to be hallmarked. I would like to get my platinum wedding ring hallmarked but am unable to find out how to set about this. Could you advise me where I should send the ring and the cost?

Hazel Gray, Isles of Scilly.

I expect quite a few people would like to have this seal of approval. If you send your wedding ring by registered post to The London Assay Office, Goldsmith Hall, Gutter Lane, London EC2V 8AQ, they will have the hallmark put on for you. However, for a private client this can take up to two months and you will have to pay a charge. The hallmark can be described as 'an orb within a pentangle' design.

Can you tell me any tips about how to tell antique furniture from fake or reproduction?

Mrs F. Watkins, Lincs.

Even experts can be fooled! Look out for the following points. Antique furniture has a good but not completely even shine; repro-

★★★★★★★★★★★★★★★★★★★★★★★★★★★★★★★★★★★

★ **Bronze** ★

★ *Bronze objects come up well if you give them* ★
★ *a rub with a cloth wrung out in warm water* ★
★ *mixed with a few drops of household am-* ★
★ *monia. A clean water rinse and a rub with a* ★
★ *dry soft cloth completes the job. Stubborn* ★
★ *tarnishes may respond better to the juice of a* ★
★ *lemon, and a bit more friction with an old* ★
★ *toothbrush reaches where nothing else can.* ★

★★★★★★★★★★★★★★★★★★★★★★★★★★★★★★★★★★★

duction is highly and evenly polished. If a piece has drawers, antique furniture will have the grain on the bottom lining running from front to back. If you can, examine any nails or screws, which should be hand-made and uneven if the piece is old. Even with finely-carved furniture, there will be slight irregularities; modern furniture will be even. Signs of wear and scratches can be faked so these are not an infallible guide.

When synthetic materials are introduced difficulties often arise in describing them so that the distinction is drawn between the synthetic and the natural material. During the last few years the cutters of real wood veneers have been worried about the plastic, paper and printed surfaces which have been applied to furniture and, because they look like wood, have actually been called oak, teak, rosewood and so on. They do understand that synthetic finishes certainly have their uses, but feel that the public have a right to know what they are buying. To distinguish furniture with real wood veneer finish manufacturers can now obtain a 'Touch Wood' label to affix to their products. So the message when buying furniture is to look for the label or ask about the finish if you want a real wood veneer.

Mrs W. G. Potter, Timber Research and Development Association, High Wycombe, Bucks.

Thank you for this invaluable information. I think everyone has a right to know exactly what they are getting for their money, and it is easy to fall into the wrong description trap.

Last year I brought back a musical box from Germany. A few weeks ago it was dropped on the floor and I think the spring has broken. I don't want to send it back to Germany to get it repaired, and an experienced clock-mender I know said he can't mend it. Do you know of any place where musical boxes can be mended?

Miss Brenda Pullen, Gravesend, Kent.

Write to Keith Harding, Clocks and Musical Boxes, 93 Hornsey Road, London N7 6DJ. He has a great knowledge and love of musical boxes and will be prepared to mend one. As he is alway busy, be patient, as he may take a little time to deal with your request. And do always remember to ask beforehand for an estimate of the cost.

I have a glass decanter of which the stopper is firmly stuck in the bottle. Is there any way to remove it without breaking the decanter?

Mrs E.G. Yes, Reading.

Drop a little oil - preferably edible, as the decanter's contents are edible - around the base of the stopper. Put the decanter in a warm place (in front of the fire - not too close - and keep turning it). The heat will cause the oil to work down, so after a short while, tap the stopper gently with a wooden spoon (upwards and sideways) and repeat until the stopper is loosened. By this time you will have earned a drink!

I remember reading about lemon-scented bookshelves. How is the scent applied, and is there any other way to keep books fresh and stop that musty smell that comes with the years?

Mrs P. Dunn, Wellington, Salop.

There is a lemon-scented furniture polish by Johnson's; alternatively, try a scented paper from Mary Chess, which I use myself. It's expensive, but lasts a long time and after two years my dressing table and linen drawers still smell sweet. Mary Chess supply only a limited number of stockists and they have no distributor in Shropshire, so write direct to: Mary Chess, 7 Shepherd Market, Curzon Street, London W1Y 7HR. Another reader who wrote to me about an unpleasant smell in her sideboard, after ridding it of termites, might find this to be her solution, too.

Visiting a friend's house I was attracted by a large bowl filled with what appeared to be a mixture of dried flowers. This mixture gave off a most delightful aroma. I would love to have some of this but I don't know how to make it.

Mrs J. Stokes, Manchester 20.

This sweet-smelling mixture goes under the inaccurate and I always think rather unattractive name of pot pourri *which means literally 'pot of things gone bad'. It is made from a collection of dried flowers, petals, leaves and herbs blended with special oils. A prowl around your local library, or well-stocked book-shop, will unearth books with old recipes, but there are endless mixtures you can make yourself from already packaged basic ingredients to be bought at most health-food stores.*

You can become more adventurous as you go along but remember to make a note of your favourite combinations. If you want to dry your own petals and herbs make sure they are picked in healthy bloom and dry them -

away from the light to keep their colour – between newspapers in a not-too-warm airing cupboard or under the bed. A sprinkling of salt, borax or silversand will help to dehydrate them.

China containers can be open or closed as long as the closed ones have generously sized holes for the perfume to come through. Here's a basic recipe to fill one large bowl: 1 pint rose petals, with some buds; 1 pint lemon verbena; half pint peony petals or larkspur flowers (for colour); one quarter pint dried rosemary or lavender; 1 tablespoon crushed spice; 1 tablespoon orris root, broken small; 10 drops of geranium oil; 10 drops bergamot oil; 10 drops of rose or sweet orange.

Allspice, cloves, cinnamon, cardamom, coriander, juniper berries, etc, are some of the more aromatic spices suitable for crushing and adding to pot pourri. Liquid measures are given as weights are deceptive, but the most convenient measure is probably a pint.
P.S. Further details about pot pourri making will be found in the chapter on Gardening.

We have a fitted carpet in our lounge over which we have a rug which will not stop 'walking'. Can you help me with this problem? No one else I have asked knows of a cure. The continual task of straightening the carpet is driving me potty.

Mrs M.E. Rutland, Southend-on-Sea, Essex

Foam rubber tacked under the rug does help, but the only cure for my 'walking' rug in front of the fireplace was to have it sewn on to the fitted carpet. Have this done professionally, though or you could ruin both rug and carpet.

How do you turn a bottle into a lampstand?
Miss A Sidebottom, Leeds.

Use a fine Durilim-tipped drill, and with great care and very little pressure, bore a hole in the

bottle. If the bottle has a flat base, make a hole in the side near the bottom. If it has a ridged base you can bore right through the centre of the base, because the flex will slot into one of the ridges without upsetting the lamp's firm stance. Insert a hollow rubber plug in the hole to prevent the flex rubbing against the glass. Slip the flex through the hole and thread upwards to meet the adaptor which will fit into the neck of the bottle. Then with plug connections, frame, lampshade and bulb you're all set. Your first attempt might well end in a smash-up, so spread a sheet of plastic on the floor to collect the debris and be prepared to empty another bottle. That's the best excuse that I've ever heard. You'll be lit-up!

We have just moved into a new house and have discovered that the previous owners had a dog who did quite a lot of damage to the sapele doors which are fitted throughout the house. Could you please tell me of the best way to start renovating them, and the best materials to use.

Mrs Barnes, Hucclecote, Glos.

I'm afraid you'll have to call in a top-class professional revarnisher and carpenter if your African mahogany (that's what sapele is) doors are really badly damaged. If it's a matter of surface scratchings, wash them down with a mixture of warm water and vinegar (a tablespoon of vinegar to a large mixing bowl of water), leave them to dry, then start building up a new surface skin by applying a thin, plain, colourless wax and rubbing in vigorously. Thicken this skin gradually day by day with more elbow grease than actual wax. Why don't people train their dog's properly? Each finds it happier and easier to live with the other when both learn to agree on how to behave.

★★★★★★★★★★★★★★★★★★★★★★★★★★★★★★

Copper

Half an onion or half a lemon works well on copper: shake some salt on to the cut lemon to make it extra-effective. If you prefer to use a proprietary cleaner, you can avoid blackened polishing dusters by simply dipping the object into warm water with detergent once you have applied the cream. The grime floats off, and all you have to do is dry and buff the cleaned piece. Dry newspaper is an excellent material for this.

A mixture of salt and vinegar also works wonders on copper. If the mixture is heated up so that the salt dissolves, it is even more powerful, and will remove those green spots.

★★★★★★★★★★★★★★★★★★★★★★★★★★★★★★

As I have recently decorated one of my rooms, my sister-in-law gave me a beautiful real goat-skin rug, white and brown with long 'fur'. As the carpet in that room is deep red, it looks smashing – except that the hair comes off the rug terribly. This rather spoils the effect and it's driving me potty. The rug has been beaten, vacuum-cleaned and even washed to try and stop it moulting but still with no success. Any solutions, please?

Mrs A. Gibson, Ward End, Birmingham.

Oh dear! I have asked the experts but apparently there is no home treatment that will stop that lovely goatskin from shedding its hair. You have one of the most decorative but tricky rugs there is.
P.S. Nissim and Company, 23 Charlotte Road, London EC2A 3PB (01 739 5051) specialise in cleaning and caring for carpets and although they do not deal with skins, they can help with other special carpet problems.

Recently, I read the letter concerning a sheep-skin rug and how to clean it. I have had two sheepskin rugs for about 18 months. After I had bought them my dog decided they were for him and has hardly moved from them, so they need continual cleaning. I found the best way of cleaning them was to put them in my washing machine, set on the 'woollen' pro-gramme, with a low suds powder and a little disinfectant. On the last rinse pour in a large amount of fabric softener and then spin twice to remove as much water as possible. When they are dry I brush them all over with a plastic hairbrush or comb. Do not worry if the backs go slightly stiff because they will soon soften and remain so as long as you continue to use the fabric conditioner.

Mrs A. Jackson, Coleshill, Birmingham.

In answer to the inquiry about cleaning sheep-skin rugs, I have been washing those with cured skins every year for 30 years. I come from a family of Yorkshire wool merchants and this is my recipe. Wash by hand in very warm, but not too soapy water. Squeeze out excess water – or better still put the rug in a spin dryer, with the woolly side on the out-side. Shake the rug well and hang outside. If the skin is not cured then it has to be cleaned by a professional operator.

Mrs Kathleen Atherton, Barnt Green, Worcs.

It's a matter of finding out whether or not your particular rug is washable and this de-pends not only on whether it has been cured, but on how it has been cured. If it has not been cured, but just dried out with methylated spirits (this is done a great deal on the Conti-nent), then it will return to its raw state if soaked. There are curing processes that do not leave a rug washable and one example is the alum and salt method, which can be de-tected if you drop a tiny piece of your sheep-skin into boiling water for 30 seconds. If it shrivels up tight, then don't risk the rest of the rug. Many rugs on the market are chrome-cured and this means it is perfectly safe to wash them, so long as the water is not too hot and a low suds detergent product such as Stergene is used. The only other advice I can add, which comes from an expert, is from time to time to 'massage' glycerine into the back of the sheepskin while it is hanging out to dry. This will help to keep it soft and supple.

My husband left a hot water bottle on the arm of our Dralon settee. I have tried to bring the pile back, but it remains flat and unsightly. Have you any suggestions?

Mrs Y. Hill, Cambs.

Try dampening the whole arm and then dry off as quickly as possible with a hairdryer, while teasing the surface upwards, with a small, fine-bristled brush.

I have two nice bamboo tables, but although I dust them regularly, they have begun to look very grubby and I'm longing to give them a good scrub with soap and water: But I have a nagging worry that bamboo shouldn't be washed. I don't want to spoil the tables. What shall I do?

Miss D'Isle, Tiverton, Devon.

Go ahead and wash them with pure soapsuds and a dash of ammonia. Natural bamboo, cane and wicker furniture should be wiped over regularly with a damp cloth, to stop it drying out and cracking and, particularly if you have central heating, it should be soaked about once a year. Either hose it down in the garden or leave it under the bathroom shower until it's completely wet. After this, let it dry out thoroughly, then coat it with shellac – a very fine varnish. This will cleanse, rejuvenate and protect your furniture.

Why do shops use such tacky labels? I spend hours trying to get them off pretty containers of shampoo and hand cream. I have tried cooking oil, but it does not always work.

Mrs V. Burden, Stoke-on-Trent.

Try a touch of meths next time. It usually removes all remains of sticky labels.

Home: cleaning, decorating and general care

Everyone has her (or his) own method and ideas when it comes to dealing with household chores. And over the years I have found it fascinating to try out other people's 'tried and tested' remedies. Here is a wide-ranging medley of your tips and mine on caring for the home.

Cleaning

I've done a silly thing. I washed our dining-room carpet and then while it was still damp I rolled the armchairs back into it without using plastic to protect it from the metal castors. How can I get rust marks out of a pale green carpet?

Mrs Doris Longden, Enfield, Middx.

If the marks haven't had time to set in, coax them out with neat lemon juice on a cloth or with a slice of lemon. If the stains are stubborn, leave a few drops of lemon juice on them overnight and wash off in the morning. Even if they haven't disappeared, they should have lightened considerably.

I have used a lot of exposed wood in decorating my kitchen and bathroom and I want to give this a good protective finish. I'm not keen on varnishes and sealants, they're too shiny. A friend recommended a mixture of beeswax and benzine – as used on coffins! Do you think it would work, and where do I get it?

James Affleck, London SW12.

Waxine is ready-mixed beeswax and turpentine for amateurs who hanker after the professional look to their furniture. Most hardware stores either stock or can order this for you. The large tins are more economical as they contain enough for several wide-surface jobs.

I dropped a hot dish on my teak dining table and badly marked it – have you any suggestions for removing the marks?

Mrs E.B., Helston, Cornwall.

First, wash your table with a mixture of warm water and vinegar (a tablespoon of malt vinegar to a soup bowl of water). Dry the surface, then 'tease' out the mark with a little methylated spirit on a clean cloth – it usually comes out after one or two attempts. Then a coating of Waxine (mentioned in my previous answer) and some elbow grease should leave the surface stain-free.

Please could you tell me a cheap way to remove terrible tea stains from the inside of plastic, unbreakable tea cups?

Mrs Conrad, Ilford, Essex.

A drop or two of bleach diluted into half a cup of hot water should do the trick. You can swill the mixture from cup to cup so a little bleach will clean up after a big party. Naturally, wash the cups well afterwards.

My bathroom is much tidier since I bought a soap dispenser, which is economical too. But where is the genius who will devise a toothpaste dispenser on the same principle? I get so sick of those half-mangled tubes which my children leave about. It would also prevent my husband's early morning profanities when the missing cap embeds itself into the sole of his naked foot.

Genista Bale, Scunthorpe, Humberside.

I am all for anything that encourages children to clean their teeth. You can buy toothpaste dispensers in several designs from The Bathroom Shop, 3rd Floor, Harrods, Knightsbridge, London SW1 (01 730 1234). They are made by Paul Corbett and are available by mail order from the above address, but check with the store about the price and postage costs.

Some friends who emigrated gave us a freezer. Unfortunately it was left shut up for some time and now smells stale. Is there any cleaner we can use which will not affect food when we begin to use it?

Mrs F.S., Somerset.

Wash it out thoroughly with a solution of bicarbonate of soda. When dry, use a freezer deodoriser, available from a freezer shop. Leave the door open overnight. When you plug the freezer in again it should be quite odour-free.

None of the dry-cleaners in my area will accept electric blankets. Can I wash or clean them myself?

Mrs Foster, Catterick Camp, Yorks.

It is not advisable to wash or clean electric blankets yourself. Return them for cleaning to the manufacturer at least every two years. Their name and address is often sewn on to the label. Charges vary for servicing an under-blanket or an over-blanket, but it is worth the money to avoid the danger of a job improperly done.

How can I stop a cellulose bath sponge from becoming 'slimy'? I find that even rinsing it out well in clear cold water is not sufficient after a few weeks of constant child-washing.

Mrs T. Humm, Urmston, Manchester.

My sponge became so slimy that I poured on some detergent and cleaned the bath with it. Rinsing it out, I noticed that the slime seemed less, so I washed it really well in detergent, finally rinsing it out in cold water. I found that I then had a totally 'de-slimed' sponge which gave up its brief spell of hard labour and returned to my own personal use. This method should work with your child-washing sponge.

Here's an idea for busy wives who are irritated by condensation on windows. To stop it for a few days rub soap on to a damp cloth, use it to wipe the window, rinse cloth and wipe over the glass.

Mrs B. Williams, Caterham, Surrey.

My tip for steamed-up windows is to put a very tiny drop of shampoo on a piece of newspaper and give the windows a good wipe with it. They do not steam up again for the rest of the day.

Mrs R. Darragh, Cookstown, Co. Tyrone.

I find methylated spirits ideal.

My friends and I are are office cleaners and wonder if you have any quick and easy methods for cleaning very greasy windows – not by using a chamois or window cleanser, but by using something we could add to water, so that the windows would need only a wipe over with a cloth, dry without leaving streaks, and only need rubbing up with a duster afterwards.

Mrs Johnstone, Glasgow.

I've had a go with these two tips and find they work well:
1. Add four tablespoons of vinegar to a bucket of water and wash with usual loose-knit cloth. 2. Crumple newspaper and dip it into a bucket of water, wring out and pat into a pad for washing windows. In both cases allow panes to dry before giving them a final wipe-over with a chamois leather. Sorry, but that can't be replaced and I think firms should issue them to you important ladies.

My mother helps pluck ducklings in her spare time, and as I am getting married soon we thought it a good opportunity to save the down to make pillows. We bagged it and put in a low oven to dry out, and have now made up one pillow using the special feather-proof case. The problem is that it still smells strongly of duck. What can we do to lose the smell?

Caroline Wheadon, Wells, Somerset.

Maybe this well-tried method for spring-cleaning pillows will do the trick. Fill the bath half full of warm water, add a handful of soapflakes and whip up a good lather. Put two pillows in this and walk up and down on them in the bath, pressing the suds right through (just as they tread grapes in a vine-yard). If the water becomes scummy, run it out and repeat the process. Rinse thoroughly, treading out the water and in the final rinse, sprinkle the water lavishly with eau de col-

ogne. Dry the pillows in the open air – in sunshine if possible – shaking frequently. Here's hoping the skies stay blue for you.

Do you know of anything that might remove tea stains from tablecloths? I don't see too well, and stain rather a lot of them – no problem with white linen, but I don't want to risk spoiling coloured materials.

Mrs F. Bailey, Morecambe.

A fresh stain of tea or coffee can come out if you soak it in hand-hot detergent and water. If the stain is set and the fabric is washable, soak it first then wash it at a high temperature in water and borax (1 oz of borax to 1 pint of water). I've found that when all else has failed on an elderly stain one part hydrogen peroxide to 9 parts cool water seems to do the trick. Soak the article until the stain has lifted, and rinse well.

For years I have used solid polish on my table, and then last week I thought I'd save myself some trouble and bought spray polish instead. Now my table is patchy and dull. Can you tell me how I can get all the polish off and start again?

Mrs Townton, W. Yorks.

Whip up some pure soapflakes in some warm water, squeeze out a soft cloth in the mixture, then wash and wipe a small area of your table, taking care not to saturate the wood. Do a small area at one time, and allow the wood to dry thoroughly before you start polishing up the surface again. Another way to remove the build-up of polish is to use half a breakfast cup of vinegar to two of warm water, and work over the table using the same technique as for soapy liquid.

I recently had some visitors from America with very badly behaved children. The worst thing the children did was to stick their well-chewed gum under the seats of my dining-room chairs. Is there any way I can remove this from the wood, material and carpet?

R. Walters, London SW6.

It isn't only children who have this disgusting habit. A theatrical producer I know often complains about chewing gum galore under theatre seats. Holloway's Chewing Gum Aerosol will remove the gum from most surfaces, but if the gum is left on a carpet for more than 24 hours it is impossible to shift. The aerosol can be ordered from G. E. Holloway and Sons, 12 Carlisle Road, London NW9 0HL (01-200 0066). They can also supply a list of distributors. Do make sure you follow the directions carefully.

I find that I often get ink on my clothes but it comes out easily if I soak the area in a little milk in a saucer. I cut my finger recently and I couldn't get the blood stains out of my handkerchief by washing it in the ordinary way. Would milk have worked for this too?

Jacky Graham (aged 11), Huddersfield, Yorks.

Yes it would. I know this little trick and it is most useful for shifting ink, blood or fruit stains so long as you put the soiled area into the milk straight away. I don't know why milk works. Neither does the Milk Marketing Board, the chemistry department of a London hospital, nor a leading ink manufacturer, although they all agree it is effective. Just a word of warning – do make sure you wash the milk out of the garment thoroughly, because milk itself can leave a stain.

My young son has spilled half a bottle of royal blue ink on my brand new carpet, and I am at my wit's end about how to remove it by next week. My husband is going to re-decorate the bedroom where the carpet is and if he finds out about it he'll go mad.

Mrs M. Bolt, London SW8.

There's a new all-purpose cleaner called Kimbo – contact Kimbermont Ltd, 3 Beeston Place, London SW1 (01-828 9111-9114), who will put you in touch with your nearest representative. The price is about £1 for a concentrated bottle which makes five gallons – but follow the instructions carefully, so you don't fade your carpet.

When I spilled ink on my carpet, my mother told me of a cleaning remedy she picked up in South Africa. It is to squash very ripe tomatoes on to the stain, leave overnight and then wash off. The lady who told my mother had often used this method on school clothes when ink had leaked into pockets, and so on, and she had always had success.

Mrs M. Lambert, London SE18.

Before I lose all my friends and neighbours, please help. I've split milk on my sculptured Bri-nylon/wool carpet and the odour is indescribable. Everyone who comes through the door backs out again, nostrils pinched. I've tried scrubbing the carpet with detergent, soap suds and even scented bath-powder, all to no avail.

Mrs Elsie Jones, Bangor, Co. Down.

This problem is a stinker because the milk has seeped through to the underlay of your carpet and turned to cheese. The first rule to fight carpet stains is prompt and speedy action, even it if means leaving your guests in mid-conversation while you dash into the kitchen for a cloth dipped in cold water. But now that the milk has sunk in, nothing will be effective till you cut out the cheesed-off section of underlay and replace it. Then, if there is still a

slight stain on the surface, squirt the area with Johnson's Aerosol Glory carpet shampoo.

My grandson was sick on the floor and carpet and I just can't get rid of the smell. Do you know of a remedy?

Mrs Nina Mitton, Stockport, Greater Manchester.

Either a strong solution of bicarbonate of soda wiped sparingly over the carpet, or a generous sprinkling of it dry and left on a while, should solve this problem. You can dip car rugs and any other washable 'victims' into this solution after a travelling accident of this kind and restore a nice fresh smell.

Will methylated spirits remove a long-standing white stain from my mahogany sideboard? You recommended it for teak and light woods.

Mrs T. Johnson, Stockport.

Friar's Balsam is the answer with dark woods such as mahogany or oak. Wash the surface with a solution of a teaspoonful of malt vinegar in a saucerful of warm water – dry well, then soak a piece of cotton wool with Friar's Balsam and work well into the stain. It may take a few applications before the stain disappears, but it should go completely. Then you can polish as usual.

Our piano is beginning to look shabby. The veneer is coming off, and the keys are discoloured. Is there any way of improving it?

Mrs M.C., Wellington.

A good tip for veneered furniture is to mix up a pint solution containing one third linseed oil, one third vinegar and one third methylated spirit. Dust the piece of furniture, then rub on the mixture liberally and leave for 24 hours. (You can repeat this process if the furniture is really bad. And don't worry if the solution bubbles, here and there.) Finally, wipe off the solution and polish in the normal way. You can improve piano keys by wiping them with a milky cloth, but do remember to wash them carefully afterwards.

Although wiping piano keys with a milky cloth is an old-fashioned remedy, it should never be used on ivory piano keys because the fat in the milk soaks into the ivory and discolours them permanently. The best home remedy is to rub them with Brasso. This will clear them of all grease and dirt and leave a highly polished surface. Very old piano keys are best renovated by professional repairers.

R.G. Lloyd Owen, Director, Harris Ivory Works, St Ives, Cornwall.

Readers' tips on cleaning

Many years ago I splashed hot fat on to a newly-papered wall. I was advised to make a paste of Fuller's Earth and carbon tetrachloride, apply it to the spot and brush away when dry. Two applications and the mark was gone. The person who told me this trick later used it to remove a hair-oil stain too.

Mrs J.P. McKernan, Woodingdean, Brighton.

I had to break up a fine relationship with a boyfriend years ago on my mother's order, because he kept leaning his oily head against my parents' wallpaper! In the end, my mother found a solution: she mixed some Fuller's Earth with cleaning fluid like Dabitoff or lighter fluid. It must be on the dry side. Then she spread it on the stain, with a knife, like butter on toast and let it dry. In the morning we would find the mixture all dried up, in pieces on the floor and the wallpaper stain gone. Buy the time we were through with the process my boyfriend was dating someone else!

Lucy G., London.

I think that dusting lavishly and immediately with talcum powder would have done the trick too. But just between you and me you're probably better off without that particular beau anyway!

Stainless steel kettles and water taps can be polished beautifully with some toothpaste – it doesn't take much of your time.

Mrs Michiko Kilfoyle, Bridgwater, Somerset.

Old toothbrushes: there must be hundreds of uses for them. They can reach all the awkward corners. I use them most around windows, sinks and the bath, cleaning the cooker, between the studs of muddy football boots, between tiles either on a fire surround or the bathroom and kitchen walls; ornaments with lots of indentations . . . I could go on, the list is endless.

D. Hobson, Leven, Hull.

I think the following should be very useful to mothers with young children. My young son tramped over the kitchen with mud and tar on his shoes and left tar marks on the cushions and carpet. I tried everything I could to remove the marks, so much so that my husband made a joke of it. 'You've tried everything except toothpaste!' he said. So I put some on a piece of cotton wool, rubbed, and the marks disappeared! I have found the remedy works with oil and similar stains.

Mrs Dowie, Midlothian.

With reference to the inquiry about brown marks round the bath, the simplest way to cure this is to mix cream of tartar and peroxide to a thin paste. Spread on thinly and leave for 15 minutes. Rinse off and the bath wil be left smooth and shiny, and it will last for about six months without need for a further application.

Mrs K. Thompson, Ramsey, Isle of Man.

After washing my net curtains, I add fabric softener, plus a sprinkling of starch, to the final rinse. My friends always ask if they are new.

Mrs D.B., Bucks.

Yellowing net curtains respond to a final rinse with fabric softener plus a touch of old-fashioned washing blue. I have used this on white socks and hankies with good effect.

Mrs F.W., Plymouth.

Snowy white curtains are a joy and thanks for the tips, but if you don't soak them overnight in a tub full of cold water (with a fistful of cooking salt added if they are really grubby) you may as well not bother to wash them. If I machine wash, I use the coolest setting. I also use Dylon Curtain White, if the curtains are really grey.

My mother visited me recently while I was trying to clean my stainless cooker hob. She advised me to use vinegar which made the metal sparkle like new again.

Mrs M. Painter, Essex.

Here is a tip for getting stains off a highly-polished surface. I put a hot mug down on a table and it left a ring. So I covered the mark with cigar ash then rubbed it with a cloth that had a drop of metal polish on it. It disappeared. I'm told it works on other stains too.

D. Shore, Ches.

I also use cigar ash as a stain remover, but I mix mine with a little olive oil. In France they use a paste of olive oil and salt.

Like many other housewives I do not relish the thought of cleaning my oven but a friend of mine told me an easy way to do it. After 'scrubbing' the oven with whatever cleaner you use put a heaped dessertspoonful of bicarbonate of soda into four pints of hot water. Wipe the oven clean with this solution and leave it. When you next use the oven just wipe it with a damp cloth and while warm repeat with the solution.

Marilyn Owens, Leicester.

Most of us at some time inherit, or buy at an auction, a piece of furniture which seems ruined by built-up dirt and polish. The following mixture will simply and cheaply restore the wood. Mix equal parts of turpentine and vinegar, add a little powdered starch and shake well. Rub this on with a succession of clean cloths, then give all surfaces a final rub with a dry cloth.

Mrs H. Fletcher, Southport, Lancs.

As an inveterate polisher I am particularly interested in this problem. Starch and turpentine is something I hadn't heard of and wouldn't recommend to get rid of a build-up of wax. White spirit used very sparingly on a soft cloth will do the trick, as will vinegar and water, and there are various kinds of 'Antiquax' polish that will help. The dark variety will help to fill in small indentations and camouflage blemishes, but in time will darken the surface of the wood, so it should be used only occasionally and very lightly. The clear kind won't darken wood, but won't hide deep marks either.

Here are a few handy household hints I've picked up over the years that may interest other readers. To brighten the colours of a dull, faded carpet, simply wipe over with a mixture of three parts water to one part vinegar. To make windows shine, clean them with stale tea – this also keeps the flies away. To remove smells from a knife after cutting onions or fish, just plunge the blade into fresh earth. I hope you find these tips useful as I have.

Miss Clare Knight, Cheltenham, Glos.

Three good tips – but before setting about the carpet make sure you wring out your cloth, otherwise you will make the carpet too wet. Methylated spirits shines up window panes, too, and you can wipe a cut lemon over a smelly knife to freshen it up. It is fun to discover just how many ways there are of getting identical results. Remember to dab rather than wipe at the spot.

If you are as lazy as I am about polishing brass or copper (not silver) here is a marvellous recipe which my mother, who lives in Denmark, gave me. 1 cup water, 1 cup flour, 1 cup vinegar, 2 teaspoons of citric acid (from a chemist) 2 tablespoons salt. Mix it all, brush it on to the metal thickly, rinse off and wipe dry with a soft cloth. For someone like my mother who has rheumatism in her hands this must be a great help as you don't need any elbow grease at all.

Mrs Inge Keis, Stourbridge, W. Midlands.

I was interested by your correspondence with a reader having difficulty in cleaning very

dirty brass. One unfailing remedy is to moisten a piece of Duraglit wadding with ordinary household ammonia, and then polish in the usual way. This lifts out the ingrained dirt, and after cleaning once or twice the brass is as good as new. If you want to give brass that pale, golden look, use Duraglit Silver Wadding, which imparts a less 'brassy' look.

Mrs N. Healey, Stockport.

Cleaning the interior of bottles which have become discoloured and stained causes a problem. As bottle-cleaning brushes often fail to reach right inside a bottle, we have devised a cheap and easy method of cleaning. Tear newspaper into small pieces, and put in the vessel with hot water. Give it a good shake, and 'hey presto', one clean bottle!

Mrs L.M. Asplin, Farnham, Surrey.

Another extremely useful tip for cut glass vases or decanters is to use dry rice: pour in a handful, add cold water to cover, and as the rice swells, it will lift off the build-up of calcium or other staining impurities from the glass surface.

I have just discovered a marvellous and cheap window cleaner, which also keeps flies at bay. Equal parts of water, paraffin and methylated spirits – shake well and rub on with a cloth; the results are fantastic.

Mrs D. Williams, Bolton, Lancs.

I read with interest Mrs Williams' idea for a cheap window cleaner. Your readers may be interested in a similar cheap cleaner which gives a fine polish to furniture, brass or chrome work, mirrors, fridges and even washing machines. Put one egg-cupful of vinegar, and the same quantity of paraffin in a jar, shake well to mix. Soak a cloth in the mixture until all the liquid has been absorbed.

Use as required. When the cloth becomes dirty, wash out and use again before re-soaking.

Mrs M. Mortimore, Great Bookham, Surrey.

I have tried many ways of removing scratches from furniture and this one is successful. To remove surface scratches from a polished table, rub lightly with a cork dipped in camphor oil. When the oil has worked in, polish and the marks will completely disappear.

Mrs M. Wurk, Angus, Scotland.

Ordinary iodine is great for touching up scratches on dark wood furniture. Apply with a toothpick or tiny pointed brush. Let it dry before you wipe over with furniture polish. Do a trial application first, and if the iodine looks a bit darker than the furniture, dilute it with alcohol.

Deana Boulton, Newcastle-upon-Tyne.

I've also managed to erase scratch marks from lighter wood by rubbing with a fresh, shelled and halved Brazil nut. Water marks still come off my furniture with a half mixture of olive oil and cigarette ash – though cigar ash seems to work more quickly.

Readers' ideas on decor

When I fixed a chain to my front door I discovered that the wall prevented me from seeing callers, so I bought a mirror tile with a self-adhesive back and placed it so that I can see the reflection of the caller without having to undo the chain.

Mrs A.D. Tarpey, Pontefract, W. Yorks.

My 12-year-old daughter made herself a beautiful patchwork quilt, so we gave her bedroom a face-lift to match. From old wallpaper pattern books, we chose the most attractive plain and patterned pieces and pasted them all over one wall to make a lovely chequer-board design, which echoed the quilt and contrasted with the plain colours of the other walls, carpets and curtains. It looks so nice that my other two children have decided to give their rooms a similar face-lift.

Sylvia Lockett, Goldalming, Surrey.

It sounds great – but I'm glad you stressed only one wall should be papered in this way and everything else kept plain, otherwise it would be too overpowering. It certainly is a good way of using up those old wallpaper pattern books which so often end up cluttering the attic.

My son was married a few weeks ago. I bought a white tablecloth, and at his reception I collected everyone's signatures. Now I am embroidering them and I shall give the finished article to the happy couple on their first wedding anniversary.

Mrs B. Wakerell, Dover, Kent.

To make a fitted sheet out of a flat one, just tie a knot in the corners. It's simple, but very effective.

Mrs Rosemary White, Middx.

Discussing carpet prices with a friend in the building trade we thought of using carpet tiles on the stair treads only and painting the risers in a contrasting colour. This removes the danger of loose stair-carpet and saves having carpet up the risers where it is really wasted. Has this been done before?

Mr J.J. Rowell, Newcastle-upon-Tyne.

In principle your idea sounds good but make sure you stick the carpet tiles very securely. Consult the carpet tile supplier about a really strong adhesive and use it all over the tile, not just at the four corners. A carpet-laying firm I consulted considered that tiles would be just as safe as stair-carpet if properly fixed to the treads. I would choose a blending rather than contrasting paint for the risers to give a 'pulled together' look. A zebra effect could be very garish.

Instead of leaving a step light on and wasting electricity I have painted the edges of my steps with white paint. It shows them up beautifully in the dark and prevents accidents.

Mrs S. Clark, Ware, Herts.

How can I brighten up a plain wall mirror? I answered an advertisement for an 'attractive' old mirror in our local paper, which unfortunately turned out to be a case of poetic licence! However I bought the mirror as the old lady who owned it obviously needed the money. Is there any way I can frame it to make it more decorative? It is 27 inches long.

Mrs B. Brennan, Aldershot, Hants.

I have padded a strip of my curtain material with some foam rubber, then stuck it round the edge of my dressing-table looking-glass. But it's easier and can look just as good, with the material stuck straight on to the glass without the padding. Then again, you could make some Victorian-style bobbles and bumps with Barbola plaster, and paint the lot gold. A tin of Barbola can be obtained from a good art and craft supplies shop, or write to Winsor and Newton, 51 Rathbone Place, London W1P 1AB (01 636 4231).

My family tease me about the uses I find for old junk, but even they consider the use I have found for a broken umbrella a handy hint. After the cover has been removed, the frame makes an ideal mini-rotary clothes-dryer for 'smalls'. I hang it by its curved handle on the branch of a tree and can remove the whole thing instantly if there's a shower.

Mrs V. Jones, Cardiff, S. Glamorgan.

You're the kind of person to be marooned on a desert island with – in no time at all you'd be improvising an escape raft and sailing triumphantly home.

Last Christmas my mother gave my husband and me two luxurious single divan beds to replace our old double bed. We were delighted with our separate sleeping arrangements – for three months! Now we find we can no longer sleep as well as we did before. Last week, out of sheer desperation, we tied the two beds together to make a super six-feet-wide double. Now our nights are sheer bliss, or would be if the mattresses didn't part in the middle. I once saw an advertisement for a method of joining twin divans but I cannot remember what it was. Can you help?

Glenys Jones, Swindon, Wilts.

I do so sympathise: there's no point in married couples sleeping apart when two beds can be as one. Rest Assured, who make zip and link beds, tell me that they will adapt divan beds which have come from them and that other manufacturers do the same with their products. So find out the manufacturers of your beds, contact the firm, and see if they will join them for you.

While browsing through my records I came across one I'd never played and never liked. I sprayed it with gold paint, glued on my favourite pop-star's name in black felt and framed it. It looks great on my bedroom wall.

Kay Duggan (aged 14), Abertillery, Gwent.

Whenever I open my chest of drawers I find myself smiling. I have lined each one with the picture side of recent birthday cards stuck together with tape. They are firmer than wallpaper and remind me of my friends and relations.

Mrs L. Jones, Gwent.

Anything that brings back happy memories is fun. My bathroom dressing table and a circular table in my bedroom are both smothered in photographs of family and friends, human and animal, under sheets of plate glass. They are both excellent talking points and reminders of the highlights and loves of my life.

To make original embroidery transfers, find a suitable subject in a book or magazine and, using a ball-point pen, trace this on to grease-proof paper. Then place the tracing face down on the material and press with a hot iron. If you do a lot of embroidery this certainly cuts the expense.

Mrs Rosemary Murray, Shotts, Lanarks.

I am always losing my jewellery so one Saturday I decided to make something to keep it together. First I got a large wooden spoon and then asked my father to put some hooks down the stem. After this was done I painted the stem green and on the base of the spoon I painted a face. Then father hung it on the wall, and now I hang my jewellery on it.

June Shepherd, Godalming, Surrey.

I recently broke the lid of an expensive teapot. I'm not usually a hoarder, but I just couldn't throw this particular piece away. It sits on my kitchen windowsill containing a beautiful plant, along with a chipped mug holding a tiny cactus. Pretty china that gets chipped or cracked can be used to such advantage in this way, and I won't be throwing any away again. I have also used other household items in the garden – an old coal hod is full of foxgloves, pinks have flourished in a pedal bin no longer fit for its proper use, and I have a flowering shrub in a cracked dishwasher lid. These unusual plant-pots are not only attractive and cheap, but they make good conversation pieces with visitors.

Mrs N. Beken, Southall, Middx.

I love hearing about alternative uses of objects that have outlived their original purpose. I'm a great hoarder myself and believe that everything, however inappropriate it may seem, will eventually become useful. I was recently given a beautiful Sukiyaki bowl and though I doubt I'll ever get around to preparing that dish, it has become a beautiful flower bowl for overblown roses and broken-off rhododendrons.

When painting and decorating I find these tips very useful. Wear your old clothes inside out, inevitably you get a few smears of paint somewhere, but these are not so bad on the wrong side of the material and do not show when the clothes are turned right side out again. Also a paper handkerchief worn on top of the head underneath a hair net prevents you from touching the wet ceiling and having a crown of paint to get rid of.

Mrs M.E.P., Anglesey, N. Wales.

Recently I read in *TV Times* about a housewife who is allergic to the smell of paint. This was a problem in our house, too, until we discovered Petal. This is a mildly perfumed liquid which is added to paint in the can, and kills all the unpleasant odours. It is made by Easy-Do-Products Ltd, 382 City Road, London EC1V 2QA (01 837 8083).

Anon.

Thank you so much for passing on the hint about Petal killing the strong smell of paint. In am 72, and being a widow do all my own decorating now. I thought you might like to hear my hint for keeping paint-brushes in good condition. Often when they are left for cleaning, they get forgotten and go stiff and hard. However, put the bristles in a container and cover with a strong solution of Jeyes Fluid. It cleans the brushes of all dried paint if left to stand for a day or two. This saves paint brushes and coppers!

Mrs G. J. Duncan, Luton, Beds.

Peg up long curtains when freshening up window paint or skirtings. You can pull them along as you go.

Mr L. A. Walker, Rhyl, Clywd.

A polythene circle laid on the surface of a half-used tin of paint keeps it from drying up when the lid is firmly replaced.

Mrs N. Turner, Stoke-on-Trent.

A dab of white soap is a quick filler for drawing-pin-holes when decorating.

J. Wagstaff, Henley-on-Thames.

To remove paint from glass, dip a razor blade in turps.

Mrs Mackay, Moray.

Decorating materials are expensive. After cleaning paint-brushes in white spirit, don't throw the liquid away. Pour it into a large screwtop jar and leave undisturbed for a few weeks. The paint will solidify at the bottom and you can pour the spirit back into its original container. Although discoloured it works just as well. You can also use the screwtop jar many more times for the same job.

Mrs N. Fentum, Tyne and Wear.

To make grouting an efficient and much cleaner job, just fill a nylon icing bag with ready-mixed grouting, insert the nozzle used for writing and proceed to fill in all the crevices. Work the grouting in with a rounded stick as you go along and I assure you that most of the grouting ends up in the crevices and not on the face of the tiles as it usually does.

Mrs P. Hoe, Prescot, Merseyside.

General care

Worried about the safety of the electrical equipment and wiring in their new home, my parents tried to get a list of correct fuses to use with various appliances. They also wanted advice as to whether the house needed to be re-wired. The local Electricity Board had no list of necessary fuses. To establish what was necessary would cost £12.70, they said. My parents are old-age pensioners. Surely this kind of inspection, where safety is involved, could be offered free to pensioners?

Mrs B. Castle, Ruislip, Middx.

People do need some guidance and the Electrical Association for Women, 25 Foubert's Place, London W1V 2AL (01 437 5212) will supply two free leaflets, Act Now – Check Your Wiring *and* Electrical Protection in The Home *if you send them a sae. They say that many pensioners who own their houses have not had wiring checked for 30 or 40 years, but it should be done every 10 years or so. If your parents rent their home, the landlord, whether council or private, is probably responsible for checking that electric installations are safe. If they own their own home, but, like many pensioners, are short of ready cash, they could try to apply for advice to the Improvement Grants department of their local council, though nowadays funds are scarce, and regulations about grants tend to vary tremendously from area to area, and from year to year. But it is possible that they could be helped under the 1974 Housing Act.*

Would you say that I am an unusual parent? I can cook, sew, knit, embroider, make clothes from paper patterns, wash, iron and turn my hand to all household chores. People often ask me as a one-parent family how I cope with three children, but when they come home from school I realise what a godsend my interests are, as I have made all my girls' dresses, cardigans and jumpers. Those same people make me smile when they say how expensive clothes are these days, because it seems to me they haven't the time or the patience to make their own. I have to stay home to care for my children at the moment, but when I go back to work I will resume my job as a heavy goods driver handling trucks up to 30 tons in weight. I would say that I'm a man with envied talent.

S. Barret, Walsall, Staffs.

I read your letter with admiration, but didn't feel you were unusual until I got to the end. I expect everyone reading this page will be as surprised as I was. What a real gentleman you must be!

There can hardly be a more useful fruit than the banana. Not only does it have culinary, wine and rum-making properties, but the inside of the skin, when rubbed on leather, gives a beautiful finish to shoes, belts, handbags and furniture. Once used, the skin can be dried in a warm oven and stored for future burning on an open fire. The ash should be collected and used to plant hyacinths and other bulbs, because they thrive on the chemicals in the ash.

Anthony Coombs, Cheam, Surrey.

I'm so thrilled with my discovery I just have to pass it on. I thought that if a fabric softener such as Comfort takes the static out of synthetic fabrics, why shouldn't it take it out of

***

Foil – Extra Uses

After using a heat lamp on my bad back, I wrap myself in foil to keep in the warmth, I crackle a bit but at least the treatment has enabled me to stand upright again!

Mrs A. Jelves, London N5.

Wrap soap-filled pads in foil after use. It saves them going rusty and gives them a longer life.

A. Sharrock, Leicester.

To direct more heat into a room during Winter, tape foil behind your radiators. It cuts down the size of electricity bills.

Mrs H. Lise, Dyfed.

Foil placed under rings on our gas cooker saves my Mum mess and money.

T. Connaughton (aged 15), Clywd.

I line my milk pan with aluminium foil. It never burns, keeps the pan clean and heats the milk more quickly.

Mr N. Wragg, Tonbridge.

Mrs Jelves' backache cure sounds too good not to be true. I would use Blu Tak or something similar to fasten foil behind radiators, as tape could bring off the paint. Do not be tempted to line the tray under the elements on an electric cooker. The manufacturers do not recommend it.

***

polythene surfaces that attract dust? So I dipped a cloth in the solution and wiped it over my bread bin, tea caddy and sugar container. Now instead of feeling a bit sticky to the touch and needing to be cleaned every day, they feel smooth and slippery. I also use it on the telephone, the children's toys, the venetian blinds, the TV screen and all white melamine surfaces. The amount of work saved is fantastic.

Mrs R. Winstanley, Preston, Lancs.

An old lady living alone gave me this tip for people in a similar situation. After she has turned the handle to drop a coin into her electricity meter she puts an extra coin in, but does not turn the handle. Then when the lights do go out she has only to turn the handle instead of fumbling for another coin. A spot of luminous paint on the meter box guides her straight there.

Mrs V. Burriss, Bedworth, Warwks.

I find the best way to get rid of summer flies is to pick some fresh mint from the garden and put it in each room. Result – no flies and a pleasant 'minty' smell around the house.

Mrs Bernie, London N21.

This does seem to work. Also, mint grows profusely, so it is ideal to grow in pots and window boxes, where it will also provide you with delicious fresh mint for sauces and salads.

When washing the floor, I wear bed socks over my shoes or slippers to avoid muddy or dirty marks being made by footprints. It really works. I'm sure your readers must have experienced the annoyance caused when they have to retrace their steps over a wet floor.

Mrs Margaret Jones, Southsea, Hants.

To prolong the life of a hot water bottle, before using a new one rinse it out with about a tablespoonful of glycerin.

Mrs Rae Whiteford, Glasgow.

Face flannels are so expensive and of such poor quality that I bought a yard of towelling to make myself three. However I find that while I'm washing the ends flap about, so I am now making circular flannels which are so much more convenient that I wonder why all flannels aren't this shape.

Violet R. Bushell, Southampton.

Here's a shopping tip which is quite a money-saver. We live in a small village and although the nearest town is only five miles away, the single bus fare is 35p so my wife has to use the village supermarket. I work in the town and now from time to time during the lunch hour I tour the town supermarkets picking out the moneysavers. I recently spent £21.72 for items that would have cost £27.09 in the village. A saving of 20 per cent. As my wife uses up items from our stock she puts money in a box for my next bulk-buying spending spree.

Frank Richards, Flackwell Heath, Bucks.

I get a nice soapy sponge for the bath by putting all those left-over little pieces of soap that mount up after a while into a sponge 'pouch' about four inches square. Fold an oblong piece of sponge into two and then sew up the three open sides after the bits of soap have been placed inside.

Mrs Clare Walton, RAF Northolt, Middx.

I never throw away old bits of soap. I keep them in a big jar. Can you tell me how to remake them again into usable blocks?

Mrs A. Jones, Wrexham.

Shred the soap into small empty plastic containers and cover with boiling water. Stir the mixture well and put in a plastic bag in the fridge to solidify. The bag prevents the smell from getting into the food. Then you will have a brand new tablet of soap. If you have children, sew the soap ends between two bits of foam cut in an animal shape. This makes a lovely soapy sponge for the bath. Incidentally, soap lasts longer if it is dry, so buy as much as you can afford each time and store it in the warmth of a linen or airing cupboard. It makes the cupboard smell sweet, too.

My husband recently changed from cigarettes to smoking a pipe. This was all right as far as I was concerned, although in cold weather when it wasn't possible to open a window I found the smoke affected my weak lungs. But I heard that lighting a candle each time a smoker lit up would burn up the smoke and clear the air. I was very sceptical at first but it really does work and I soon found that my husband was passing on the matches for me to light my candle.

Mrs O.N.F., Northolt, Middx.

P.S. A lighted candle will cancel out the smell of fresh paint too.

To protect your precious china and cut glass, place a folded tea towel in the bottom of the washing-up bowl before adding the water. Place another tea towel on the draining board to stand the articles on before drying carefully.

Mrs M. Hurst, Rochdale.

★ **What people do with . . . denture tablets!**

A fizzy denture tablet in warm water freshens my dishcloths and flannels.

Sue Jackson, Cheltenham.

Once a month I soak my teapot with one overnight and in the morning the inside is like new.

Mrs S. Parker, Crewe.

I leave half a denture tablet overnight in my flask with warm water. It gleams in the morning.

Mrs P. Cash, Thetford.

When I take down my curtains I soak all the grubby curtain hooks in a bowl of warm water and a denture tablet. You don't even have to rub them.

Mrs Doudican, Darlington.

All white enamel pans, casseroles, plastic and china cups and coffee pots come clean if you put two tablets in very hot water and soak for four minutes.

Mrs J.G. Mottram, London W9.

To clean nylon hairbrushes and combs, place them bristles uppermost in a container and add half a denture tablet. The dirt rises to the surface and the objects come out like new.

Mrs D. Worringham, Woodley, Berks.

The Good Housekeeping Institute tell me that one should not put denture tablets in a metal pot of any kind; apparently it may induce pitting of the surface. Since receiving this advice I have cleaned my metal teapots by adding a spoonful of detergent powder, pouring on boiling water and leaving it to soak for 3–4 hours. I rinse out first with hot then cold water, and no unpleasant taste remains.

Mrs Anne Baxendale, Fareham, Hants.

If your bathroom scales look shabby, carefully remove the top layer and replace it with a cork tile cut to the same shape and glued on.

Miss C. F. Moorhouse, Barnstaple.

P.S. A layer of Fablon freshens them up, too.

If you save all the scoops out of the baby milk tins and make holes in the end of the handles with a hot needle threaded with strong cotton or wool, and join them together, and make a good strong knot at the end, you have a safe but strong rattle for your baby to play with. I did it with my last two babies and will do it for the next one, when we have enough scoops.

Mrs C. Johnson, Plaistow, London E13.

Clothes and Home Maintenance: useful addresses

Clothing

John Lewis (for unusual haberdashery inquiries),
Oxford Street, London W1.

The Handbag Services Co,
16 Beauchamp Place, Knightsbridge, London SW3 1NF. (01 589 4975)

Permutit Boby Ltd (water softeners, washing problems),
632 London Road, Isleworth, JW7 4E2. (01 560 5199)

Guillaume (specialist cleaners),
59 Davies Street, London W1. (01 629 0868)

E. R. Howard Ltd (makers of Woolite),
Gippeswyk Avenue, Ipswich, Suffolk IP2 9AD. (Ipswich 56446)

Association of British Launderers and Cleaners,
Lancaster Gate House, 319 Pinner Road, Harrow, Middx HA1 4HX. (01 863 7755)

Suède Services
2A Hoop Lane, Golders Green Road, London NW11 8JS. (01 455 0052)

Lewis and Wayne (specialist cleaners),
13 Elystan Street, London SW3 3NT. (01 589 5730)

Lilliman and Cox (specialist cleaners),
34 Bruton Place, London W1X 7AA. (01 629 4555)

Leslie Fogel (dressmaking service and pattern cutting),
5 South Molton Street, London W1Y 1DH. (01 493 2541)

Paul Craig (hat-making service),
15 D'Arblay Street, London W1. (01 437 5467)

The Frock Exchange (for top quality second-hand clothes),
450 Fulham Road, London SW6 (01 381 2937)

Household and Cleaning

Mr K. J. Trayler (re-caning),
Fir Close, Frostenden, Wangford, Suffolk. (Wangford 261)

Mr F. W. Groce (re-caning),
104 Godley Road, London SW18. (01 870 2897)

Mr Louis Rich (restoration of furniture of all kinds),
13 Crescent Place, London SW3. (01 589 4077)

Mary Chess (perfumed shelf paper),
7 Shepherd Market, Curzon Street, London W1Y 7HR. (01 629 5152)

China Repairers Ltd,
64 Charles Lane, London NW8 7SB. (01 722 8407)

Nissim and Company (carpet repairs),
23 Charlotte Road, London EC2A 3PB. (01 739 5051)

Permaclean (UK) Ltd (carpet cleaning),
103-105 Brighton Road, Coulsdon CR3 3NG. (01 668 5421)

Servicemaster (GB) Ltd (carpet cleaning),
Head office: 48 Fingeringhoe Road, Colchester, Essex. (Colchester 66699)

Winsor and Newton (art supplies such as Barbola),
51 Rathbone Place, London W1P 1AB. (01 636 4231)

Easy-Do Products Ltd (manufacturers of Petal paint smell remover),
382 City Road, London EC1V 2QA.
(01 837 8083)

Harrods (stockists of Paul Corbett toothpaste dispensers),
Knightsbridge, London SW1. (01 730 1234)

G.E. Holloway and Sons Ltd (makers of a chewing-gum remover),
12 Carlisle Road, London NW9 0HL. (01 200 0066)

Kimbermont Ltd (makers of Kimbo all-purpose cleaner),
3 Beeston Place, London SW1. (01 828 9111-9114)

Other Useful Adresses

National Association of the Launderette Industry,
Guardian House, 92-94 Foxberry Road, London SE4 2SH. (01 692 8622)

International Wool Secretariat (information on care of wools, carpets, etc),
6 Carlton Gardens, London SW1. (01 930 7300)

British Man-Made Fibres Federation,
24 Buckingham Gate, London SW1E 6LB. (01 828 0744)

Good Housekeeping Institute (information on household products, cleaning, etc),
National Magazine House, Broadwick Street, London W1V 2BP. (01 439 7144)

British Standards Institution,
2 Park Street, London W1A 2BS. (01 629 9000)

Dylon (Annette Stevens, Consumer Advice Bureau),
Dylon International Ltd, Worsley Bridge Road, Lower Sydenham, London SE26 5HD. (01 650 4801)

The Monarch Shield Co (for protection of silver, pewter, brass, or other precious objects),
10 Shacklewell Road, London N16 7OA. (01 254 6362-6365)

The Furniture Hospital (will accept work sent from out of London),
14A Ravenscourt Avenue, London W6. (01 741 0940)

7
Gardening

Gardening is one of those wonderful things that an amateur can enjoy as much as the professional. It can be just as much of an enthralling hobby as a full-time occupation and there is nothing on which one can put a more individual stamp than one's own plot, whatever its size.

I acquired a lovely garden when I married Peter Saunders. Laid out originally by his first wife Ann, it includes a magnificent mimosa tree grown from a few seeds she picked up on the pavement and brought back from the South of France. Amongst other clever ideas of hers there is also a waist-high double wall with plenty of earth filling the space between which enabled her to go on gardening without bending down in her last years when she became very ill.

It was a great thrill for me to discover that I have a set of reasonably green fingers and now I enjoy this three-quarters of an acre to the full through each season. It is fun being able to bring back cuttings from holidays abroad (not rooted ones of course, they are illegal). In this way, Peter and I have growing reminders of happy times spent far from home, too. I find my intense love of colours still influences me when choosing what goes where, so there are masses of 'Just Joey' roses in the beds outside the drawing-room windows to recapture the apricot of the curtains inside – and 'Superstars' line the drive. But whereas red, white and blue seemed to dominate over all for the year of the Royal Wedding, my choice has now turned to shades of blue, in the hyacinth bulbs which are just beginning to peep through the earth below my office window as I write, darkest purple to palest sky. These shades will fade out into the mass of white busy lizzies which run riot as soon as the weather gives them a chance – and after which I have named a snow-white and very active toy poodle! My 'Picking Patch' in the garden is coming on well, too. In that I keep a cacophony of colour because the drawing room calls for all shades of coral and red, the dining room and hall positively beam when full of all rays of yellows, while the bedroom reflects calm in pinky-mauve hues.

Although I have always been very enthusiastic about arranging flowers, it was Julia Clements who harnessed and trained my enthusiasm. Julia is a legend in gardening club circles throughout the world as a teacher, speaker, author and judge of flower arranging. She and I travelled together the length and breadth of Britain over many months in a 'Hostess with the Mostest' show. I introduced it and of course it included a section about flowers. What I enjoyed most during those events was standing in the wings while Julia Clements, with what appeared to be effortless skill, filled vase after vase of all shades and sizes with perfectly balanced arrangements. Invariably working from the back and out towards the audience, the results, viewed from the front, were always enchanting and incredibly varied. She used leaves, flowers, fresh and dry, sometimes added fruit and often based an arrangement on bits of driftwood – but whatever the ingredients she always ended up with a flourish by waving, like a magician, an enormous coloured scarf so as to give each arrangement a perfect backcloth. Most effective!

A still beautiful woman, she combines great dignity with humour and infinite knowledge of her subject. She shares lots of her secrets in her many books but after travelling with her I shall never be able to face a vase from the front when I start an arrangement and will always hear her soft voice saying: 'Remember, my dear, proportions are all-important – the highest point for a tall arrangement *must* be one and a half times the height of the vase, and on the same principle the width must be one and half of the vase for low ones.' Another excellent tip of Julia's which I use without fail and which keeps my foliage fresh much longer than usual, is to cut up the centre of the stems to let them drink up the water ('Never mash them, Katie, you'll just encourage bacteria to develop') and if you have the chance, submerge the leaves in sugar-laced water for a few minutes before shaking and using them. As a general rule for the small branches which can lie flat in a basin, use a couple of teaspoons of sugar to two inches of water, and go to two dessertspoons when you are soaking bigger branches in the bath.

Looking over my thoughts on the subject of gardens and flowers, I think you can see exactly what I meant when I said at the beginning of this book that I have been very lucky to meet and learn from experts on all kinds of subjects.

My husband is English, I am Italian and I miss the gay, laughing colours of my native Liguria Riviera. Although I realise how lucky we are to have a house, I get depressed because all the houses look alike in this part of London. I thought of planting lots of different coloured flowers, though I can't spend much money. Also, a few yards from my kitchen door there's a dreary old wooden fence, belonging to our neighbours, and I'd like to grow something to cover it. The fence is always in the shade so it would have to be a really hardy plant. Have you any ideas?

Amelia Dowling, Haringey, London.

I understand so well how you feel, because most of my childhood summers were spent in our villa between Rapallo and San Michele in Italy. Remember 'busy lizzies' love the shade, spread energetically, and with care you can take cuttings from them year to year. You could also paint the outside of your house a pale yellow or pinkish terracotta to brighten it up. Runner beans grow amazingly quickly too, and are easily coaxed in various directions; they would give both that old fence a very attractive face-lift, and you a few home-grown vegetables into the bargain. But make sure your neighbours don't mind your using the reverse side of their fence – maybe you could promise them a share in your first home-grown picking celebrations.

Here are a handful of gardening tips which I have found, tried and tested.

Having had a complete crop of potatoes ruined by slugs, the next year we dug the potato trench, put a good layer of sea-sand along the bottom and planted the 'sets' into this. Then we added sand to the soil which was to cover them, so they had sand all around them, and not one potato was attacked by slugs or any other pest. Sea sand should not be used when preparing seed compost but a little can be lightly sprinkled over and around annuals to deter slugs.

When blackcurrants are ripe, it's much easier to cut the branches bearing the fruit and pick the berries off at some convenient seat, indoors or out. The fruiting branches need pruning anyway, so this is good for the bush.

In the coldest weather, many plants in an unheated greenhouse may be protected by a single sheet of newspaper (exchanged when damp for a dry one). For instance, parsley rooted in a large pot will stand the Winter this way as will many tender plants.

A good garden shrub which has large clusters of red berries, which birds for some reason will not touch is *Skimmia*. You need to plant two bushes, one male and one female, the latter providing the berries, the former, heads of cream-coloured flowers early in Spring. The flowers also have a lovely scent,

159

so you get two colourful additions to your garden scheme. (The shrubs can be propagated by seeds, cuttings, or layers.)

Mrs O. Bush Fron, Gwynned.

The reason your sea sand remedy works is because it contains salt: slugs can't abide it. Apparently a sprinkling of soot will do the same trick. Another tip on the subject of salt: if you're a keen kitchen gardener, try to rotate your vegetables on a three-year plan to prevent a build-up of salt in the soil. Too much will do your plants no good.

You could also use your newspaper as protection not only in the coldest weather, but when the sun is high. Spray your greenhouse stock with warm water, before the sun gets up, and cover the plants with newspaper, to keep them shaded and moist during the hottest part of the day.

My wife and I own an allotment which is quite a distance from our home and because of this we do most of our work there on Sundays. We are a newly-married couple and we save by growing our own vegetables, but as we have to stay at the allotment all day we get very hungry. We take a flask of tea, coffee or soup, but we get sick of sandwiches. We have tried taking pies and pasties to the allotment, first heating them in foil, but they are cold when we are ready to eat them. Do you know a way in which to keep pies and pasties hot for say up to one and a half hours?

Robert and Jean Hedley, Hebburn, Northumb.

Apart from the insulated shopping bag there's a 'no-power' cooker called The Hot Box. It works on the principle of retaining heat. You put very hot food in it and it continues to cook stews, hot pies, or rice puddings, thus saving fuel. After eight hours or so you would have to re-heat the contents, but it would

certainly keep food piping hot for the one and a half hours you mention. Write, enclosing a sae for further details to Stearns (Shipton Green) Ltd, Shipton Green, Itchenor, Nr Chichester, West Sussex PO20 7B2 (0243 512823).

Can you help me? I have just bought a small garden flat, but garden isn't the right word for it, as it's really a concrete patch with one flower bed. Being a country girl, I would love the green grass look, but what can I do with concrete? Is there anything on the market which will go over concrete and won't involve too much work?

Teresa Clarkson, London N6.

You could try Monsanto Astro-turf. There's a choice of three surfaces; patio, landscape and action, and you can lay it yourself (just like a carpet) or have it permanently fixed by specialists. Once it is down it is non-slip and quite happy about all kinds of weather. Although I am not a fan of fake lawns they are quite realistic – and will save you both

weeding and mowing. For a list of national distributors, write to Monsanto Ltd, Telford House, 14 Tothill Street, London SW1H 9LH (01 222 5678).

We are always hearing how schools are so short of money so don't you think it would be a good idea if all schools used a small plot of their land to cultivate a few vegetables? The produce could be sold to the children at break-time – a raw carrot is cheaper than a bar of chocolate. Apart from encouraging the children's interest in gardening, think how many trips to the dentist it would save.

Mrs M. Taylor, Wednesfield, Staffs.

Many schools do run gardening projects for the children, but perhaps those that do not will now start putting your idea into practice.

Please could you tell me how to preserve gourds for decoration? I grew some last year and covered them with a layer of clear poly-urethane varnish but they went bad after a while.

Mike Morley, Doncaster, Yorks.

Perhaps you didn't allow the gourds to dry out thoroughly. Let them ripen on the plants until they are hard and the leaves begin to die, then cut them from the plant with a sharp knife. Wipe clean and allow them to dry out for at least six weeks, either in really warm sun or a well-heated airing cupboard. Only when they are bone dry should you varnish them. If you follow this method I think you'll find you have better luck this year.

A few years ago I married an American stationed in this country. Since my wedding day I have kept my bouquet in the freezer and it is as fresh as when we were married. We are leaving for the United States this year and I

do so want to keep it. Do you know of any way I can get my bouquet over there in a freezer container?

Barbara Wawrin, Mildenhall, Suffolk.

Wouldn't it be more convenient in the long run to keep your bridal bouquet just as fresh, but more visible? Sprinkle it generously with borax (available at any chemist) and leave it in a dry place for two to three weeks, or until it has dried out. Then keep it in a transparent box, with clear adhesive tape around the edges. This preserves single flowers, too.

I had so many roses in the garden this year I thought it would be a good idea to make a pot pourri. I tried drying the petals in the airing cupboard, but they just lost all their scent. Where can I find out how to make pot pourri?

Mrs J. Wales, Norwich.

I'm quite sure that the ideal book for you is Pot Pourris and other Fragrant Delights, *by Jacqueline Heriteau, published by Penguin. I found out that making a simple English pot pourri involves a lot more than picking and drying plain rose petals. You mix three cups of dried, scented rose petals – which have to be picked at the right time of day to keep their smell (as explained in the book) – two cups of dried lavender flowers, one cup of dried lemon verbena leaves and one tablespoon of coarse-ground cloves with 7 oz. of gum benzoin. Put all this in an airtight container – a glass jar with a screw top secured with sticky tape will do – and put it in a dry, dark place, shaking it every day, for six weeks. Only then can you put the mixture in your pot pourri container.*

Where can I buy a shrub called Honesty? I have seen it only in a vase and that was many years ago. Then recently I saw sprays of it on a television programme. Having always been fascinated by its transparent silvery look, I would love to buy one for the garden to brighten the winter months and to use in my own indoor arrangements.

Mrs V. J. Baudier, Enfield, Middx.

Honesty is not really a shrub but a hardy biennial with the lyrical name of Lunaria biennis. *If seeds are planted this year, the silvery diaphragms around the seeds, for which the plant is grown, will be produced next year. They can be bought through stockists of Garden Pride seeds (Packet No 2124) or if in difficulty write to the suppliers, Hurst Gunson Cooper Taber Ltd, Avenue Road, Witham, Essex CM8 2DX.*
P.S. Hursts have recently launched a 'Garden Gro-Plan' scheme which helps you to select and plan a vegetable patch suited to your garden size and consumption needs. Write to the above address for full details.

In a television programme recently we were shown a coffee plant which appealed to me very much, and perhaps to other viewers. I would be most grateful if you could tell me where I could order such a plant.

Mrs N. T., Purley, Surrey.

Coffee plants may figure in the stock of your local plant shop but they are fairly rare. One place which sells the plants and is more than helpful is Garden Care, 88 Broadway, London NW7 3TB. (01 959 4292). The plants cannot be sent by post but the seeds can. If you have a heated greenhouse or propagator you can sow your seeds at any time of the year. They must have moist warmth. Germination often takes four to five weeks so don't give up hope. Sow the seeds about half an inch deep in pots and transfer the seedlings to bigger pots as they grow. Eventually they will be quite big (about two to three feet) and will need six-inch pots. The plants prefer a sandy, loamy soil and like plenty of water. Wavy-edged leaves and white flowers make them very attractive and coffee berries follow the flowers if the plants are kept warm and moist enough.

For years I have tried to grow the Christmas Orange Plant from seed and the plants have grown but no orange berries have set. This year I sprinkled dried blood on the flowers, from the heart and liver I give my dogs and any meat we had ourselves. Every flower has produced a healthy-looking berry.

Mrs Joyce Kindra, Bournemouth, Dorset.

I have heard how successful an infusion of diluted blood can be. In fact an enthusiastic gardener in a London basement patio treks out to the nearest slaughter-house for blood for his vine. Knowing this, I never could taste the grapes, though I must admit they looked succulently fat and juicy even though they grew in - of all places - Paddington. A short cut to the same results is to buy a packet of dried blood at your nearest garden supply shop. It is the quickest tonic there is.

I am lucky enough to have a fairly large garden and would like to pass on a few tips. Nylon tights, cut across in strips, are good for supporting plants and bushes and in a strong wind don't chafe the stems. Half egg-shells

filled with soil are ideal 'pots' for starting off seeds. Vending-machine cups and yoghurt pots, after having a hole pierced in the bottom, are ideal for cuttings, etc. Hot detergent water from the washing machine is ideal for killing weeds in cement paths or asphalt, and I find it brings the cement paths up with a nice, clean bleached finish after a few wash-downs. I leave my large dahlia tubers in the ground all winter, and cover them with a blanket of fluff from my vacuum cleaner to keep them warm.

Dorothy Potter, Hayes, Middx.

I have had an avocado pear stone suspended half in water since Christmas, in the hope of encouraging it into a small plant. To date, I have a white stem of four inches which has grown into the water with shoots off it. The stone has split across the top slightly, but I cannot see any sign of growth there. Please could you tell me whether I should trim the stem at this stage and plant it in soil, or leave it until little shoots have grown larger and there is some growth at the top?

Mrs P. Devall, Street.

You're in too much of a hurry! Avocados take a long time to grow. You can keep watching it grow in water (mix five drops of Baby Bio to a pint of water to feed it every time you change the water) but it should do better in soil. As the roots are terribly brittle at this stage, do not touch them if you transfer it. Just add, very gradually, John Innes' No. 1 potting mixture to the container until all the water is forced out. Keep the avocado in a warm greenhouse temperature because they come from tropical climes!
P.S. I've seen them thrive in a warm kitchen, and in a sitting room, too—maybe they like company!

As a senior citizen (I am 88 years old) I have recently moved into a bed-sitter with a lovely view of a garden with a clump of flowers which look like poppies in full bloom. I left my room for a while and when I returned all the blooms had disappeared. Next morning they had reappeared. I hadn't realised that they went to sleep at night and woke when daylight came. Can you give me a reason for this and recommend a book on the subject?

Miss E. Cossless, Windlesham, Surrey.

Flowers, like humans, have a life rhythm, but a few of them, such as poppies, have more obvious waking and sleeping times. Just as we suffer from 'jet lag', they don't like their rhythm to be disturbed. If gardeners try to force flowers into bloom by keeping them in perpetual artificial light, it upsets the plants. The opening and closing of flowers seems to be partly controlled by phytochrome, a chemical in the leaves which reacts to light. This works in different ways in different plants. Over and above the mechanical action of the phytochrome there is the life rhythm called the circadian cycle, which helps them to close at the natural time, even if they are in a lighted room. Electric light, though, is not always strong enough to activate the phytochrome. Julia Clements mentions this in more detail in her Gift Book of Flower Arrangement, *published by Hamlyn. But if you are so interested in flowers you should read* The Secret Life of Plants *by Peter Tompkins and Christopher Bird, published by Penguin. You will be surprised how actively they share our lives. It is nice to see that your curiosity about life around you has not abated with the years. Nobody is ever too old to learn.*

Having two small children I find it impossible to keep my small garden in good shape without banning all ball games and general romping about. I don't think this is really fair as we don't have a playground near us, but I do want to grow my flowers and teach my children to enjoy them. Friends say it's impossible to have a garden that's a playground as well as a pleasure to look at. Have you any ideas that might help?

George Henley, London SE18.

This is a chance to divide and rule – literally. Get some cheap hurdle fencing, which looks nice and rustic, and fix the hurdles about 10 yards from the house. Use the area that is enclosed near the house for your flower beds and let the area farther away go wild as a play area for your children. Let them do what they like in their patch under the strict understanding that your flower area is out of bounds. They'll soon learn that because you are respecting their needs, they must respect yours. Before long, with encouragement, they will be using their bit of the garden for their own flowers – or even vegetables, such as lettuces and radishes, which are easy to grow and can be enjoyed by all the family. There's nothing like giving children responsibility to get them to behave responsibly.

I am retired and for the first time in my life have a small garden. Gardening books, though beautiful, are so expensive and not really suitable for a small garden. So now I keep all gardening hints from newspapers and magazines and stick them into an old holiday brochure. I thought perhaps others might benefit from this idea, and it makes an ideal, simple-to-read gardening book.

Mrs M. Tagger, London E3.

I have used this tip for many years with good results. When growing tomatoes, as soon as they are of a fair size put the whole truss, on the growing plant, in a clear polythene bag. Fasten the top of the bag with a clothes' peg for its easy removal and make sure there are some small holes in the bottom to drain off any condensation. This gives each plant its own little greenhouse and they ripen very quickly.

Mrs I. Marche, Goring-by-Sea, W. Sussex.

Your useful tip reminds me that for everyone wanting to grow things in a restricted space, or even indoors, whether it's just a collection of cooking herbs or a little herbaceous border, Gro-Bags are a most practical answer. They are the method now being used by many commercial growers of tomatoes. The bags contain a growing compost with plant foods that, when watered, will last the young plants until they are seven weeks old, after which they must have a liquid feed such as Tomorite. Gro-Bags are made by Fisons and can be bought at garden centres and at many supermarkets, including Woolworths.

P.S. Green tomatoes will ripen well if you wrap them individually in newspaper and leave in a drawer for two or three days.

★★★★★★★★★★★★★★★★★★★★★★★★★★★★★★★

★ *A few tips to repel several kinds of pest: if you are plagued by slugs in the garden, set little pots into the soil (a yogurt cup is ideal) and fill them to the earth's surface with beer. The slugs hate the smell and will soon disappear. A similar trick to keep ants away from rose bushes or even to cut off an invading track leading to the house or patio, is to sprinkle a little fresh urine on the ground. Ants have a highly efficient bush telegraph system and the message will soon pass down the line.* ★

★★★★★★★★★★★★★★★★★★★★★★★★★★★★★★★

In view of the rising costs of vegetables my mother, who is 77, decided to have a go at growing her own. But she found she couldn't afford cloches or a cold frame out of her pension. We solved her problem with this idea, which may be a help to other 'home growers'. We used an old wooden two-sided clothes horse. I undid the sides and loosely taped it together along the top rail. I then covered both sides with polythene (it looked a bit like a small tent, with an opening at each end) leaving the feet free to go into the ground. My mother now has a miniature greenhouse which will take many plants.

Miss Christine Barker, Bradford, W. Yorks.

I am a wife and mother, and having grown sick of the price of vegetables, decided to grow my own. My husband and I wanted to start our plants in seed trays, but the price of these was so high that instead we improvised. We used things we would normally throw away, which was very economical and I felt your readers might like to know some of our ideas. The first was plastic egg cartons. For every dozen eggs you buy you have a dozen separate seed pots. Yoghurt cartons made nice plant pots for lettuces until they were ready to plant outside and cottage cheese,

margarine and other plastic cartons are ideal for radishes, spring onions, and cress. You can also cut up empty washing-up liquid bottles three inches from the bottom, but make sure they have holes for drainage.

Mrs M.M. Mulvery, Wooton Basset, Wilts.

As flowers such as freesia are so expensive, try putting them in lemonade instead of water. They do last longer.

Mrs Joan Brown, Bexleyheath, Kent.

It's probably the sugar in the lemonade that does the trick and you'd have the same longer life results if you melted a generous dessert-spoonful of sugar in a pint of water before arranging your flowers in the mixture. I always want freesias to last forever, they smell so good.

How do you get rosebuds to open up after putting rose cuttings into a vase? I've tried all manner of additions to the water, tried fresh water every day or left it two or three days before changing the water. I hammer the stems as advised but it's all to no avail and so disappointing.

Mrs M. White, Walker-on-Tyne.

Try cutting the stems shorter than you have been doing and then make a 1 inch slit up the middle – do not crush the stems – and soak them right up to their necks in water for a few hours. Maybe the buds need an extra long drink and the water has not been reaching them. This method seems to open most flowers. It is always good to change the water each day but if you do not have time at least add some fresh to every vase.

When my husband was in hospital recently I bought him 10 red roses from a local florist. The next day I found to my chagrin, just one surviving rose. I have now found that the stems of newly-cut roses should be placed in two inches of boiling water for about 20 seconds, then plunged into cold water. This apparently dispels any air bubbles in the stem, allowing the roses to drink.

Mrs W. Benson, Liverpool.

Writer and floral arranger Julia Clements taught me to revive droopy roses by cutting their stems obliquely and plunging them, as you say, in boiling water. But she suggests you then wrap them tightly, blooms as well, in newspaper and lay them overnight in a bath, submerged in cold water. Next morning unwrap them carefully and they will be as good as new.
P.S. Incidentally, Julia Clements has written a number of books about flowers and flower arranging, which I find so instructive and helpful. Keep an eye out for her name when you are browsing in the bookshop, and look for the titles listed at the end of this chapter.

As my old plastic dustbin was rather the worse for wear I measured 12 inches up from the bottom of the bin and carefully cut round it with a fine saw. I then made holes in the bottom for drainage, put in a few small stones, filled it with some earth and planted some bulbs. I am now waiting for a nice show of hyacinths.

Mrs E. Rowe, Exeter.

My old rubber gloves, cut out at the thumb and fingers, are made into rubber rings which I then use for tying up plants after they have finished showing in Spring. Ordinary rubber rings are so expensive, and not very strong.

Mrs H. Eccles, Lowton, Warrington.

P.S. These are two tips of the kind I always enjoy – transferring something from its normal use to a new and equally helpful one.

I would like to share this tip with your readers as it really does work. To rid your garden of slugs prop the peel of oranges or grapefruit around the garden so there is room for the slugs to crawl underneath and you will find that they crawl into them rather than under stones, and so may be disposed of easily. It is safer than using slug pellets as you can be sure you are not harming other animals or birds.

Mrs M. Pilgrim, Rayleigh, Essex.

For anyone who has trouble finding a 'plant-minder' while they are away on holiday, perhaps they'd like to share my secret: place an old towel in the bottom of the bath, fit a length of rubber tubing from the cold tap to the far end of the bath and soak the towel. When it is thoroughly soaked, place all the plants on the towel at the far end of the bath, leaving the plug hole free. Leave the tap dripping very very gently through the rubber hose on to the towel. There's no danger of flooding and the plants get the water they need.

Mrs M. Herring, Spilsby, Lincs.

Useful Addresses

Stearns (Shipton Green) Ltd (for the Hot Box),
Itchenor, Near Chichester, West Sussex PO20 7BZ. (0243 512823)

Monsanto Ltd (for list of stockists of Astro-turf),
Telford House, 14 Tothill Street, London SW1H 9LH. (01 222 5678)

Hurst Gunson Cooper Taber Ltd (for Honesty seed inquiries and vegetable 'Gro-Plan' scheme),
Avenue Road, Witham, Essex CM8 2DX. (0376 516600)

Garden Care (suppliers of coffee plants),
88 Broadway, London NW7 3TB.
(01 959 4292)

Thompson and Morgan Ltd (stockists of coffee plant and other seeds),
London Road, Ipswich. (0473 218821)

Oat Farms House (pot pourri ingredients by mail order),
Felmingham, North Walsham, Norfolk NR28 0LD. (026 373 2772)

Useful Reading

The Fragrant Garden, Kay N. Sanecki (Batsford).
The Scented Garden, Rosemary Verey (Michael Joseph).
Reader's Digest New Illustrated Guide to Gardening (Reader's Digest Association).
Reader's Digest: The Gardening Year (Reader's Digest Association).
Gardeners' Question Time, Ken Ford, Alan Gemmell, Fred Loads, Bill Sowerbutts (Robson Books).
The **Colour in Your Garden** Series by Octopus. Titles include:
Beautiful Bulbs, H.G. Witham Hogg.
Beautiful Shrubs, J.R.B. Evison.
Greenhouse Gardener, David Shelton.
Handyman Gardener, David L. Bebb.
The Rose Expert
The Houseplant Expert, Dr D.G. Hessayon (pbi publications).
Flower Arrangements, Julia Clements (Leisure Days Publications paperback).
The Gift Book of Flower Arrangement, Julia Clements (Hamlyn).
The Secret Life of Plants, Peter Tompkins and Christopher Bird (Penguin paperback)
The Well-Tempered Garden, Christopher Lloyd (Penguin paperback)

8
Pets

Animals in general and dogs in particular have played a very important part in my life ever since I can remember, and although I am certain that those of you who do not share my enthusiasm on this subject will save yourselves a lot of trouble and heartache, I am equally sure you are missing out on some of the fun, companionship, unquestioning devotion and loyalty that a well-trained dog can bring.

And those words 'well-trained' are all-important because I must admit I put the blame firmly on to the irresponsible behaviour of certain dog owners for encouraging the often understandable antagonism of the anti-dog brigade.

I speak as someone who, over many years, has shared her life at very close quarters with a number of breeds ranging from a Great Dane, a St Bernard, through assorted mongrels to a minute sleeve peke weighing about 4 lb, to my present West Highland Terrier and a rescued white toy poodle called Bizzie Liz. In fact I consider my first duty to my pets, friends and neighbours, as well as myself is to be a responsible trainer-owner. There is nothing more annoying to live with than a badly-behaved dog, except perhaps a badly-behaved child, but in both cases they have to be taught what is expected of them before they can start to develop their own personality – and a badly-behaved dog is usually a bewildered one who is often the butt of an impatient swipe or shout just because time and patience have not been spent on explaining the house rules from the first moment it became a full member of the family.

My first rule would be: *do not have a dog unless you really want one.* Do not be influenced by either children's pleadings or the fluffy charm of a small pup. Keep in mind that you are taking another individual into the home, who will be as demanding as the rest of you put together and will share your life for 10 to 14 years to come. Surprise giving or receiving, particularly at Christmas, is cruel to everyone concerned: harassed, unprepared parents, untrained, frightened animals in the hands of enthusiastic but rough children produce nothing but frayed tempers and overall frustration. Apart from anything else a new puppy should be welcomed with a lot of forethought which must include a bed, blanket, food and drinking bowls – plus a generous supply of white vinegar to counteract those inevitable puppy puddles before it realises that outside is the place to piddle (or on a newspaper on a lino floor in an emergency). Yes, white vinegar has superseded soda water for scientific alkali-versus-acid reasons, see page 184. The name and telephone number of your nearest vet should have been checked before the arrival of any pet.

My second rule is this. If you DO want a dog, please go to the trouble to choose a breed which will fit into your lifestyle. Even though Great Danes need much less exercise than you would expect because their hearts are too small for their build and get easily strained, their size and ever-waving tail will cause havoc and destruction in restricted spaces – just as a long-haired dog, however small, is going to need frequent and regular grooming whether you live in a town or the country if you don't want it to smell doggy. What's more, some dogs moult more than others and this does not go hand in hand with the length of their coat. So really mull over the books which sum up the pros and cons of various breeds before you make your choice. And once you have decided, follow up your selection by reading books which go into more detail about a specific breed. Should you pick a cross breed or a mongrel, it is fun to check up on the various characteristics you can 'see' in him or her.

My third rule ties up with what I feel is the overall and perhaps repetitive 'message' between these pages: remember to *use* WORDS *to communicate* with your pet. So often I watch and want to cry out when I see a dog owner tugging or jerking back at a lead, or pulling an obviously terrified animal across a busy street in silence. *Use your voice:* to reassure, to praise, to scold, to teach. You will be astonished what a wide vocabulary a dog can build up. Repeat certain phrases daily: 'I'm coming back!' – every time you leave him; 'We're nearly home' – after a walk; 'DON'T do that' or 'STOP it'. All are quickly docketted in a dog's mind – but only if you change the tone of voice to match their meaning. 'Stop it' said in the cooing way of 'Good dog' is useless, and when you praise, which should be as often as possible because an owner's pleasure is a mainstay of a pet's life, make it sound a real joy: 'WHAT a good boy/girl.' And then smile! You will be amazed and amused how many dogs will, in time, smile back, revealing a whole set of teeth and a crinkled nose of delight!

The most vexed question which recurs in readers' letters over the years is whether a dog can be left on his own all day. Many people want to own a dog but try to overlook the commitment this involves in terms of time. To leave a puppy alone from dawn to dusk on the basis that it has to get used to it amounts to downright cruelty. Just because you do not see how it behaves does not mean it is not thoroughly distressed by this sudden solitude and silence, having not long been taken away from its brothers and sisters. A dog's brain can become literally addled, physically, by being left alone for hours on end, and the animal will never develop its intelligence as it should and could.

It is also unfair to the dog and yourself to get back dead beat from a day's work and not have the energy to walk or play with this creature who has spent so long in silence. Similarly I am appalled how many people scold a pet that has messed all over the place after a whole day alone. Would you not burst? If you have no garden, make sure you keep the dog paper-trained if you have to leave it for a short while when it is still a pup. And when fully-grown, remember, a male dog needs to empty his bladder more often than a bitch does, and will suffer serious discomfort and eventual damage if this is not taken into consideration.

Remember, too, that dogs, more than any other animals, want to please, but they are not mind-readers and they have to have the rules explained with patience and clarity. Of course we want to be able to leave a pet alone for a few hours and I find one of the best ways to get them used to this is to leave them in one room and close the door while you get on with something elsewhere in the home. Set her up with a toy, her bed and perhaps a cast-off of yours, tell her you will 'Be back' and harden your heart against the odd whimper. If she persists in crying go back and tell her she's very 'NAUGHTY' and to 'GO TO SLEEP', then leave her again. After a quarter of an hour or so of silence go back and praise lavishly and add a choc drop or something similar as a bonus.

Cats incidentally *can* be trained not to scratch the furniture, curtains and carpet to pieces while you are away. If you do not want to invest in already made-up scratching boards and are good at do-it-yourself, get a thick log about three feet long, still with the bark if possible, then cover half of it with cheap velvet. Then, every time the cat makes for your best armchair, tap him firmly with a rolled newspaper and redirect him to his own scratching ground. This rolled newspaper works well for dogs, too, as it makes a noise but a rap with it does not hurt bones or innards. That look of indifference and disdain is far from stupidity … and you will win the day if you are that much more determined than he is.

I have emphasised these early days in pet care because they are so important in successful pet-owning. Be persistent, consistent, kind and firm from the moment this new character arrives and you will have laid the most solid of foundations of a wonderful and I hope very long-lasting relationship which will give you both tremendous pleasure.

Please, please help! My dog has just eaten two £1 notes. I have salvaged one rather nibbled one; but of the other only one half remains. Where do I send the pieces to get replacements?

Mrs Lynn Higgs, London N2

Get to a bank quickly ... with the remains plus culprit. The left-overs sound decipherable enough to get you two brand new replacements. If the bank manager is a dog-lover, the sight of a cash-hungry pet might win sympathy as well.

I have adopted a beautiful little Sheltie dog from the RSPCA. She has had a rough deal from five homes, yet she is only 11 months old. There is a lot we shall have to give up financially to keep her properly but we are determined to make her feel secure. Her name is Kiki. I would love to know the meaning of this name. Our other little dog is Cara, which is Irish for 'friend', which is why we chose it.

Mrs D. Bowden, Hillingdon, Greater London.

It's wonderful to watch an animal who has been badly treated blossom under loving care. I have a little bitch we rescued off the beach in Kenya, complete with an attempted decapitation scar. She is waiting in quarantine right now (Freedom Day is August 21) so I know exactly how you feel about your Sheltie. I'm afraid I cannot discover the origin of Kiki as a name. I know a magnificent bull mastiff who could only be called by his made-up name of Baroof – but Cara is Italian for 'dear' as well as Irish for 'friend'.
P.S. All you dog-lovers who enquired will be glad to know that Kippy lived five happy years after her term in quarantine and died at what must have been a ripe old age.

I am 14 and have a two-year-old black Labrador, Joe. His worst fault is his friendly attitude. He loves all other dogs and always rushes towards any he sees. I was taking Joe for a walk when I met a woman with an ankle-high canine. I did not notice the tiny dog, but Joe did. With his usual friendliness he made for it, round behind my legs. I was knocked flat on my face. Can you do anything about over-friendly Joe?

Catherine Murphy, Maidstone, Kent.

It sounds as if Joe could do with some professional training. The National Canine Defence League, 10 Seymour Street, London W1H 5WB (01 935 5511), will send you a list of your nearest dog-training centres on receipt of a sae.

My grand-daughter keeps pestering me to get her a mongrel puppy for Christmas. She is eight years old. Her Dad thinks she is too young and her Mum says she knows who will end up looking after it! Shall I or shan't I?

Mrs Leonie Horne, Liverpool.

If there is the slightest doubt, the answer is no. Training a puppy takes endless time and patience from both the parents and the child.

Unless the dog is accepted as a full member of the family, the venture will only lead to daily frustration, rows and, worst of all, cruelty to the poor dog. Remember, you are not playing with a toy. To help make up your mind, get hold of a leaflet A Puppy for the Family? It is free if you send a sae to Sherley's Pet Care Leaflet Offer, Ashetree Works, Kingston Road, Leatherhead, Surrey KT22 7JZ. Please state the title as it is one of six leaflets available. You could also read Jilly Cooper's marvellous book Intelligent and Loyal: A Celebration of the Mongrel (published by Eyre Methuen) before you decide, as there are as many different types of mongrel as there are pedigree dogs.

I have a small nervous dog who loves exercise but is regularly terrified by large dogs who chase her. I am tempted to invest in one of those long Flexi-leashes but they seem expensive for my budget. I wondered what you thought of these leashes?

Joan Clubber, Hampstead, London.

If used with care a Flexi-leash is worth its weight in gold as I have found with a previously badly-treated highly nervous poodle. But I find it preferable to switch to an ordinary lead when walking a dog through traffic as the lock can easily unclick. May I plead, though, with owners of large breeds to have consideration when they see their dogs causing distress. A playful paw can injure, and sheer size literally panics a small nervous dog. I speak as one who has in the past owned large dogs as well as small.
P.S. Flexi-leashes are available from most reputable pet shops, or alternatively from Flexi Co, 311 West End Lane, London NW6 1RD. They are available in various lengths and strengths.

On choosing a dog: this advice comes from the Battersea Dogs' Home, and I endorse it completely. Before buying a dog for anyone in your family or for yourself, ask the following questions.

1 Can I afford the upkeep of a dog? (A medium-sized dog will cost between £3 and £4 per week at current prices to feed, plus veterinary fees, or insurance scheme.)

2 Is my accommodation suitable for an animal to live in? (Many private landlords and councils do not permit tenants to keep animals in flats.)

3 Have I space near my home where I can exercise the dog on a regular basis, off the lead?

4 Can I make arrangements for the dog to be looked after when I go away on holidays?

5 Is there someone at home during the day to look after the animal?

If you cannot answer yes to the above questions – all of them, quite realistically – then perhaps you should think seriously about whether you ought to have an animal at all. Once you acquire an animal you are acquiring another member of the family, and there is a continuing responsibility to look after it.

My daughter, aged eight, would dearly love a puppy for Christmas. The problem is that since birth she has had an allergy to cats, dogs, birds and horses, which affects her chest, makes her eyes run and makes her sneeze. As a child, her father suffered from asthma, but now is affected only in the same way as our daughter, with animals. Are there any drugs available or anything which would enable us to have a dog in the house without ill-effects?

Mrs B. Burns, Manchester 9.

Doctors seem to be unable to counteract this allergy some people have to animal fur – it would not be kind either to your daughter or to a puppy to bring them together. I suggest she approaches all animals occasionally, to see if she grows out of this condition – it happens sometimes. But your daughter might be interested in having a pet without fur or feathers, such as goldfish, terrapins or a tortoise.

I was interested to read in your page about natural veterinary products for dogs, so I would be grateful if you would say where I can get them as I want to get the garlic one for my little dog. Ideas on how to feed dogs have much improved over the years. I should know, as I have been a dog owner for 40 years. They are the most lovable creatures and mine has been a great comfort to me since I have been living alone.

Mrs K. Kilburn, Mirfield, W. Yorks.

You should be able to get a selection of Denes Veterinary Herbal Products at your local pet shop. If not, send a sae to 14 Goldstone Street, Hove, E. Sussex BN3 3RL, for a list of distributors. Incidentally, Denes make a tinned pet food called Healthmeal which is free of all chemical preservatives and colouring. Although I don't believe in feeding animals solely out of tins, you might want to see if your dog likes this as a change. When you can't buy the garlic tablets, most pooches enjoy a fresh clove of garlic crushed in their meal, plus a few drops of corn or sunflower seed oil. My pets have a daily dose of two to three Denes All-in-One Tablets which I'm certain helps to keep them fit and lively.

I am single and live alone. While I am out at work I think it unfair to keep a dog. However, I shall soon be retiring and am considering getting one then. There is no doubt that giving a home to a stray would be of benefit to both dog and myself. But in a family there is always someone around if one member is ill or away and I am concerned about making a dog wholly dependent on one person. I know I shall want to have the occasional 'lie in' in the morning, and when I feel off-colour or have a cold I retire to bed so what about the poor dog then? I wouldn't mind – indeed I would welcome the daily walks so long as I am fit – but I can't think of a solution to the problems which would arise if I were not. I wouldn't want a cat in case it killed birds in the garden. Any ideas, Katie?

Miss M. Walton, Manchester.

There is no doubt you have to keep active and energetic to give a dog a really good home. Even family or friends, who may be willing in principle to help you at times, may be obliged to let you down at the last minute. As you obviously care for birds, would you not consider having a budgerigar? You would be sur-

WALKIES

prised what a good companion a small bird can be if you take the time and trouble to develop its personality. You can get advice about how to train and look after them from Pedigree Petfoods Education Centre, National Office, Waltham-on-the-Wold, Melton Mowbray, Leics. LE14 4 RS (0664 64171). In an emergency perhaps a friendly pet shop owner might be prepared to take your pet as a paying guest for a few days.

I am looking for somewhere different to go for a holiday where we could take our Alsatian dog, which is very much part of our family. We found a lovely spot on the west coast of Scotland where the people we stayed with were happy to accept the dog, but now we feel like a change. We don't mind whether we are self-catering or in a boarding house, as long as the dog is welcome.

Mrs M. Scott, Tyne and Wear.

I agree, a holiday is incomplete without one's dog, and they appreciate the change as much as humans. There's a useful holiday brochure available from W. H. Smith and Sons Ltd, Pets Welcome, published by Herald Advisory Services, which lists the sort of addresses you need.

Having just acquired a dog which will be travelling frequently in the car with me, I need some help. I believe there is a gadget on the market which allows the car window to be open without fear of the dog jumping out. Do you know where I can get one of these?

M. Black, Shifnal, Salop.

Most pet shops stock or can order a Lever Gap. This is a criss-cross trellis which fits into the frame of any window. The diamond pattern enables it to stretch or become narrower. There is a groove which fits along the window and the window can be wound up to form a solid thief-proof grid. If you have any problems in obtaining a Lever Gap, write to Freeline Ltd, 11 Brook Gate, South Liberty Lane, Bristol BS3 2UN. But even with one of these fitted to a window on either side of the car it would be cruel to leave an animal there in hot weather. Even on a warm sunny day an open car can get uncomfortably hot. Sit in it yourself for quarter of an hour and see what I mean. Always carry cold water in a vacuum flask when travelling with a dog.

I was interested in your letter about natural veterinary products for dogs, but you did not say which you thought the ordinary dog-owner should keep at hand, or give us any tips about natural feeding. Could you explain a bit further, please?

Mrs R. Darwinson, Newport Pagnell, Bucks.

I am glad you asked this. The main remedies in powder or tablet form are garlic (the strongest of internal disinfectants), iodine-rich seaweed to put a gloss on the coat and Naturebone, which replaces the calcium a dog would get in his wild state from gnawing bones. Thick slices of wholemeal bread, dried out in the oven, make good dog biscuits. One main evening meal is plenty for an adult ani-

mal but a puppy needs to be fed more often. A lot of people believe meat should be given raw, but only two of my many dogs have liked it. It is important that, according to the animal's size, the pieces should be big enough for them to chew. Not only will this keep their teeth clean and strong but it will also keep the digestive tract active. Never give them mince or sloppy food. The occasional fast day is healthy, but add honey to the drinking water on those days and if the dog becomes really anxious hand out an oakcake or a couple of sweet biscuits.

I know you believe in natural health and beauty as I do, and now I've bought a puppy, I want to bring him up this healthy way too, with all necessary minerals, vitamins and proteins. Is there a range of natural veterinary products, and if so, where do I get them?

Mrs F. Panton, Cardiff, S. Glamorgan.

Animals instinctively prefer natural foods and, if left to themselves, know what they need to eat to prevent, as well as to cure, illnesses. Juliette De Bairacli Levy's The Complete Herbal Book for the Dog is published by Faber and Faber and will give you all the information you need. The products are available from Natural Rearing Products, 1 Coopers Heath, Hempstead, Holt, Norfolk NR25 6LA (026371 2874). Their Herbal Compound Tablets are very effective for virus fevers. If you have difficulty in finding this book, as I have, your library might come up trumps. Then there is Denes Veterinary Herbal Products Ltd, 14 Goldstone Street, Hove, E. Sussex BN3 3RL, where you can write for their introductory booklet A Full Life for Your Pet, plus a list of distributors.

My Alsatian dog is a bit big for bathing. I remember a TV programme once in which

you told how you cleaned the coats of your own dogs. How do you do it?

E.E. Taylor, Gloucester.

Boots Bay Rum (the greaseless kind) is what you need. Either sprinkle it neat on to the dog's hair, then wipe over with a flannel wrung out in hot water – or pour some bay rum into a bowl of hot water and apply with a wrung-out flannel. In both cases a light towelling-over and a good brush will complete this almost dry-clean.

At the age of 42, I am thinking of taking up poodle-clipping. I feel sure I would have a flair for it once properly trained.

Mrs June Allwork, Southport, Lancs.

What a good idea! The Kennel Club suggest you get in touch with Mrs Rita Gee, Beritas Kennels, 137 Woodlands Road, Crumpsall, Manchester 8. She is the nearest person to you who can give the best advice on training.
P.S. Mrs Gee no longer trains people herself but is well-known in poodle-showing circles and could refer anyone to another trainer.

The Power of the Dog

There is sorrow enough in the natural way,
From men and women to fill our day;
But when we are certain of sorrow in store,
Why do we always arrange for more?
Brothers, and sisters, I bid you beware,
Of giving your heart to a dog to tear.

Buy a pup and your money will buy
Love unflinching that cannot lie –
Perfect passion and worship fed
By a kick in the ribs or a pat on the head.
Never-the-less it is hardly fair
To risk your heart for a dog to tear.

When the fourteen years which Nature permits
Are closing in asthma, or tumour, or fits,
And the vet's unspoken prescription runs
To lethal chambers or loaded guns,
Then you will find – it's your own affair,
But ... you've given your heart to a dog to tear.

When the body that lived at your single will,
When the whimper of welcome is stilled (how still!)
When the spirit that answered your every mood
Is gone – wherever it goes – for good,
You will discover how much you care,
And will give your heart to a dog to tear!

We've sorrow enough in the natural way,
When it comes to burying Christian clay,
Our loves are not given, but only lent,
At compound interest of cent per cent,
Though it is not always the case, I believe,
That the longer we've kept them, the more do we grieve;
For, when debts are payable, right or wrong,
A short-time loan is as bad as a long –
So why in Heaven (before we are there!)
Should we give our hearts to a dog to tear?

Rudyard Kipling

I have a young Chihuahua which I find most difficult to feed. The only things she likes are rusks and Ostermilk. I don't know much about these dogs. We have no children, so she's like a child to us.

Mrs Down, Aberdare, Glamorgan.

I suggest you buy The Chihuahua, *a book in the Popular Dogs Series, written by Thelma Gray. I'm sure you'll find it invaluable. Chihuahuas are usually little dogs full of character and vitality, so ask your vet to give yours an injection just to boost her appetite. (I presume she has had her two Epivax inoculations.) Here are a few ideas which may also help: 1) Put a little Brands Essence on your finger and let her sniff and lick – if she likes it, put a teaspoonful daily either in jelly or liquid form over her food. Then 2) seal some rabbit in a frying pan with vegetable oil or margarine and onions, then take out the onions and boil or bake till well-cooked. Pie veal cooked the same way is very tempting, too. 3) When you have steak, as a special treat let her have a tiny bit of yours. 4) Ostermilk is nourishing, but so is Complan – try some. I'd suggest switching from rusks to digestive biscuits. 5) Goodboy vitaminised chocolate drops for dogs (the mini ones) usually meet with great approval, especially if you throw them to her as a great game when she has eaten some dinner, but do read the instructions on the tin about quantity. 6) When you go out to dinner, take her, too, if dogs are welcome, and give her a tit-bit. She may be a society girl at heart! And being so small even giving her the best food is not going to be all that expensive.*

Why do poodles have wool, and not hair like other canines? Can you also tell me please where they originate from? I know they were once hunting dogs, but that's all.

Mrs M. Lord, Childwall, Liverpool.

177

The standard poodles are by origin part German, part Russian. They were used as water hounds, and the name in fact does come from the German pudeln, *to splash in water. There are records of poodles in Italy and Holland back in the 15th and 16th centuries, and they appear in 17th and 18th-century paintings, but they did not come to Britain until much later. As for the poodle's coat, it is no more wool than frizzy hair, is, but it can be woven, as can the undercoats of the Samoyed and Keeshond breeds. Though it will take a mountain of clippings to make a scarf and beret set, at least it's a shaggy dog tale you can make come true.*

We have a marvellous Labrador who is really part of our family (we have three children) and would be lost without him because he is so gentle and intelligent. I can understand why they are used as guide dogs for the blind. Can you please explain a little about the 'puppy-walkers' used by the Guide Dogs for the Blind organization? We should like to take part in this work but I don't know how the walkers are selected or where to apply.

Mrs E. Blackshaw, Hyde, Ches.

*There is a puppy-walking scheme run by the Guide Dogs for the Blind Association. Members of the public can take young puppies into their home and rear them until they are 10 to 12 months old when they go to a centre for training as guide dogs. Because puppy-walkers need supervision the scheme is limited to the following areas: 1) Within a 30-mile radius of Leamington Spa including Birmingham and Coventry. 2) Parts of Surrey and North Hampshire especially near Basingstoke, Farnham and Guildford. 3) The Staines and Watford areas. 4) Within a four-mile radius of Leicester. 5) In Lancashire based on the Bol-*ton Training Centre. 6) 30 miles around Exeter. 7) In Scotland based on the Forfar Training Centre.

The type of home required is one where a puppy is welcomed and understood by the whole family; children are a help as are family pets – cats and other dogs especially. Homes in built-up areas are also preferred because in general the puppy-walker's job is to prepare a dog for its future work by getting used to all the sounds and smells of everyday life.

But remember, puppy-walking is a job which demands a most unselfish attitude – I know it would break my heart every time I had to part with an animal I had grown to love.

For further details write to: The Breeding and Puppy-Walking Manager, Guide Dogs for the Blind Association, Tollgate House, Banbury Road, Bishop's Tachbrook, Leamington Spa, Warks. (092 685 226).
P.S. It would save a lot of work for the Association if you looked up your local training centre, in the telephone directory, if you fall in one of the areas listed above, and contact them directly.

Many people will receive pets as Christmas presents, and while they might be able to afford the general upkeep of the animal, they might not have considered the expense of medical treatment. Vets are expensive and as there is no equivalent of a National Health Service for dogs, I wonder if there is a private insurance scheme to cover veterinary fees. This would be a good present for someone who has a treasured pet and a small budget. I'm sure such a scheme would be welcome.

Mrs Hicks, Sandwich, Kent.

There is such a scheme in operation Mrs Hicks. I think it is an excellent idea and agree it would make a marvellous present. Pet Plan Ltd, 32 Wood Lane, London W12 7DU (01 743 1841), specialise in insurance for cats and dogs. You use the vet of your choice and pay him in the usual way, but the receipted bill and completed claim form is forwarded to Pet Plan who reimburse you. Even so, you do have to pay the first £6.50 of any treatment. For details of how the scheme works write to Pet Plan, enclosing a sae.

A number of people in our road are elderly and live alone. Although many of them have dogs I have noticed that if their pet dies they don't replace it. This is becuase they are afraid the day will come when they are no longer able to exercise the animal, or fear they may die first. It is sad to see them walking alone, until they gradually stop going out altogether. A neighbour of mine solved this problem by 'adopting' a dog while its owners were at work. It occurred to me that there must be many people who have dogs which are left alone while they are at work and would welcome someone taking them out during the day. This would give an elderly person the company of an animal for a good many hours, without the strain of the ultimate responsibility for it. Obviously this wouldn't work with a puppy, but an older dog might appreciate it.

Daphne Hughes, Bristol.

I think this is a splendid plan. Never mind the ifs and buts. It is cruel to leave a dog – puppy or adult – alone day after day. Even puppies would learn the difference between their 'real' home and their 'foster' home. But in case of accident it would be wise to insure the animal. The National Dog Owners' Association at 39–41 North Road, Islington, London N7 9DP (01 609 2757), has a good scheme which insures up to three dogs belonging to one

person for a yearly payment (half price for OAPs and the registered disabled). Write, enclosing a sae for full details.
P.S. The NDOA also runs an advice service for the choice of a pet, kennelling information, breeding and any other dog-owning queries.

We are moving to a lonely spot in the country and have bought an Alsatian as a guard dog. But I am told that even if a notice warned intruders of a dog at large and they were attacked by it, we might be liable for heavy damages and could be told to have the dog destroyed. Is this so? With a young family I would certainly feel safer if I had the protection of a dog.

Mrs C.A. Dickinson, Leeds, Yorks.

I understand your wish to have a large dog on your property. We are all entitled to take action to protect ourselves and our property, but if your dog attacked the milkman or a friend, that person could claim damages and ask for the dog to be destroyed. It is unwise to have a notice saying Man-eating dog at large *because that advertises the dog as dangerous. But there is nothing wrong with* Guard dog patrolling. *Under an Act of 1971, owners are liable for the damage done by their dogs on the highway – such as causing an accident. The Canine Defence League recommend owners to take out an insurance to cover third party accidents. For a few pounds you can take out a third party cover for £500,000 which will also indemnify you against vet's fees up to a certain sum. This can be obtained from The Dog Breeders Insurance Co Ltd, Beacon House, Landsdowne, Bournemouth BH1 3LE. The National Canine Defence League (address at the end of this chapter) have a similar scheme, but for members only.*

Please help. I have an adorable tabby cat aged four, but I'm having terrible problems with her clawing the furniture. I have just bought a beautiful suite of furniture. It took me a long time to save up for it and now I find her clawing along one arm of the couch. I have tried a scratching post and a recommended repellent which keeps kittens away from furniture, but it doesn't deter my cat. Is there anything available to keep older cats at bay?

Mrs Sylvia Wilkinson, Catford, London.

I doubt whether you will be able to discipline your tabby now she's four. If a cat doesn't learn certain rules when it's a kitten or at least within the first year, it will never get out of bad habits. You could try a firm whack with a rolled newspaper when she starts to scratch, but perhaps it would help more to have her claws clipped regularly by the vet. Don't try to do this yourself in case you cut too deeply, but once they have been done you can smooth them off with an emery board. She might need gentle persuasion to let you do this the first few times, but she'll soon trust you.

We are moving soon from the country to a town house and I hope to take my cat with me. I have heard tales about cats not liking a break with their old surroundings and that they tend to return 'home' again. I would like to know if this is true, and if there is anything that would prevent this happening?

W. Campion, Lighthorne.

Although cats are supposed to be more attached to places than people, really loved family pets I've known have moved very happily from home to home. The cat should travel in a comfortable closed basket with soft bedding, and should not be fed before the journey, as it may feel sick. When you arrive at your new home, put out the litter box and fresh food and water (or milk) and keep it indoors for 48 hours. But, and this is most important, keep stroking and talking to it to get it over that first feeling of strangeness and disorientation.

How can I tell my cats apart? This may seem stupid, but they are mother and daughter, coal black and exactly the same size. They come in separately for their food and I never know which has been fed. I cannot put collars on them as they are great tree climbers and might get hitched up.

Mrs H. Craft, Chertsey, Surrey.

To a sensitive animal owner, different personalities usually show through eventually even in pets of almost identical appearance. I think you'll find in time that you can tell your cats apart even though you might not be able to say how. But I consulted The Pet Shop of 286 St Paul's Road, London N1, where they have different plastic pet collars, or an all-elastic pet harness and lead. Collars can always be put on cats very loosely so that they can wriggle out in an emergency. I think you will find your local pet shop can show you the kind you need.

I have a lovely black cat with a white chin which has a beauty spot right in the middle. But she has one problem – bad breath. I don't think it could be the food I give her because she always has a varied diet. She always wants to be cuddled and this makes matters worse. What should I do?

Christine Ruscoe, Llanmaes, Glamorgan.

Veterinary Amplex should be the answer. Read the instructions concerning quantity, and if you can't give her the pill whole, you can crush it into her food. If her breath still smells after a few days, take her to a vet. Her

This is a tip I shall try myself. If you are thinking of putting up a nesting box, or a food tray for birds, remember to put it somewhere where you will not encourage rats or squirrels. For this reason, make sure nesting boxes do not have a wide rim around the edge – a narrow one will ensure feathered friends get the pickings without rodents getting in first.

P.S. Do remember also a most useful address, John E. Haith Ltd, Park Street, Cleethorpes, South Humberside DN35 7NF. Mr Haith supplies economy packs of pigeon foods and bird seeds most efficiently and reasonably.

teeth could be causing the trouble, and giving her some pain.

Our cat has fleas, and they seem to have taken over our carpet as well as his coat. Please tell us the best way of dealing with this because of the embarrassment when the fleas leap out and land on our visitors.

B.A., Sussex.

I think the best thing for you to do is obtain some Nuvan Top, available only from your veterinary surgeon, to deal with animal fleas quickly and efficiently. Nuvan Top also make a spray to treat carpets and furniture to leave your home flea-free.

If you are a bird lover, I have found a novel way to make a feed hopper to use in the garden. Several household fresheners come in openwork plastic containers. When they're empty, wash them thoroughly and fill with nuts, then hang them on the washing line. We now watch a number of wild birds feeding every day and it gives us enormous pleasure.

Mrs L.W., Yorks.

Last January I had my hair cut at home and was left with a large pile of hair. I put it out in the garden thinking it might be useful for the birds for lining their nests. As a child, my great-aunt used to teach me that St Valentine's Day is the birds' wedding day, and sure enough, the hair lay untouched for three weeks, until February 14th. During the ensuing week all the hair was taken and the last lock went on February 21. Maybe the charming old story of St Valentine's Day is true.

Mrs P. Bond, Solihull, W. Midlands.

I have two pet budgies and they are free to fly about the house all day long. The problem is that they sit on the pelmets and throw the ornaments off. So we have had to remove these. Then they took to eating the wallpaper off the walls. We are running out of patience! Can you help?

Miss J.W., Knebworth, Herts.

A switch from wallpaper to paint might be your answer. I have heard the expression, 'bird brain' but a number of stories appear to disprove this, so it could be worth your while trying to train your birds by putting them back in their cage every time they misbehave. They may learn . . . .

I love my budgie but I'm getting a bit impatient with him pecking and chewing my wooden furniture, not to mention stripping my wallpaper. The vet says there's nothing wrong with him but if he goes on like this there's going to be quite a lot wrong with my home. Any suggestions gratefully received.

Mrs Agnes Leigh, Liverpool.

Apparently this gnawing and chewing is an instinct left over from the wild state when the birds needed to hollow out a nest for themselves. Just divert these activities to his cage. Instead of a sandsheet (which he might peck to pieces) sprinkle the floor with clean loose sand and if you give him a block of soft wood or a twig from a fruit tree this may be just as acceptable to him as your furniture or wallpaper.

When my grandchildren presented me with a beautiful blue budgerigar for Christmas – complete with cage, toys and a little mirror – I was delighted. I call him Peter and he has settled down well, spending ages twittering to his reflection in the mirror. He 'talks' to himself, but not to me – that's the problem. The pet shop told my family he must be about three months' old. Is he too young to talk properly yet?

Mrs F. Graham, Plymouth, Devon.

Peter is just the right age to learn to talk – but he won't start unless you teach him. Has he settled down enough yet to sit on your finger? If not, start by making friends that way first. Put your hand in the cage and encourage him to sit on your index finger, talking quietly to him and using his name. Soon you'll be able to bring him out of his cage on your finger and he'll be ready for school. Teach him simple phrases, one at a time. Keep his lessons short, and repeat the same words over and over again – in about six weeks, Peter should reward you with his first words. You might find the Pedigree Petfoods Education Centre useful. They issue a free leaflet for pet budgie owners, which you can obtain from the address supplied at the end of this chapter.

How does one explain death to children, and especially with regard to their pets? My eldest daughter (now aged nine) walked around and around the house for ages holding her dead guinea pig, talking to it and stroking it. I kept telling her it was dead, but she didn't seem to understand, and nothing I could say would console her. We now have another guinea pig – a lovely little thing that she loves dearly – but I'm dreading the day when it dies.

Mrs J. Gardiner, Stourbridge, Worcs.

I have found it works well to establish in children's minds that all of us, humans and animals, have an allotted span of life, after which our bodies go to sleep for good, which we call 'dying', although we are sure our minds, hearts and souls go on living elsewhere. I tell them that unfortunately animals have shorter lives on Earth than we do, so it is very important to find out from the vet, and from books, how to look after them as well as possible so that they have a happy time with us, and the better we take care of them, the longer we can prolong their lives. I always add that we believe that when we die we meet up again with the people and animals we have loved, so it is not a 'forever' parting.

My trouble is noisy goldfish. The other evening we were wakened by our dog barking, and we found the goldfish were taking a piece of stone from the bottom of the tank up to the top and dropping it. This echoed in the wall fitment and sounded like a stone thrown at the window which was what alarmed the dog. How do I train the fish to sleep at night?

Mrs L. Barlow, Leigh-on-Sea, Essex.

Your goldfish could be dropping hints with those stones. A midnight snack sprinkled in their tank before you go to bed might solve the problem. If not, make a 'bedroom' for them, with a partition, and make sure that area has rocks and not tiny pebbles on the

floor. If your goldfish still prove night-time playmates get in touch with the nearest aquarium manager.

Is it possible to have my rabbit boarded out while I go on holiday?

Ian Hibbert, Aylesbury, Bucks.

I'm glad you raised this point because now so many families take Winter holidays, the problem of what to do with pets is an all-year-round one. If you cannot get a friend to look after your pet while you are away – and, of course, you can't take it with you abroad because of quarantine regulations – then place your pet in a good kennel. Some of them take rabbits as well as dogs and cats. Your local library will have a list of registered boarding establishments for animals. The Royal Society for the Prevention of Cruelty to

Animals have published a leaflet called Pets at Holiday Time *which is available on receipt of a sae. Write to the RSPCA, Causeway, Horsham, Sussex RH12 1HG.*

I saw a programme on ITV called *Horses, Heroes and Hard Cash.* On it was shown the slaughter of old racehorses and also of two- and three-year-olds who proved unmanageable and of no value on a race course. I have one horse and am thinking of buying another. I wonder if it would be possible to buy one of those destined for an untimely end at the abattoir?

Mrs E.C. Pritchard, Ynys Mon, Gwynedd.

I think you may have got hold of the wrong end of the stick. The Racing Information Bureau assures me that if a racehorse is not good enough for flat racing in this country it is still a most valuable property and unlikely to end up in an abattoir. It can be sold for flat racing abroad where the standard is not quite as high as in Britain, or bought for jumping on National Hunt courses or for show jumping. Sometimes a horse is retired after its three-year-old season to go to stud. I quite understand your wish to give another horse a happy home and you could certainly go along to one of the sales. You can find out when and where they are if you write to the Racing Information Bureau, Winkfield Road, Ascot, Berks SL5 7HX (0990 25912), enclosing a sae for a reply.

Could you please tell me the address of the Horses and Ponies Protection Society? Do they ever sell any of the horses in their care?

Denise Hallard, Warrington, Lancs.

The Horses and Ponies Protection Association, Green Bank Farm, Fence, Near Burnley, Lancs (0282 65909), runs two homes, one at Capel House, Bullsmore Lane, Waltham Cross, Herts, and a second one at Fence. Most of the animals are ageing mares, small ponies, yearlings or donkeys. Many of these animals are in the care of families. The Association will part with them only if they know the animals are going to homes which are regularly inspected and to people who have proper knowledge and facilities, but once given a home, the family becomes fully responsible for the animal, although the Association will take it back into care if you move abroad or have some other major reason for not being able to continue 'fostering'. Even when the animals are released as stable and grazing companions, the society emphasises the need for adequate facilities. It is always grateful for offers of help, but it never sells its protegés.

Cat and dog owners may notice that carpets give off an unpleasant animal odour after vacuuming. A small lemon-scented deodorant block, fixed inside the dustbag before cleaning, will leave the room smelling sweetly. A single block lasts for several weeks and the cost is trifling.

Mrs E.C. Bowman, Stockport.

This reminds me that a half and half mixture of water and vinegar (more vinegar if it's an old dog) dabbed on the remains of a mopped-up puddle will remove both traces and smell, as the acid neutralises the alkaline. The technique is to dab, not rub, and dry as quickly as possible by gently treading a pile of tissues on the spot to absorb the moisture. Renew them regularly as they soak up the mess. Leave a dozen or so under a heavy weight to complete the process. For overall professional cleaning with a high-powered suction machine, contact Permaclean (UK)

Ltd, 103–105 Brighton Road, Coulsdon, Surrey (01 668 5421) which offers an on-the-spot carpet-cleaning service all round Britain, but ask for a free estimate first. The Carpet Cleaners Association, 97 Knighton Fields Road West, Leicester LE2 6LH, provides invaluable leaflets on carpet care if you send a sae.

I am sick and tired of animal lovers who keep their pets indoors all day and then put them out at night, causing accidents and annoyance to everyone. Why do people imagine that just because they enjoy having an animal, everyone must share it? My climbing plants and rose bushes have been broken by fighting cats; while dogs – one the size of a pit pony – have trampled and broken plants in my front garden. When I complain to their owners they say meekly: 'It's their instinct to chase birds and kill them, and damage plants in the process.' What can I do? Form a Society for the Prevention of Damage to Plants?

Mrs J. G. Atkinson, Newcastle-upon-Tyne.

People who allow their pets to behave badly have neither love for their animals nor the slightest modicum of good manners. And when such people talk of suffocating their animal's 'natural instincts' the reply to them is that as children we all have our wilder instincts curbed so why not discipline a pet? I have always had a dog of one kind or another (right now I get enormous fun from a very lively Yorkshire terrier), but I've trained them not to be a nuisance to anyone. The trouble is, it seems much easier to teach pets good manners than the people who own them. Have you tried using dog- and cat-repellent powders which you can sprinkle round the borders of your garden to keep out these unwelcome night visitors? These products are available from most pet shops, and cost less than a £1.

Useful Addresses

The National Canine Defence League,
10 Seymour Street, London W1H 5WB.
(01 935 5511)

Sherley's Pet Care Leaflets,
Ashetree Works, Kingston Road,
Leatherhead, Surrey KT22 7JZ.

Flexi Co (for Flexi-leashes),
311 West End Lane, London NW6 1RD.

Natural Rearing Products,
1 Cooper's Heath, Hempstead, Holt, Norfolk
NR25 6LA. (026371 2874)

Denes Veterinary Herbal Products,
14 Goldstone Street, Hove, E. Sussex BN3
3RL.

Pedigree Petfoods Education Centre,
National Office, Waltham-on-the-Wold,
Melton Mowbray, Leics LE14 4RS. (0664
64171)

Lever Gap (for car window protection),
Freeline Ltd, 11 Brook Gate, South Liberty
Lane, Bristol BS3 2UN.

Guide Dogs for the Blind Association,
Tollgate House, Banbury Road, Bishop's
Tachbrook, Leamington Spa, Warks. (092
685 226)

Pet Plan Ltd (insurance for animals),
32 Wood Lane, London W12 7DU. (01 743
1841)

The National Dog Owner's Association,
39–41 North Road, Islington, London N7
9DP. (01 609 2757)

Dog Breeders' Insurance Co Ltd,
12 Christchurch Road, Landsdowne,
Bournemouth
BH1 3 LE. (0202 295771)

Dog Breeders Associates (a useful
organisation if you wish to buy a pedigree
puppy or breed them)
1 Abbey Road, Bourne End, Bucks SL8 5NZ.
(06285 20943)

The Pet Shop (for plastic pet collars),
286 St Paul's Road, London N1.

John E. Haith Ltd (for bird seed in bulk),
Park Street, Cleethorpes, S. Humberside
DN35 7NF.

Watmoughs Ltd (for monthly magazine *Cats
and Rabbits*),
Idle, Bradford, W. Yorks BD10 8NL. (0274
612111)

British Rabbit Council,
Purefoy House, 7 Kirkgate, Newark, Notts.
(0636 76042)

The Budgerigar Society,
57 Stephyns Chambers, Bank Court, Hemel
Hempstead, Herts HP1 1DD. (0442 56873)

Caperns Advisory Service,
Spillers Foods Ltd, New Malden House, 1
Blagdon Road, New Malden, Surrey KT3
4TB. (01 949 6100)

Cage and Aviary Birds Magazine,
Surrey House, 1 Throwley Way, Sutton,
Surrey. (01 643 8040)

The Zoological Society of London (for those
interested in exotic pets),
Regents Park, London NW1 4RY. (01 722
3333)

Centre for Educational Zoology,
7 Carson Road, W. Dulwich, London SE21
8HT.

The RSPCA (for useful leaflets),
Causeway, Horsham, Sussex RH12 1HG.
(0403 64181)

The Racing Information Bureau,
Winkfield Road, Ascot, Berks SL5 7HX.
(0990 25912)

**The Horses and Ponies Protection
Association,**
Green Bank Farm, Fence, Near Burnley,
Lancs. (0282 65909)

Permaclean (UK) Ltd,
103-105 Brighton Road, Coulsdon, Surrey.

The Carpet Cleaner's Association,
97 Knighton Fields Road West, Leicester
LE2 6LH.

Further Useful Addresses

The People's Dispensary for Sick Animals,
PDSA House, South Street, Dorking, Surrey.
(0306 81691)

Battersea Dogs' Home (membership for
young people is offered, which entitles a
child to a newsletter and a visit to the home
for the member and a friend),
4 Battersea Park Road, London SW8 4AA.

Pro-Dogs (a charity to encourage responsible
dog ownership: I love their slogan 'Dogs
deserve better people'),
203 London Road, Aylesford, Kent ME20
7PZ. (0622 78102)

The Kennel Club,
1 Clarges Street, London W1Y 8AB. (01 493
6651)

Humane Education Centre,
Bounds Green Road, London N22 4EU (889
1595)

Wings Haven (Birds Protection Association),
Sheffield Park, Near Uckfield, Sussex.

Royal Society for the Protection of Birds,
The Lodge, Sandy, Beds SG19 2DL.

Feline Advisory Bureau,
350 Upper Richmond Road, Putney, London
SW15. (01 789 9553)

Useful Reading

**Intelligent and Loyal: A Celebration of the
Mongrel,** Jilly Cooper (Eyre Methuen).
Pets Welcome (Herald Advisory Services).
The Complete Herbal Book for the Dog,
Juliette de Bairacli Levy (Faber and Faber).
The Chihuahua, Thelma Grey (Popular Dogs
Publishing). Popular Dogs Publishing also
do many other titles concerned with parti-
cular breeds, the following titles being a
selection of what is currently available. For
the full list, write to Popular Dogs Publish-
ing Co Ltd, Hutchinson Publishing Group,
17-21 Conway Street, London W1T 5HL.
The Collie, Margaret Osborne.
The Dalmatian, Eleanor Frankling.
The Cairn Terrier, S.W.H. Beynon and
Alex Fisher.
The Family Beagle, Thelma Grey.
Keeping Rabbits, Elisabeth Downing (Pelham
Books).
All About Your Cat's Health, Geoffrey West
(Pelham Books).
Astrology for Dogs (And Owners) William
Fairchild (Elm Tree Books).
An Illustrated Guide to Dogs, Joan Palmer
(Salamander Books).
The Dog's Guide to London, Sandy Molloy
(Garnstone Press).
**In Touch. Aids and Services for Blind and
Partially Sighted People** (a handbook for
the visually handicapped), Thena Heshel
and Margaret Ford (BBC Publications).

Index